PENNSYLVANIA OVERLOOKS

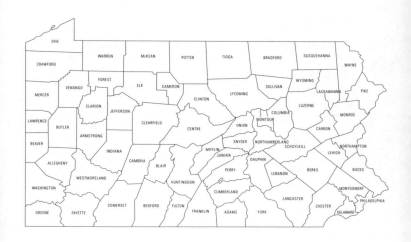

ART MICHAELS

PENNSYLVANIA OVERLOOKS

A Guide for Sightseers and Outdoor People

THE PENNSYLVANIA STATE UNIVERSITY PRESS

UNIVERSITY PARK, PENNSYLVANIA

A Keystone Book

*is so designated to distinguish it from the typical scholarly monograph that a
university press publishes. It is a book intended to serve the citizens of Pennsylvania by educating them and others, in an entertaining way, about aspects of
the history, culture, society, and environment of the state as part of the Middle
Atlantic region.*

THE OUTDOOR RECREATIONAL ACTIVITIES described in this book are
potentially dangerous by their very nature. By engaging in the activities described herein, participants are assuming full responsibility for
their own actions and for the actions of those in their care or under their
supervision. This book is not intended to educate or inform the reader
on the possible dangers and risks involved in outdoor recreational activities. Conditions at or near the various overlooks described herein
can change as a result of natural conditions or other conditions without
the knowledge of the author or publisher of this book. Therefore, the
author and publisher disclaim any liability whatsoever for the condition of places named and described in this book and any occurrence at
or near the places named and described in this book. In addition, nothing in this book is intended to substitute for the reasonable judgment
of individuals while they are participating in outdoor recreational activities described herein.

Library of Congress Cataloging-in-Publication Data
Michaels, Art, 1948–
Pennsylvania overlooks : a guide for sightseers and
outdoor people / Art Michaels.
p.   cm.
"A Keystone book."
Includes bibliographical references and index.
ISBN 0-271-02231-0 (pbk. : alk. paper)
1. Pennsylvania—Guidebooks.   2. Natural areas—Pennsylvania—
Guidebooks.   I. Title.
F147.3 .M53 2002
917.4804'44—dc21
2002012191

It is the policy of The Pennsylvania State University Press to use acid-free
paper. Publications on uncoated stock satisfy the minimum requirements
of American National Standard for Information Sciences—Permanence
of Paper for Printed Library Materials, ANSI Z39.48–1992.

CONTENTS

EASTERN PENNSYLVANIA

ACKNOWLEDGMENTS

This book required more than two years of preparation, research, writing, revising, and photographing—and some ten thousand travel miles throughout Pennsylvania. In its planning stages, many people helped me clarify the book's purpose and structure, and many others provided me with a wealth of information. Still others read and critiqued parts of the manuscript. I am grateful to everyone who answered a question, sent me information, suggested an overlook, gave me directions, identified a distant landmark, and critiqued my work at various stages.

Researching this book and gathering the information called for a staggering amount of detailed material from an equally huge number of sources. Thanks go to all the Pennsylvania Department of Conservation and Natural Resources (DCNR) employees in the bureaus of Forestry, State Parks, and Topographic and Geological Survey for their excellent cooperation in answering my questions and providing precise information.

Some people helped me much more than I expected, and I am delighted to be able to thank them by name. First, special thanks to my wife, Cathy, who helped with the organization of this project, served as navigator on our overlook trips, and posed in many of the photographs. Thanks also to Sam and Jamie, our children, who became models at some of the overlooks and tolerated our absences to research and photograph the book.

The following people deserve particular appreciation. I am grateful to John L. Bearer, Matt Beaver, Terry Brady, Robert Davey, Helen L. Delano, Rick Keen, William Sevon, Steve Shaffer, Cory Wentzel, and Jody Zipperer from the DCNR; Tom Ford, Pennsylvania Fish and Boat Commission; Frank Hoover, Bob Mitchell, and Regis F. Senko from the Pennsylvania Game Commission; Samuel W. Berkheiser Jr. and Rodger T. Faill from the Pennsylvania Geological Survey; Gladys Grubb and Susan E. Kline, U.S. Army Corps of Engineers; and Charles Bier, Julie Lalo, Michelle Merlo, and the resource conservation staff of the Western Pennsylvania Conservancy for their help. From the state parks, thanks to Andy Hinson (Blue Knob), Dale J. Luthringer (Cook Forest), and Ron Dixon (Tobyhanna), as well as Don

Holdren, PennDOT; Scott Leeds, Delaware Water Gap National Recreation Area; and Katie Lawhon, Gettysburg National Military Park.

I would also like to thank Jim Fisher and Janice Hartman, Altoona Railroaders Memorial Museum; Anne Bleistine, Holtwood Environmental Preserve; Gina Padilla, Kings Gap Environmental Education and Training Center; Jason Bell, Loyalhanna Watershed Association; Merri Lisa Formento-Trigilio, Penn State University; William Blewett, Shippensburg University; and Albert Filemyr, Wyncote Audubon Society. Thanks to Tina King, City of Harrisburg Parks and Recreation; Clyde Gamber and John Gerencser, Lancaster County Department of Parks and Recreation; and Michael Fobes, York County Department of Parks and Recreation, along with Robin L. Smith, Athens Township; Karen Wertz, Cambria County Transit Authority; Marty Hinton, Deep Wood Vacation Home Rentals; Emily Beck, Erie Area Convention and Visitors Bureau; Joyce Simile, Greater Pittsburgh Convention and Visitors Bureau; Ken Bunneil, Honesdale Borough; Pam Prosser, Huntingdon County Visitors Bureau; and Leigh Anne Sperry and Annie Urban, Laurel Highlands Visitors Bureau.

Thanks also to my fellow writers and photographers Mike and Jeri Bleech, Wes Bower, Jeff Knapp, and Joe and Mary Ann Workosky, as well as Greg Grove, Reverend Karl Heckert, Charlie Hoyer, Mark A. McConaughy, Jeff Mulhollem, Dave Padula, Brian Reedy, Ron Seeley, Tom Thwaites, Tim "Screaminghawk" Vechter, and John Wiseman. Finally, I thank Laura Reed-Morrisson, my editor at Penn State Press, for her expertise and care with the manuscript.

All of the photographs included in this book are my own.

At Hawk Point Overlook in Susquehannock State Park on a clear, sunny Saturday in June, a family took in the view from the 400-foot-high promontory. One of the adults, walking hand in hand with a youngster about seven years old, said to the child, "Well, Enrique, how do you like your first day in America?" I did not hear the child's response, but I did see him smile.

It is no wonder that on the child's first day in this country, the family took him to a Pennsylvania overlook. Such magical places inspire awe in those who view the landscape from their heights. Surely those parents wanted not only to instill a sense of wonder in the child but also to provide an optimistic beginning to his visit—and perhaps to his new life in America.

A natural overlook is a cliff, mountaintop, ridge, or other high vantage point that affords a vista of the surrounding terrain. The elevations of some overlooks in this book may not seem impressive at first, but overlooks truly are majestic. They provide a wealth of opportunities, attracting sightseers and outdoor people in every season. Government agencies, private conservation groups, tourist promotion agencies, and sporting clubs spotlight them in their publications, Web sites, and promotional literature. Even so, overlooks are often "overlooked" by many people who would treasure them. My wife and I discovered overlooks largely by trial and error. Some trips were disappointing; many were tremendously rewarding.

We have been avid anglers, boaters, wildlife watchers, and sightseers for years, but we have increasingly sought out overlooks. They have offered us a different understanding of the outdoors. We learned that a Pennsylvania overlook—Mt. Pisgah in York County—almost became our nation's capital. From High Knob Vista in Wyoming State Forest, Sullivan County, we reveled in the intense reds, yellows, and oranges of fall spreading to the horizon. We gained a new appreciation for a snowy, leafless forest or a formation of tundra swans when we saw them from High Rocks Vista (Ralph Stover State Park, Bucks County) and Breezyview Overlook (Chickies Rock County Park, Lancaster County). We identified myriad colors in a sunset behind the panorama of Hyner View State Park (Clinton County), and we reconnected with the freshness of spring as the forest at Jakes Rocks Overlook (Warren County) once again turned green.

Aspects of Pennsylvania geology became clearer when we witnessed—from Lower Overlook, Chimney Rocks Park, Hollidaysburg—the unmistakable division between Pennsylvania's Ridge and Valley physiographic province and the Allegheny Front of the Appalachian Plateaus province. We rediscovered the meaning of hallowed ground when we surveyed the site of North America's bloodiest battlefield from Little Round Top at Gettysburg National Military Park. Even city lights sparkled with unusual brilliance from the Duquesne Incline in Pittsburgh.

Overview of Site Listings

My wife and I are middle-aged, not in top physical condition, and hardly handy with advanced technical outdoor skills. But we have found each of the following overlooks very accessible: you can drive to them, or you can park near them and reach them in an easy walk. The longest "hike" to an overlook in this book takes about fifteen minutes. (We have noted some overlooks and facilities that are accessible to people with disabilities: please call ahead before your visit to find out what specific accommodations are available.) The overlooks detailed here are also located on public land, such as federal government land, state parks, state forests, state game lands, county parks, and local parks, or they are open to the public. Access to most of these overlooks is free, and most day-use activities are free. Several overlooks charge admission fees, however, and some opportunities at or near these sites may also require fees. In the overlook descriptions in this book, the symbol [$] means that participating in the opportunity (or part of the opportunity) involves a fee.

This book provides a glimpse of the overlooks in Pennsylvania. Some spectacular overlooks can be reached only by hiking vigorously or climbing over rough terrain, and these are not described here. We omitted still others for reasons of safety—certain roadside vistas offer great views, but parking may be scarce at best or may be dangerously close to traffic. Other overlooks may no longer be maintained as overlooks by their owners. Some overlooks that appear to be public places are actually privately owned; matters of liability and respect for landowners' rights prevent their inclusion in the book. In state forests, overlooks may be accessible by car, but some of the forests' unimproved dirt roads make for treacherous, very bumpy rides.

The overlook at Hyner View State Park is a whopping 1,300 feet above the West Branch Susquehanna River.

Such sites, therefore, have been omitted. (Check the Pennsylvania state forest public use maps for these overlooks.)

Each overlook listing includes vital information: a general description of the overlook and its area, the overlook's distinguishing features, its height (above sea level, a valley floor, or a waterway) when known, the compass direction and width in degrees of the view, and features visible from the overlook. The "Administration and Amenities" section of each entry gives information on hours of operation, entry fees, rest rooms, availability of water, and other administrative details. The "Opportunities" section highlights the wealth of activities at and very near a particular site. Check the "Nearby Overlooks" section to locate other area vistas and the "Nearby Opportunities" section for recreational options. (The symbol preceding each opportunity indicates the main feature of interest, but the choices are endless.) Watch birds and other wildlife; boat, camp, ski cross-country or downhill; visit environmental education centers or view fall foliage. Fish (or ice fish), golf, go hang gliding, or hike. See historical sites, ride a horse or a snowmobile, hunt, or ice skate. Fly a kite—or a model airplane. Visit natural or wilderness areas, shoot photographs, and picnic; enjoy playground and playfield facilities, rappel, sled, snowshoe, stargaze, swim, or discover new wildlife refuges. This book details only a few of the many opportunities and attractions near these overlooks, and it largely focuses on outdoor pursuits. (Consult the General Internet

Resources section for additional ideas.) Each listing offers driving directions and contact information, including the Web sites and phone numbers of nearby federal projects, state parks, state forests, and park facilities, as well as the Pennsylvania Game Commission and the Pennsylvania Fish and Boat Commission. Call these offices for current information on programs and activities.

Some of these overlooks are easy to find. Some are not. For this reason, in addition to the directions provided for each overlook, visitors should get the appropriate map for the park, state forest, or game lands. Check each overlook's contact information for these resources. U.S. Geological Survey quadrant maps are also helpful in pinpointing these sites. You can obtain USGS maps over the counter statewide in a variety of outlets, or you can download them from a Web site (see the General Internet Resources section). I also found the DeLorme *Pennsylvania Atlas and Gazetteer* and PennDOT's official Transportation Map useful.

Advice for Visitors

Drive slowly on backwoods forest roads, and keep a camera handy. Wildlife abounds in many areas, and unanticipated photo opportunities can occur at any moment. Binoculars or a spotting scope are similarly essential, as they will help you see some of the distant landmarks from an overlook more readily. And on your way to an overlook, if you travel on interstate routes or on the Pennsylvania Turnpike, be sure to stop at a PennDOT rest area or welcome center and peruse the pamphlets and maps. In the area of your destination, you will find useful published material on other opportunities, attractions, activities, accommodations, and discount coupons.

A few words of caution are in order. To reach many of these overlooks, you have to drive on "improved" dirt roads. They often have only one lane, and they are steep-sided and narrow. There is little room for error. Drive carefully on these narrow roads, and do not attempt to tow a trailer or other unit on them. For many of the roads, a high-axle four-wheel-drive vehicle is best.

Dust can cover your vehicle after driving on these dirt roads. I have found that the dust collecting on my vehicle's liftgate window—even in state forests on clear, dry days—is often so thick that the rear-windshield wiper works to clear it as if it were a light coating of snow.

In addition, after significant rainfall, these roads can be slippery and muddy. In winter, they may be impassable. Some of the parks simply close in winter, and even if state forest main roads and state parks are open, you might discover closed gates on access roads leading to overlooks. In the winter, then, be sure to call ahead to confirm access.

Do not venture beyond designated overlook areas or cross fences, railings, and other barriers. Do not climb onto cliff barriers and precipices. Supervise children diligently.

Furthermore, know an area's rules and regulations. Hunting may or may not be permitted in certain park areas in certain seasons. The same applies to fishing, boating, trail use, and other activities: when they are permitted, state laws apply. (Obtain an area's rules and regulations by contacting the owner or managing agency listed in the overlook's contact information or in this book's General Internet Resources section.) State game lands are managed mainly for wildlife habitat and hunting, even though they are open to other kinds of recreation. If you venture onto game lands during the spring and fall hunting seasons, wear regulation blaze-orange. Stay on established trails and roads, and do not mark or forge new routes.

The elevations of some of these spots are the highest in the state, and the weather there can be very different from that in lowlands. For example, Jersey Shore and Lock Haven—both in the West Branch Susquehanna River Valley—might experience calm conditions with temperatures in the mid-70s in the summer. At the same time, the air temperature at Hyner View State Park might be recorded in the low 60s, with winds of 20 to 25 miles per hour. Even in the summer, conditions like these will make it feel much cooler. For this reason, be sure to take an extra sweatshirt, jacket, or sweater to be prepared for cooler (and sometimes downright colder) conditions at overlooks.

With overlooks of such varied value and beauty, do not hold out for an overlook trip only in spring or summer! Overlooks are inviting year-round. Some are historically or culturally significant; at others, the main interest may be geological or environmental. Pick several overlooks in the same area and create your own auto tour. Getting out to these places renews the spirit, as a good night's sleep refreshes the body. Pick a bright, crisp day, in any season, choose an overlook in this book and go there with a picnic lunch and a best friend, a loved one—or an entire family. View a sunrise. Observe a sunset. Experience a nighttime view of a city skyline from a vista. A majestic overlook will leave you breathless, enveloping you in delight, wonder, and hope.

STATE GAME LANDS #314
AND DAVID M. RODERICK
WILDLIFE RESERVE

State Game Lands #314, in Erie County, spans 3,131 acres. The Ohio state line is the western border of these game lands, and the Lake Erie shoreline forms their northern border for about 1.5 miles. This segment of the shoreline is the longest undeveloped reach of Lake Erie's south shore between Toledo, Ohio, and Buffalo, New York. The overlook spot, the site of the David M. Roderick Monument, offers a nearly unspoiled view of the lake and its natural shoreline, except for the westward sight of the Conneaut, Ohio, breakwater and the occasional seagoing vessel entering or leaving the area.

The David M. Roderick Wildlife Reserve was dedicated in July 1991. The United States Steel Corporation (now USX) owned the property, which it had bought from Andrew Carnegie early in the 1900s. (Carnegie intended to build a steel mill on the site, but those plans were changed in the 1960s.) David M. Roderick—for whom the reserve is named—was chief executive officer of USX from 1979 to 1989 as well as an avid outdoorsman,with an abiding interest in conservation. During Roderick's tenure as CEO, the property was sold to the Mellon Foundation, which turned it over to the Western Pennsylvania Conservancy. The Conservancy sold the reserve to the Pennsylvania Game Commission.

The most common species here include woodcock, rabbit, grouse, and white-tailed deer. Indeed, wildlife-watching—and bird-watching in particular—is the main attraction at this tract, which covers 4 square miles. The lake and its shoreline mark a major north-south migration route for birds, including raptors such as hawks and eagles, waterfowl, and some one hundred documented songbird species. Upland ground birds, such as grouse, pheasant, and wild turkey, are also abundant. In spring, birds flying north use this area as a rest stop before they take wing over the lake, and in the fall, birds flying south rest in this area after their journey over the water.

The overlook is a cleared, grassy area about 100 yards long at the David M. Roderick Monument, and the site stands about 100

Northwest view from the David M. Roderick Monument.

feet above the water. The peaceful view is due north, 300 degrees west-northwest to about 75 degrees east-northeast. Visible to the east is a clifflike stretch of undeveloped Lake Erie shoreline; to the west, more shoreline and the Conneaut breakwater. You can enjoy this view from the benches that face the lake.

The shoreline cliffs here are part of present-day erosional processes. They are not Ice Age remnants of a former high lake shoreline. (The retreat of the last glacier to reach this area left the cliff's sand and gravel.) Today's lake level has been relatively steady for the last three thousand to four thousand years; earlier lake levels were different from modern levels. You can see the remnants of ancient shorelines—sandy, gravelly ridges about 10 to 15 feet high—in several places in Erie County. Many, however, have been altered or removed by building and regrading, so they are not obvious.

The lake erodes the shoreline at a rate of about 3 feet annually, but this rate varies according to elements such as storms in the area, lake levels, and whether the shoreline has a beach.

OPPORTUNITIES: Hiking, hunting, sightseeing, and wildlife-watching.

ADMINISTRATION AND AMENITIES: There are no services at this overlook.

DIRECTIONS: From U.S. Route 20, where Route 20 and PA Route 5 meet at West Springfield, turn north onto Rudd Road, which is

Easterly view along the lakeshore at the David M. Roderick Monument.

clearly marked with a street sign. Drive 2.6 miles north on Rudd Road to its end at Lake Road. Turn left (west) onto Lake Road and drive 1.4 miles to the monument's parking area on the north side of Lake Road.

FOR MORE INFORMATION: Contact the Pennsylvania Game Commission, Northwest Region Headquarters, PO Box 31, 1509 Pittsburgh Road, Franklin, PA 16323 (814-432-3187 or 1-800-533-6764), or visit its Web site at www.pgc.state.pa.us.

NEARBY OVERLOOKS: Allegheny National Forest overlooks (Warren County); Seneca Point Overlook (Clarion County); and Beartown Rocks Vista (Jefferson County).

OTHER NEARBY OPPORTUNITIES

Presque Isle State Park (Erie County). Activities include bicycling, boating (with unlimited horsepower), ice boating, fishing for trout and other species, ice fishing, hiking on 19 trail miles, hunting, picnicking, ice skating, cross-country skiing, lake swimming, and wildlife-watching. The park also offers boat launching and mooring [$], boat rental [$], environmental education, a food concession, a marina, pavilion rental [$], a playfield, a playground, and a visitors center.

Pymatuning State Park (Crawford County). Activities include boating (with 10hp limit), ice boating, tent and trailer camping [$], organized group tent and trailer camping [$], fishing for warm-water species, ice fishing, hiking on 2 trail miles, hunting, picnicking, ice skating, cross-country skiing, sledding, snow-mobiling on 15 trail miles with trailhead, lake swimming, and wildlife-watching. The park also offers boat launching and mooring [$], boat rental [$], modern cabin rental [$], environmental education, a food concession, a marina, pavilion rental [$], a playfield, and a playground.

In Crawford County, the Pennsylvania Fish and Boat Commission's *Linesville Fish Culture Station* has a visitors center (814-683-4451), and Erie County's *Fairview Fish Culture Station* also welcomes visitors (814-474-1514).

Erie National Wildlife Refuge (Crawford County). Activities include boating (in boats without motors), fishing, hiking, hunting, cross-country skiing, and wildlife-watching. It also offers boat launching and environmental education. Call the Refuge (814-789-3584) for complete information on regulations.

2

ALLEGHENY NATIONAL FOREST

Tidioute Overlook, Jakes Rocks Overlook,
and Rimrock Overlook

The Allegheny National Forest encompasses more than 513,000
acres in Elk, Forest, McKean, and Warren Counties. This
enormous area and its overlooks constitute part of the High
Plateau Section in Pennsylvania's Appalachian Plateaus province.
The High Plateau Section—one of five divisions in the
province—includes most of Elk, Forest, Venango, and Warren
Counties as well as most of the Allegheny National Forest. Large
flat or rounded upland areas and deep valleys characterize this
area. Elevations range from about 1,000 feet to some 2,500 feet
above sea level. Jakes Rocks Overlook, for example, is 2,000 feet
above sea level and 700 feet above the Allegheny Reservoir; Rimrock Overlook is 2,020 feet above sea level and 700 feet above the
reservoir. The Tidioute Overlook is 1,540 feet above sea level and
440 feet above the Allegheny River.

The river between Kinzua Dam and Emlenton, a distance of
some 107 miles, is the Middle Allegheny River Water Trail—
a partnership among the Pennsylvania Fish and Boat Commission,
Pennsylvania Department of Conservation and Natural Resources,
USDA Forest Service, Allegheny National Forest, Oil Heritage
Region, and Venango Museum of Art, Science, and Industry.
Water trails were first proposed by the Pennsylvania Fish and Boat
Commission to provide information on access, to promote day use,
camping, and boating, and to encourage resource stewardship.
(For details on Pennsylvania water trails, water trail partnerships,
and current water trail maps, visit the Pennsylvania Fish and Boat
Commission's Web site, www.fish.state.pa.us.)

Three sections of the Allegheny River (a total distance of 86.6
miles) between Kinzua Dam and Emlenton were designated part
of the National Wild and Scenic Rivers System. The Clarion
River, which forms part of the Allegheny National Forest's southern border, was also designated a national Wild and Scenic River
from near Ridgway to Piney Dam's backwaters, a distance of
some 52 miles. (For more on the Clarion River, see Chap. 4.)

River view at Tidioute Overlook.

Tidioute Overlook

Tidioute Overlook actually comprises two overlooks connected by a trail—the Town Overlook and the River Overlook. From the Town Overlook, the Allegheny River and the town of Tidioute are visible. There are two benches and a picnic table. The view at the Town Overlook is north-northwest from 300 degrees west-northwest to about 45 degrees northeast.

At the River Overlook, a wayside exhibit describes the Allegheny River Islands Wilderness. Between Buckaloons and Tionesta are seven islands that Congress designated part of the National Wilderness Preservation System, a program designed to save the remaining parts of rare riverine forests. The 1984 designation created the Allegheny River Islands Wilderness. At 368 acres, the islands constitute one of the Wilderness System's smallest components. The seven Wilderness Islands are managed by the USDA Forest Service, Allegheny National Forest. One of the islands—Courson Island—is visible from the River Overlook; the overlook's view is east-northeast from about 0 degrees north to about 90 degrees east.

Jakes Rocks.

Jakes Rocks

Jakes Rocks stands about 700 feet above the reservoir. This massive form is composed mainly of conglomerate, a hard rock that resists erosion more than the surrounding rocks. The view is mainly north from about 300 degrees west-northwest to about 60 degrees east-northeast. Visible to the north on the reservoir's eastern side is its Kinzua Creek arm; the next inlet on the eastern side is Sugar Bay. Visits here during the second or third week of

Northwest view from Rimrock Overlook.

October often provide a view of magnificent fall color. Jakes
Rocks is also what geologists call a "rock city." (For more on rock
cities, see the description of Beartown Rocks Vista in Chap. 5.)

Walk west along the trail to another formal overlook offering
views of Kinzua Dam. (You can also reach this overlook by
following the trail at the south end of the parking lot near the
rest rooms.) The view is mainly west-southwest from about 180
degrees south to about 270 degrees west. Continue south on the
trail to reach more informal overlooks.

On the exit road, there are two more parking areas with
formal overlooks from which you can see Kinzua Dam. Each of
these overlooks has a parking lot with a stone fence. The second
(more southerly) overlook provides an excellent view of Kinzua
Dam, the Allegheny Reservoir, the Allegheny River, the Kinzua
tailwater boat access, and the Allegheny National Fish Hatchery.
These panoramas are extraordinary in the fall.

Rimrock Overlook

Rimrock Overlook is another rock city. The view at Rimrock is
westerly, over Kinzua Bay, from about 210 degrees south-

southwest to about 330 degrees north-northwest. On the other side of Kinzua Creek, the mouth of Dewdrop Run is visible.

Rimrock Overlook is a gigantic rock with a formal overlook about 50 yards long built on top. Like Jakes Rocks, it is composed of conglomerate. A narrow, catacomb-like stairway leads through a fracture in the rock to its base, where there are more trails and areas to explore.

OPPORTUNITIES: Auto touring, boating and canoeing (seven accesses), camping [$] (eleven campgrounds ranging from highly developed sites to remote areas with no facilities), fishing (Allegheny Reservoir, Allegheny River, East Branch Lake, Tionesta Lake) and ice fishing (Allegheny Reservoir with safe ice), hiking and backpacking [$] (twelve trails over 185 miles), horseback riding, hunting, photography, cross-country skiing (eight trails over 54 miles), snowmobiling, and wildlife-watching. Boat launching [$], five boat access campgrounds, National Scenic Areas (Hearts Content Scenic Area, Tionesta Scenic Area, and Tionesta Research Natural Area), off-road vehicle trails (four trails over 106 trail miles), and wilderness areas, including Hickory Creek Wilderness (8,337 acres) and Allegheny Islands Wilderness (368 acres), are also available.

Opportunities in the Allegheny National Forest can be almost overwhelming. To make the most of your visit, stop at the Bradford Ranger District Office, located at the intersection of PA Routes 59 and 321 (814-362-4613), or the Marienville Ranger District Office, located on PA Route 66 in Marienville (814-927-6628). Both offices have water and rest rooms in addition to free pamphlets, items for sale, and other informational brochures.

ADMINISTRATION AND AMENITIES: Drinking water and rest rooms are available at Jakes Rocks. Rimrock Overlook has rest rooms. Tidioute Overlook has rest rooms with access for people with disabilities. Day-use areas are open from dawn to dusk. The gate at Rimrock Overlook is closed from December 14 to Memorial Day because the access road is heavily used for cross-country skiing.

DIRECTIONS: To reach Rimrock Overlook: From PA Route 59 a few miles east of Kinzua Dam, turn south onto Forest Road 454 (at the sign for Rimrock Overlook) and drive about 2.3 miles to the large parking area for Rimrock. From the parking lot, take the path to the overlook. The leisurely walk takes three minutes, and the paved path has steps for negotiating the steeper areas.

To reach Jakes Rocks: From PA Route 59 a few miles east of Kinzua Dam, turn south onto Longhouse Road (National Forest Scenic Byway, Forest Road 262). After 1.3 miles, turn south onto Forest Road 492 at the sign for Jakes Rocks and Rimrock Overlooks. After 1.1 miles, you arrive at a T, where you turn right (northwest) and follow the sign to Jakes Rocks. Bear right in 0.6 mile and follow signs to the overlook and a large parking lot with rest rooms. Park at the north end of the parking lot and take the trail north into the woods. The walk to Jakes Rocks is about five leisurely minutes over a blacktop path.

To reach the Tidioute Town and River Overlooks: From U.S. Route 62 at Tidioute, turn easterly onto PA Route 337 and follow the signs to the overlook. After 1.2 miles, turn north at the sign for the Allegheny National Forest Picnic Ground Overlook and drive into the parking lot. The Town Overlook is on the left; the River Overlook is on the right. The trail to the Town Overlook is slightly uphill and flat, and the walk takes about three minutes. The River Overlook is about 100 yards from the parking lot on a level trail.

FOR MORE INFORMATION: Contact Allegheny National Forest, 222 Liberty Street, PO Box 847, Warren, PA 16365 (814-723-5150 or 814-726-2710 [TTY]), or visit its Web site at www.fs.fed.us/r9/allegheny.

NEARBY OVERLOOKS: Kinzua Bridge State Park (McKean County); Seneca Point Overlook (Clarion County); Beartown Rocks Vista (Jefferson County); and Elk State Forest overlooks and State Game Lands #311 elk-viewing sites (Cameron, Potter, and Elk Counties).

OTHER NEARBY OPPORTUNITIES

Chapman State Park (Warren County). Activities include bicycling, boating (with electric motors only), tent and trailer camping [$], organized group tent and trailer camping [$], fishing for trout and other species, ice fishing, hiking on 13 trail miles with trailhead, hunting, ice skating, picnicking, cross-country skiing, sledding, and lake swimming. The park also offers environmental education, a food concession, pavilion rental [$], and a playfield.

Oil Creek State Park (Venango County). Activities include bicycling, tent and trailer camping [$], fishing for trout and other species, hiking on 52 trail miles with trailhead, hunting, picnicking, cross-country skiing, and wildlife-watching. The park also offers bicycle rental [$], environmental education, a food concession, a historical center, pavilion rental [$], a playfield, a playground, and a visitors center.

The Pennsylvania Fish and Boat Commission's *Tionesta Fish Culture Station* has a visitors center (814-755-3524), as does the *Linesville Fish Culture Station* in Crawford County (814-683-4451). The Pennsylvania Game Commission's *Pymatuning Wildlife Learning Center* offers programs and exhibits on wildlife and a Hunting Heritage Room (814-683-5545).

The *Pennsylvania Lumber Museum* is located on private property surrounded by Susquehannock State Forest at Galeton (Potter County). It focuses on the history and technology of Pennsylvania's lumber industries. Contact the museum (814-435-2652) or visit its Web site at www.lumbermuseum.org for details. The museum is administered by the Pennsylvania Historical and Museum Commission: for more information, visit the Commission's Web site at www.phmc.state.pa.us.

The *Kinzua Dam visitors center* is located on PA Route 59 at the dam. The center features displays, slide programs, and brochures that explain the purpose of the dam and power plant. Contact the visitors center (814-726-0661) or visit www.lrp.usace.army.mil/projects/kin.

The *Allegheny National Fish Hatchery* and its visitors center are located just west of Kinzua Dam on the north side of the Allegheny River. The hatchery is dedicated to restoring lake trout to the lower Great Lakes; it is open to the public between 9:00 A.M. and 3:00 P.M., and tours are available by calling the hatchery (814-726-0890). Visit http://northeast.fws.gov/pa/allegny.html for more information.

Erie National Wildlife Refuge (Crawford County). Activities include boating (in boats without motors), fishing, hiking, hunting, cross-country skiing, and wildlife-watching. It also offers boat launching and environmental education. Call the Refuge (814-789-3584) for complete information on regulations.

The *Drake Well Museum* in Titusville (Venango County) occupies 219 acres on which Edwin L. Drake began the modern oil industry: in 1859, he drilled the world's first oil well. The museum includes exhibits, demonstrations, and replicas of Drake's oil derrick and engine house as well as reproductions of other early oil-field machinery. For details, contact the Drake Well Museum (call 814-827-2797 or e-mail drakewell@ usachoice.net), or visit the museum's Web site at www.drakewell.org.

The *Clarion–Little Toby Creek Trail* (Elk and Jefferson Counties) is part of the Pennsylvania Rails-to-Trails program. The trail runs 23 miles from Ridgway to Brockway. For more information, contact Love's Canoe in Ridgway (814-776-6285).

The *Warren/North Warren Bike Trail* (Warren County) is also part of the Pennsylvania Rails-to-Trails Program. Two trail miles are currently active, with 3 more miles planned. For details, contact the Warren County Planning and Zoning Commission, 33 Hickory Street, Warren, PA 16365 (814-726-3861).

Appalachian Plateaus Province

The Appalachian Plateaus province is one of seven physiographic provinces—main areas of common geologic activity—in Pennsylvania. (Geologic events, of course, occur over billions of years, and not all parts of the state have experienced the same kinds of activity.) The Appalachian Plateaus province is Pennsylvania's largest physiographic province. It includes nearly half the state, embracing all of western Pennsylvania from the southern counties of Greene, Fayette, and Somerset northward to Erie and Warren Counties; to the east, it encompasses most of Elk, Clearfield, and Cambria Counties. Curving northeastward, it also extends through Sproul State Forest as well as Lycoming, Sullivan, and Wyoming Counties and into Pike and Wayne Counties.

Millions of years ago, this enormous region was a high, flat plateau. Waterways gradually eroded the relatively even land in the province, shaping its low valleys, clefts, gorges, winding waterway cuts, and other landscape features.

3

BRADYS BEND SCENIC OVERLOOK AND KENNERDELL OVERLOOK

These two overlooks are about 25 miles apart on the Allegheny River. Both overlooks are pull-offs with ample parking, and both views include bends in the Allegheny River. Geologists call these river turns "meanders"—bends, or turns, in flowing waterways.

Bradys Bend Scenic Overlook

Bradys Bend Scenic Overlook in Clarion County is a 75-yard area that includes the parking area and two observation decks. The view from the observation deck closest to the parking lot is obscured by vegetation, but the second observation deck offers a much nicer scene. A U.S. Geological Survey benchmark records Bradys Bend Scenic Overlook's elevation as 1,351 feet above sea level. The river is 840 feet above sea level, so the overlook stands about 510 feet above the river. The view is mainly north-north-west from about 285 degrees west-northwest to about 45 degrees northeast. Views up to about 6 miles are possible from this overlook. Bradys Bend is approximately 0.5 mile across at the neck and spans about 6 river miles curve to curve.

A few miles downriver, near Rimer, Lock and Dam No. 9 straddles the Allegheny River. This lock and dam forms a slack-water pool about 9 miles long that includes the portion of the Allegheny River visible from Bradys Bend Scenic Overlook. Lock and Dam No. 9 is the last upriver structure in a series of locks and dams creating slackwater pools on the Allegheny River. Without locks and dams, the river's natural course would include sections of both high water and low water. Low water limits river commerce, however: heavy boats carrying raw materials and finished products cannot pass through such sections. Some 160 years ago, engineers solved this problem by building a series of locks and dams that ensured navigable water almost year-round. In 1841, the Monongahela Navigation Company built Pittsburgh's first lock and dam in the downtown area. The Ohio River's first lock and dam was built in 1885, and the Allegheny River's first lock and dam was built in 1902 at Herr's Island.

Northwest view from Bradys Bend Scenic Overlook.

The lock-and-dam systems on Pittsburgh's rivers contributed much to the city's rapid and steady growth as a commercial center. Today, the twenty locks and dams on all three rivers still pass commercial craft as well as pleasure boats. All the locks and dams today are projects of the U.S. Army Corps of Engineers. The Allegheny River has eight lock-and-dam systems, the Monongahela has nine, and the Ohio, three. All are open to the public, but call ahead if you plan to visit.

Bradys Bend Scenic Overlook is also a hawk watch site—and is most active during the fall migration. Volunteers count the number of raptors (birds of prey) during the migration and report the findings to organizations and institutions, including Hawk Mountain Sanctuary, Cornell University, and the Hawk Migration Association of North America (HMANA). The information helps conserve and protect these species. For more on hawk watch sites, see the separate entries on Rothrock State Forest, Hawk Mountain Sanctuary, and Fort Washington State Park (Chaps. 20, 37, and 47).

Kennerdell Overlook

Kennerdell Overlook, a small roadside pull-off in Venango County, is located on the southwest-pointing neck of a river meander. The neck is about 1 mile wide, and the meander around Kennerdell includes some 4 river miles. The view, which is mainly to the north, runs from about 315 degrees northwest to about 45 degrees northeast. The overlook stands about 1,200 feet

Northerly view from Kennerdell Overlook.

above sea level and 300 feet above the Allegheny River. To the south is Kennerdell (and another river bend), and to the north, the river's course curves yet again. The overlook is near river mile 109, the distance to The Point in Pittsburgh—the confluence of the Monongahela and Allegheny Rivers, which together form the Ohio River. (The Point is river mile 0.) The finger of land visible on the other side of the river is part of the Allegheny River Tract of Clear Creek State Forest.

OPPORTUNITIES: Picnicking, sightseeing, visiting a historic site, and wildlife-watching.

ADMINISTRATION AND AMENITIES: Aside from a picnic table at Kennerdell Overlook, there are no services.

DIRECTIONS: From either direction on PA Route 68 in Clarion County, Bradys Bend Scenic Overlook is marked with small blue signs at 0.5 mile from the overlook. If you approach from East Brady, the overlook is 2.6 miles from the Allegheny River bridge. You can drive right up to and park at the precipice.

To reach the Kennerdell Overlook: From the Allegheny River bridge in Kennerdell, follow SR 3008 northeast up the mountain and drive 1.5 miles to the overlook. The overlook, located on the west side of the road, is unmarked.

FOR MORE INFORMATION: For Bradys Bend Scenic Overlook, contact PennDOT District 10, 2550 Oakland Avenue, Indiana, PA 15701 (724-357-2800). The Kennerdell Overlook is privately owned by Scott W. Schneider, Misty Ridge, PO Box 53, Kennerdell, PA 16374.

NEARBY OVERLOOKS: Seneca Point Overlook (Clarion County); Beartown Rocks Vista (Jefferson County).

OTHER NEARBY OPPORTUNITIES

Moraine State Park (Butler County). Activities include mountain biking, boating (with a 10hp limit), ice boating, organized group tent camping [$], fishing for warmwater species, ice fishing, hiking on 27 trail miles, horseback riding on 16 trail miles, hunting, picnicking, ice skating, cross-country skiing, sledding, snowmobiling on 20 trail miles with trailhead, lake swimming, and wildlife-watching. The park also offers bicycle rental [$], boat launching and mooring [$], modern cabin rental [$], environmental education, a food concession, pavilion rental [$], a playfield, and a playground.

Two Mile Run County Park (Venango County). Activities include mountain biking, boating (with electric motors only), tent and trailer camping [$], organized group tent camping [$], fishing for trout and other species, ice fishing, miniature golfing [$], hiking, horseback riding, hunting, picnicking, ice skating, cross-country skiing, sledding, stargazing, lake swimming, and wildlife-watching. The park also offers boat launching and mooring [$], boat rental [$], environmental education, a food concession, and pavilion rental [$]. Contact the park for more information (call 814-676-6116 or e-mail twomile@csonline.net), or visit its Web site at www.twomile.org.

Jennings Environmental Education Center in Slippery Rock features exhibits and year-round indoor and outdoor programs. For details, call 724-794-6011 or visit www.dcnr.state.pa.us/stateparks/parks/jenn.htm.

A few miles east of Kennerdell is *Rockland Furnace,* which is listed on the National Register of Historic Places. The furnace—a remnant of a stone blast furnace in an area where some thirty blast furnaces once operated—stands upstream of Shull Creek and dates from the early 1830s.

Kennerdell Tunnel, near Kennerdell, is a mile-long mountain cut that once let historic railroads pass around Kennerdell. Now it serves as a hiking trail. Bring a flashlight—the tunnel curves into darkness at both ends.

4

COOK FOREST STATE PARK

Seneca Point Overlook

Virgin trees that are nearly 200 feet tall, 3 feet in diameter, and 200 to 350 years old are main attractions at Cook Forest State Park. The park includes 6,668 acres on the Clarion River and straddles the border of Forest and Clarion Counties. One area of virgin hemlock and white pine in Cook Forest State Park is called Forest Cathedral, a registered National Natural Landmark. Large hemlocks— some of which are quite old—appear throughout the park. In fact, when you first take the dirt road that leads to Seneca Point (see the directions below), you drive through an old-growth hemlock forest, even though the area was selectively cut for hemlock and pine some 150 years ago. After driving a mile or so along this road, the forest abruptly changes to mixed hardwoods. The hardwoods mark the line where the cutting of the 1800s and early 1900s stopped—but they also mark the place where a severe fire burned the area in the late 1800s.

As you walk the trail to Seneca Point, notice the apparently randomly placed boulders strewn about the area. Nearer the overlook, the massive sandstone boulders become more plentiful, forming a rock city. (See the explanation of rock cities in the entry for Beartown Rocks Vista in Chap. 5.)

Notice the cuplike depressions and the pimplelike bumps in Seneca Point's sandstone boulders. The bumps are iron ore deposits. Some of the depressions are places where Native Americans mixed and ground food and other materials. Most of the carvings in Seneca Point's sandstone are the work of vandals, but some Native American carvings are visible.

The view at Seneca Point is mainly westerly, about 315 degrees northwest to about 180 degrees south, through the Clarion River Valley. Seneca Point is approximately 1,580 feet above sea level and some 400 feet above the Clarion River's elevation. Visible to the southwest on the river are Hemlock Island and the Gravel Lick Bridge. Much logging activity occurred in this area from the early 1800s to the early 1900s, and a sawmill stood at the confluence of the Clarion River and the stream that enters it from the north at Hemlock Island. An 1878 atlas of Pennsylvania

Westerly view of the Clarion River Valley from Seneca Point Overlook.

names this stream Alsbach Run (George Alsbach was one of the area's first settlers). Log rafts and flat-bottomed boats, which lumbermen built in this area, were used in the 1800s and early 1900s to ship lumber and other equipment. The last commercial raft reportedly floated the Clarion River between 1910 and 1915.

As you look westward through the Clarion River Valley, you will find that all the mountaintops are generally the same height—a characteristic of the Appalachian Plateaus province. The Clarion River has been designated both a national and state Wild and Scenic River. Wild and Scenic River status provides the

Forest Cathedral, Cook Forest State Park's stand of virgin hemlock.

river added protection against development, and it increases the opportunities for conservation and preservation.

Hiking is a major activity at Cook Forest State Park. (For details on hiking in the park and a description of the trails, contact the park office.) Be sure to walk to the Forest Cathedral. Overlooks aside, Forest Cathedral's virgin timber is one of Pennsylvania's most magnificent sights. Drive to the main picnic area and park at the Log Cabin Inn visitors center. Take the blue-blazed Longfellow Trail to the Forest Cathedral. The trail begins on the north side of the cabin and is smooth and groomed, but steep: do not venture here if you are not physically fit for such activity. The uphill walk to the first area of the Forest Cathedral takes about twelve minutes. Gaze at the huge hemlocks, and follow their lines skyward. Trails designated A, B, and C provide different routes through the Forest Cathedral.

Actor Gary Cooper became keenly interested in this area and its primeval forest after starring in Cecil B. DeMille's *Unconquered* (1947). Parts of Cook Forest State Park appear in the movie, including Seneca Point.

OPPORTUNITIES: Boating (canoes only), tent and trailer camping [$], organized group tent camping [$], fishing for trout and other species, hiking on 30 trail miles, horseback riding on 4.5 trail miles, hunting, picnicking, ice skating, cross-country skiing, sledding, snowmobiling on 20 trail miles, pool swimming [$], and wildlife-watching. Cabin rental [$], environmental education, a historical center, pavilion rental [$], a playfield, a playground, and a visitors center are also available.

ADMINISTRATION AND AMENITIES: The park hours are 8:00 A.M. to sunset. Water and rest rooms accessible to people with disabilities are available at the parking area, and the park office has flush toilets.

DIRECTIONS: From PA Route 36, about 1 mile west of Cooksburg, turn southwest onto Firetower Road, a one-lane improved dirt road. A brown sign at the intersection reads "Fire tower and Seneca Point, 1.5 miles." After 1.2 miles, pull into the parking lot on the left and park at the south end, near the rest rooms. Follow the sign and walk on the trail toward Seneca Point. About 150 yards from the parking lot, the trail splits: take the right fork to Seneca Point. It is a leisurely three-minute walk from the parking lot to the overlook.

FOR MORE INFORMATION: Contact Cook Forest State Park, PO Box 120, Cooksburg, PA 16217 (call 814-744-8407 or e-mail cookforest@dcnr.state.pa.us), or visit its Web site at www.dcnr.state.pa.us/stateparks/parks/cookforest.htm.

NEARBY OVERLOOKS: Beartown Rocks Vista (Jefferson County); Allegheny National Forest overlooks (Warren County); Kinzua Bridge State Park (McKean County); Elk State Forest overlooks and State Game Lands #311 elk-viewing sites (Cameron, Potter, and Elk Counties); and Bradys Bend Scenic Overlook (Clarion County).

OTHER NEARBY OPPORTUNITIES

Oil Creek State Park (Venango County). Activities include bicycling, tent and trailer camping [$], fishing for trout and other species, hiking on 52 trail miles with trailhead, hunting, picnicking, cross-country skiing, and wildlife-watching. The park also offers bicycle rental [$], environmental education, a food concession, a historical center, pavilion rental [$], a playfield, a playground, and a visitors center.

Two Mile Run County Park (Venango County). Activities include mountain biking, boating (with electric motors only), tent and trailer camping [$], organized group tent camping [$], fishing for trout and other species, ice fishing, miniature golfing [$], hiking, horseback riding, hunting, picnicking, sledding, ice skating, cross-country skiing, stargazing, lake swimming, and wildlife-watching. The park also offers boat launching and mooring [$], boat rental [$], environmental education, a food concession, and pavilion rental [$]. Contact the park (call 814-676-6116 or e-mail twomile@csonline.net), or visit its Web site at www.twomile.org.

The *Drake Well Museum* in Titusville (Venango County) occupies 219 acres on which Edwin L. Drake began the modern oil industry: in 1859, he drilled the world's first oil well. The museum includes exhibits, demonstrations, and replicas of Drake's oil derrick and engine house as well as reproductions of other early oil-field machinery. For details, contact the Drake Well Museum (call 814-827-2797 or e-mail drakewell@usachoice.net), or visit the museum's Web site at www.drakewell.org.

The *Clarion–Little Toby Creek Trail* (Elk and Jefferson Counties) is part of the Pennsylvania Rails-to-Trails program. The trail runs 23 miles from Ridgway to Brockway. For more information, contact Love's Canoe in Ridgway (814-776-6285).

5

CLEAR CREEK STATE FOREST

Beartown Rocks Vista

Clear Creek State Forest encompasses three tracts in Jefferson, Venango, and Forest Counties that total more than 13,200 acres. At more than 9,000 acres, the Jefferson County tract is the largest—and it includes the Beartown Rocks Vista.

Beartown Rocks is what geologists call a rock city. Rock cities and similar structures can be found in northwest Pennsylvania and southwest New York. These curious formations and their overlooks also appear at Seneca Point in Cook Forest State Park and at Rimrock Overlook and Jakes Rocks in the Allegheny National Forest.

A layer of hard rocks sometimes caps a ridge top. These hard rocks are called caprock—and they resist erosion. At Beartown Rocks, sandstone and conglomerate form the caprock. When caprock is exposed on a mountaintop above rocks that erode more quickly, the harder rock layer soon hangs over the faster-eroding, underlying soft rocks. Widely spaced fractures in the caprock, called joints, enlarge over time and create huge blocks, and the caprock breaks into massive cubelike and rectangular chunks. These sometimes ordered, sometimes randomly placed formations resemble city blocks and buildings with "streets," crevices, and tunnel-like passageways caused by further erosion, frost heave, and "root pry."

Blocks may eventually move far from the source, so huge rock chunks may appear to be oddly placed away from the main group. You can see this kind of distant block placement at Seneca Point Overlook, in the area around Beartown Rocks, and throughout the forest near Rimrock and Jakes Rocks Overlooks.

The house-sized rocks are a natural playground for children of all ages, who climb on the rocks and wander through the crevices. Notice the trees that seem to grow right out of the rocks; the roots look like gnarled arms and hands with fingers that caress the rock formations. For this reason, Beartown Rocks has an eerie appearance. Root pry—the tree roots growing in the rock fractures—actually helps rock cities form. Along with the freezing and thawing of water in the fractures, tree roots separate the hard rocks into the large "city blocks" of a rock city.

Northwest view from Beartown Rocks Vista.

The view at Beartown Rocks is mainly northwest, about 270 degrees west to about 0 degrees north. The vista is about 1,910 feet above sea level and some 300 feet or so above the lowest terrain to the northwest. The Clear Creek watershed, a tributary of the Clarion River, and the Clarion River Valley are visible, as is Marienville at a distance of some 11 miles to the north.

OPPORTUNITIES: Boating, fishing, hiking, hunting, cross-country skiing on 5 trail miles, and wildlife-watching.

Tree roots seem to embrace the rock formations, giving Beartown Rocks an enchanted appearance.

ADMINISTRATION AND AMENITIES: No services at Beartown Rocks Vista; water and pit toilets are available in nearby Clear Creek State Park. Follow Corbett Road north to the park office.

DIRECTIONS: From Sigel, turn easterly onto PA Route 949 and drive 1.1 miles. Then turn right (easterly) onto Spring Creek Road. After another 1.1 miles, bear left at the fork in the road, continuing on Spring Creek Road for 0.8 mile. Turn left (north) onto Corbett Road; after driving another 0.3 mile, turn left (west) at the sign for Beartown Rocks. The parking lot appears after 0.2 mile. From the parking lot, the vista is a 100-yard walk up a steep, rocky path.

FOR MORE INFORMATION: Contact Clear Creek State Forest, Bureau of Forestry, Forest District #8, 158 South Second Avenue, Clarion, PA 16214-1904 (call 814-226-1901 or e-mail fd08@dcnr.state.pa.us), or visit its Web site at www.dcnr.state.pa.us/forestry/stateforests/forests/clearcreek/clearcreek.htm.

NEARBY OVERLOOKS: Seneca Point (Clarion County); Bradys Bend Scenic Overlook (Clarion County); Allegheny National Forest overlooks (Warren County); Kinzua Bridge State Park (McKean County); and Elk State Forest overlooks and State Game Lands #311 elk-viewing sites (Cameron, Potter, and Elk Counties).

OTHER NEARBY OPPORTUNITIES

Clear Creek State Park, near Sigel (Jefferson County). Activities include tent and trailer camping [$], canoeing, fishing for trout and other species, hiking on 16 trail miles, hunting, picnicking, ice skating, cross-country skiing, sledding, creek swimming, and wildlife-watching. The park also offers rustic cabin rental [$], pavilion rental [$], and playfield and playground facilities.

Cook Forest State Park. (See Chap. 4.)

Two Mile Run County Park (Venango County). Activities include mountain biking, boating (with electric motors only), tent and trailer camping [$], organized group tent camping [$], fishing for trout and other species, ice fishing, miniature golfing [$], hiking, horseback riding, hunting, picnicking, ice skating, cross-country skiing, sledding, stargazing, lake swimming, and wildlife-watching. The park also offers boat launching and mooring [$], boat rental [$], environmental education, a food concession, and pavilion rental [$]. Contact the park (call 814-676-6116 or e-mail twomile@csonline.net), or visit its Web site at www.twomile.org.

The *Drake Well Museum* in Titusville (Venango County) occupies 219 acres on which Edwin L. Drake began the modern oil industry: in 1859, he drilled the world's first oil well. The museum includes exhibits, demonstrations, and replicas of Drake's oil derrick and engine house as well as reproductions of other early oil-field machinery. For details, contact the Drake Well Museum (call 814-827-2797 or e-mail drakewell@usachoice.net), or visit the museum's Web site at www.drakewell.org.

The *Clarion–Little Toby Creek Trail* (Elk and Jefferson Counties) is part of the Pennsylvania Rails-to-Trails program. The trail runs 23 miles from Ridgway to Brockway. For more information, contact Love's Canoe in Ridgway (814-776-6285).

6

KINZUA BRIDGE STATE PARK

Kinzua Bridge was built in the late nineteenth century to transport coal, timber, and oil by rail from western Pennsylvania over Kinzua Gorge and into New York markets. For the New York, Lake Erie, and Western Railroad and Coal Company, the alternative to building the bridge across the gorge was to construct 8 extra miles of track. General Thomas L. Kane chose to build the bridge instead, and in 1882, a forty-man workforce erected the bridge—in only ninety-four days! At 301 feet high, Kinzua Bridge was then the world's highest railroad bridge; the viaduct is 2,053 feet long. It was rebuilt in 1900 to support heavier trains and bigger loads. It remains America's second-highest railroad bridge and the world's fourth highest. The last commercial train trip over the bridge was in 1959; in 1963, Governor William B. Scranton signed legislation that created Kinzua Bridge State Park. Kinzua Bridge was named to the National Register of Historic Places, and in 1982, it became a National Historic Civil Engineering Landmark.

In 1987, train traffic began again—this time for tourists. The Knox & Kane Railroad operates tourist train trips from June through October. Round-trips are available from Marienville and from Kane (96 and 32 miles to Kinzua Bridge, respectively). On both routes, the train crosses Kinzua Bridge and turns around, offering passengers magnificent views of the Allegheny National Forest's mountains and valleys. (For details and ticket information, contact the Knox & Kane Railroad at PO Box 422, Marienville, PA 16239, or call 814-927-6621.)

The Kinzua Bridge overlook, a formal decked area, provides a wonderful view of the viaduct. Seeing the train crossing the bridge transports you back one hundred years. This overlook's narrow view is mainly north-northwest from about 315 degrees northwest to about 30 degrees north-northeast.

For an even more exciting view, cross the bridge by way of planked walkways (with sturdy railings) on either side of the track. From the middle of the bridge you can take in the Kinzua Gorge in both directions; landmarks are visible for some 20 miles. Study the sea of green below to see Kinzua Creek, which slowly created

The train crossing Kinzua Bridge transports viewers back a century.

the gorge. During the summer of 2002, Department of Conservation and Natural Resources structural studies of the Kinzua Bridge revealed deterioration and rusting of the bridge's steel understructure. For this reason, the bridge is currently closed to pedestrian and train traffic, and walking under the bridge is banned. Kinzua Bridge State Park is still open, and visitors can still view the bridge and Kinzua Gorge from the observation deck. For updates, contact the state park (contact information appears below).

Wayside exhibits in a kiosk between the parking area and the overlook include "A Better Bridge," "Bridging the Gap," and "Resources and Railroads," all of which explain the bridge's history, purpose, and construction. Near the kiosk, Kinzua Concessions sells snacks in an old railroad car.

OPPORTUNITIES: Organized group tent camping [$], fishing for trout, hiking on 1 trail mile, hunting, picnicking, and wildlife-watching. Pavilion rental [$] is also available.

ADMINISTRATION AND AMENITIES: Water and rest rooms are adjacent to the parking lot. The park closes at sunset.

DIRECTIONS: On U.S. Route 6 in the borough of Mt. Jewett, turn north onto SR 3011. The turn is marked from both directions with signs to Kinzua Bridge State Park. After driving 3.3 miles, turn left at the state park entrance, and drive 0.6 mile to the parking lot. Reaching the overlook requires a leisurely walk of about three minutes on a blacktop path.

FOR MORE INFORMATION: Contact Kinzua Bridge State Park c/o Bendigo State Park, PO Box A, Johnsonburg, PA 15845 (call 814-965-2646 or e-mail bendigosp@state.pa.us), or visit its Web site at www.dcnr.state.pa.us/stateparks/parks/k-bridge.htm.

NEARBY OVERLOOKS: Allegheny National Forest overlooks (Warren County); Elk State Forest overlooks and State Game Lands #311 elk-viewing sites (Cameron, Potter, and Elk Counties); Susquehannock State Forest overlooks (Potter County); Sproul State Forest overlooks (Clinton County); Seneca Point (Clarion County); and Beartown Rocks Vista (Jefferson County).

OTHER NEARBY OPPORTUNITIES

Elk State Park, near Rasselas (Elk and McKean Counties). Activities include boating (with unlimited horsepower), ice boating, fishing for trout and other species, ice fishing, hunting, picnicking, ice skating, and water skiing. The park also offers boat launching and environmental education.

Sizerville State Park, northeast of Emporium (Cameron and Potter Counties). Activities include tent and trailer camping [$], fishing for trout, hiking and backpacking on 5 trail miles with trailhead, hunting, picnicking, cross-country skiing, snowmobiling on 2 trail miles with trailhead, and pool swimming. The park also offers environmental education, a food concession, pavilion rental [$], playground facilities, and a visitors center.

The 5-mile *Kinzua Bridge Trail* (McKean County), with a trailhead at Kinzua Bridge State Park, is part of the Pennsylvania Rails-to-Trails program. For more information, contact Kinzua Bridge State Park.

Two Mile Run County Park (Venango County). Activities include mountain biking, boating (with electric motors only), tent and trailer camping [$], organized group tent camping [$], fishing for trout and other species, ice fishing, miniature golfing [$], hiking, horseback riding, hunting, picnicking, ice skating, cross-country skiing, sledding, stargazing, lake swimming, and wildlife-watching. The park also offers boat launching and mooring [$], boat rental [$], environmental education, a food

concession, and pavilion rental [$]. Contact the park
(call 814-676-6116 or e-mail twomile@csonline.net), or
visit its Web site at www.twomile.org.

In Crawford County, the Fish and Boat Commission's
Linesville Fish Culture Station has a visitors center
(814-683-4451), and the Pennsylvania Game Commission's *Pymatuning Wildlife Learning Center* offers programs
and exhibits on wildlife and a Hunting Heritage Room
(814-683-5545).

The *Drake Well Museum* in Titusville (Venango County)
occupies 219 acres on which Edwin L. Drake began the
modern oil industry: in 1859, he drilled the world's first
oil well. The museum includes exhibits, demonstrations,
and replicas of Drake's oil derrick and engine house as
well as reproductions of other early oil-field machinery.
For details, contact the Drake Well Museum (call
814-827-2797 or e-mail drakewell@usachoice.net), or
visit the museum's Web site at www.drakewell.org.

PITTSBURGH

Duquesne Incline, Monongahela Incline, and
Grandview Avenue Overlooks

In the 1800s, Pittsburgh's location—where the Allegheny and
Monongahela Rivers combine to form the Ohio River—was the
perfect place for the iron and steel industries to thrive and grow.
Pittsburgh's steel mills occupied the flat land on the riverbanks.
Along the water, factories appeared as products and raw materials
were transported mainly by river systems. Pig iron, coal, and
other raw materials arrived in Pittsburgh from places such as the
Great Lakes, Tennessee, and Kentucky, and products were
shipped by way of the rivers to markets in Chicago, Detroit, East
Coast cities, and the South.

Pittsburgh's iron and steel industries grew rapidly in the late
1800s and early 1900s. This swift expansion, a growing population of laborers, and Pittsburgh's hilly landscape left little room
for workers to live near the rivers and mills. Laborers had to live
farther away—on Pittsburgh's hilltops and beyond.

The inclined-plane passenger car, better known simply as an
"incline," was Pittsburgh's distinctive solution to its transportation problem. A passenger car—actually a cable car powered by
steam and pulled by cables—traveled up and down a hillside on
metal rails. Laborers could thus live even atop Mount Washington and get to work by way of the incline.

For one of the first times in American history, workers com-
muted by means other than walking. The Monongahela Incline,
built in 1870, was America's first inclined-plane passenger car.
The Monongahela Incline and the Duquesne Incline (the latter
dates from 1877) are America's oldest remaining inclines.
Between 1854 and 1901, Pittsburgh boasted nineteen inclines.
These passenger cars allowed suburbs to develop. Indeed, the
new America, an industrial nation of commuters that defines us
yet today, emerged in places like Pittsburgh and Johnstown with
their inclined-plane passenger cars.

Bridges, commuter trains, highways, and the automobile
made inclines obsolete. Today, most riders are tourists, not commuters. But the Monongahela and Duquesne Inclines were a

The Duquesne Incline's observation deck provides a wonderful view of Pittsburgh.

critical part of Pittsburgh's industrial expansion. They helped industries—and a nation—grow. They remain a source of pride and a symbol of home to residents of Pittsburgh and southwest Pennsylvania. Even now, they carry passengers to some of Pennsylvania's best overlook views.

The Duquesne Incline is 800 feet long with an elevation of 400 feet above the Ohio River and a mainly easterly view from 0 degrees north to about 165 degrees south-southeast. Clearly visible are the Ohio River, the old Three Rivers Stadium, Heinz Field, the Allegheny River, the Fort Pitt Bridge, the Pittsburgh Plate Glass Building, Point State Park, and the Monongahela River. Visible on the Ohio River is the Carnegie Science Center, with a submarine—the USS *Requin,* a Center attraction—docked in front. The Duquesne Incline also has a wonderful (if modest) historic exhibit with archival photographs, newspaper clippings, and a small souvenir shop.

The Monongahela Incline is 635 feet long with an elevation at the top of about 367 feet above the Monongahela River. The view is mainly northeast from 315 degrees northwest to about 120 degrees east-southeast.

Between McArdle Roadway and the Monongahela Incline, a stroll of about 0.5 mile, are four observation decks with views similar to those at the Monongahela Incline. The decks, built in

The Monongahela Incline is 635 feet long with an elevation of 367 feet.

the 1960s, provide wonderful views of Pittsburgh and the Monongahela River. The Grandview Avenue observation decks are about 1,140 feet above sea level and some 430 feet above the Monongahela River.

OPPORTUNITIES: Hiking (walking along Grandview Avenue), sightseeing, and visiting historic sites.

ADMINISTRATION AND AMENITIES: Riding the inclines requires a small fee. No facilities at the inclines. The observation deck at the Duquesne Incline has coin-operated binoculars. Call or check the Web sites below for the current operational hours.

DIRECTIONS: To reach the Duquesne Incline: Cross the Mononga-hela River on the Liberty Bridge. Just before you reach the tun-nel, turn right onto McArdle Roadway (do not enter the tunnel). After driving uphill about 0.8 mile, you reach Grandview Avenue. Turn right, and follow the signs for the incline.

To reach the Grandview Avenue observation decks and the Monongahela Incline: From the intersection of McArdle Roadway and Grandview Avenue, turn left. As soon as you turn left onto Grandview Avenue, you can stroll on the sidewalk along the 0.5 mile between McArdle Roadway and the Monon-gahela Incline. Take in the views along Grandview Avenue, and stop at the four observation decks. Grandview Avenue and some intersecting streets allow limited street parking, some of which is metered.

Four decks along Grandview Avenue offer ample room to view the city.

FOR MORE INFORMATION: Contact the Duquesne Incline, 1220 Grandview Avenue, Pittsburgh, PA 15211-1204 (call 412-381-1665 or e-mail cablecar@incline.cc), or visit www.incline.cc and http://trfn.clpgh.org/incline for details. For information about the Monongahela Incline, contact the Port Authority of Allegheny County (412-442-2000) or visit www.portauthority.org/ride/incline.asp.

NEARBY OVERLOOKS: Ohiopyle State Park overlooks (Fayette County); Mt. Davis (Somerset County); and Bradys Bend Scenic Overlook (Clarion County).

OTHER NEARBY OPPORTUNITIES

Keystone State Park (Westmoreland County). Activities include boating (with electric motors only), tent and trailer camping [$], fishing for warm-water species, ice fishing, hiking on 5 trail miles, hunting, picnicking, ice skating, cross-country skiing, sledding, lake swimming, and wildlife-watching. The park also offers boat launching and mooring [$], modern cabin rental [$], environmental education, a food concession, pavilion rental [$], a playfield, and a visitors center.

Raccoon Creek State Park (Beaver County). Activities include boating (with electric motors only), tent and trailer camping [$], organized group tent and trailer camping [$], fishing for trout and other species, ice fishing, hiking on 13 trail miles, horseback riding on 10 trail miles, hunting, picnicking, ice skating, cross-country skiing, sledding, snowmobiling on 8 trail miles, lake swimming, and wildlife-watching. The park also offers boat launching and mooring [$], boat rental [$], modern cabin rental [$], environmental education, a food concession, a historical center, pavilion rental [$], a playfield, a playground, a visitors center, and a wildflower reserve.

Jennings Environmental Education Center in Slippery Rock features exhibits and year-round indoor and outdoor programs. For details, call 724-794-6011 or visit www.dcnr.state.pa.us/stateparks/parks/jenn.htm.

The *Allegheny Trail Alliance* is part of the Pennsylvania Rails-to-Trails program. It consists of seven trail organizations that have combined their efforts to link Pittsburgh and Washington, D.C., in a motor-free connection. Some 150 miles of this connection will run from Point State Park in Pittsburgh to Cumberland, Maryland. The C&O Canal Towpath extends 185 miles from Cumberland to Washington. For more information, contact the Allegheny Trail Alliance, 419 College Avenue, Greensburg, PA 15601 (call 724-853-2453 or e-mail atamail@atatrail.org), or visit its Web site at www.atatrail.org.

For more information on *opportunities and attractions in Pittsburgh,* visit the Greater Pittsburgh Convention and Visitors Bureau's Web site at www.visitpittsburgh.com.

8

OHIOPYLE STATE PARK

The Falls Day-Use Area, Baughman Rocks, Tharp Knob,
Kentuck Overlook, and Sugarloaf Overlook

"Wild," "beautiful"—such adjectives aptly characterize Ohiopyle
State Park's more than 19,000 acres, mostly located in Fayette
County. The park includes some 14 miles of the Youghiogheny
River and Gorge, where the river knifes through Laurel Hill. The
"Yough" (rhymes with "sock") offers breathtaking scenes of the
area's rugged beauty and some of the best canoeing and kayaking
in the eastern United States. One could spend weeks at Ohiopyle
State Park in any season and still not participate in all the park's
opportunities. One could also shoot rolls and rolls of film and fail
to capture all the park's beauty. For these reasons, Ohiopyle State
Park is one of Pennsylvania's most frequently visited state parks;
it hosts more than two million visitors annually.

The four overlooks listed below represent only a few of the
vistas offered by the park. Hiking some of its 41 trail miles will
lead you to still others. The Falls Day-Use Area is the main park
area in Ohiopyle.

Baughman Rocks

Baughman Rocks is about 2,080 feet above sea level and some
700 feet above the Youghiogheny River. The stunning view at
Baughman Rocks is mainly easterly, about 45 degrees northeast
to about 165 degrees south-southeast, and it looks down the
Youghiogheny River Gorge where the river leaves Fayette County
and enters Somerset County.

Baughman Rocks is a rock city. (For an explanation of this geological feature, see the entry for Beartown Rocks Vista in Chap. 5.)

Kentuck Overlook

Kentuck Overlook's view is mainly south-southeast from
135 degrees southeast to 185 degrees south-southeast. This
overlook, which stands about 700 feet above the Youghiogheny
River, offers another sight of the Youghiogheny River Gorge.

The observation deck at The Falls.

Tharp Knob

This overlook is a cleared, grassy field with benches and shade trees. The wonderful view at Tharp Knob is mainly southeast, about 90 degrees east to 180 degrees south. Tharp Knob's elevation is also about 700 feet above the Youghiogheny River.

Sugarloaf Overlook

The view at the Sugarloaf Overlook parking area is westerly from about 345 degrees north-northwest to about 225 degrees southwest. The site stands approximately 2,760 feet above sea level and some 800 feet above the low points of the valley to the west. Sugarloaf Knob is off to the west, about 1.5 miles away. To the southwest is Laurel Hill; to the south and southeast, mountains border the Youghiogheny River Lake.

OPPORTUNITIES: Mountain biking, white-water boating, tent and trailer camping [$], organized group tent camping [$], fishing for trout and other species, hiking on 67 trail miles with trailhead, horseback riding on 12 trail miles, hunting, picnicking, cross-country skiing, sledding, snowmobiling on 19 trail miles with trailhead, and wildlife-watching. Bike rental [$], rustic cabin rental [$], environmental education, a food concession, pavilion rental [$], playfield and playground facilities, and a visitors center are also available.

Baughman Rocks.

ADMINISTRATION AND AMENITIES: Water fountains and flush toilets are available at The Falls Day-Use Area and throughout the park. Also at The Falls are a gift shop and a snack bar. Day-use areas are open from 8:00 A.M. to dusk.

DIRECTIONS: To reach Ohiopyle State Park: From PA Route 711 at Normalville, turn south onto PA Route 381. The Ohiopyle State Park entrance sign appears after about 9 miles. Follow PA

Route 381 south into the borough of Ohiopyle. The Falls Day-Use Area is on the right. Pull into the large paved parking lot.

To reach Baughman Rocks: Follow Sugarloaf Road (SR 2012) easterly about 2.1 miles from PA Route 381. Turn left into the parking area at the sign for the scenic view. Walk up a moderately steep 75-yard path to the railed overlook.

To reach Sugarloaf Overlook: From PA Route 381, turn east onto Sugarloaf Road (SR 2012) and follow it 5.1 miles to Firetower Road. Turn left (north) onto Firetower Road to Sugarloaf Overlook. Drive up the steep, single-lane, unimproved, very rutted dirt road for about 100 yards, and turn right into the parking area at the fork in the road.

To reach the Tharp Knob Overlook: From PA Route 381 just south of The Falls Day-Use Area, turn south onto Kentuck Road (SR 2019) and drive 1.2 miles to the Tharp Knob Picnic Area. From the parking lot, follow the blue-blazed Kentuck Trail about 200 yards—a two-minute walk—to the overlook.

To reach Kentuck Overlook: Continue northeast on Kentuck Road (SR 2019) about 1.1 miles to Holland Hill Road. Turn right onto Holland Hill Road and drive a few hundred yards to the overlook, which is a marked pull-off on the right side of the road.

FOR MORE INFORMATION: Contact Ohiopyle State Park, PO Box 105, Ohiopyle, PA 15470-0105 (call 724-329-8591 or e-mail ohiopylesp@state.pa.us), or visit its Web site at www.dcnr.state.pa.us/stateparks/parks/ohio.htm.

NEARBY OVERLOOKS: Mt. Davis (Somerset County); Pittsburgh overlooks (Allegheny County); and Johnstown Incline (Cambria County).

OTHER NEARBY OPPORTUNITIES

Laurel Mountain State Park, northwest of Somerset (Westmoreland and Somerset Counties). Activities include cross-country and downhill skiing.

Laurel Ridge State Park (Cambria, Fayette, Westmoreland, and Somerset Counties). Activities include organized group tent camping [$], trout fishing, hiking and backpacking [$] on 94 trail miles with trailhead, hunting, picnicking, and cross-country skiing [$] on 35 trail miles. The park also offers pavilion rental [$].

Laurel Summit State Park (Westmoreland County). Activities include picnicking, snowmobiling with trailhead, and cross-country skiing; the park also offers pavilion rental [$].

The Western Pennsylvania Conservancy's *Bear Run Nature Reserve* provides hiking and backpacking on 20 trail miles, tent camping, group tent camping, cross-country skiing, and wildlife-watching. It adjoins Ohiopyle State Park and Frank Lloyd Wright's Fallingwater. For information about Fallingwater and Bear Run Nature Reserve, contact the Conservancy (call 412-329-8501 or e-mail webmaster@paconserve.org), or visit its Web site at www.wpconline.org. Bear Run is part of the Pennsylvania Scenic Rivers System.

The *Allegheny Trail Alliance* is part of the Pennsylvania Rails-to-Trails program. It consists of seven trail organizations that have combined their efforts to link Pittsburgh and Washington, D.C., in a motor-free connection. Some 150 miles of this connection will run from Point State Park in Pittsburgh to Cumberland, Maryland. The C&O Canal Towpath extends 185 miles from Cumberland to Washington. For more information, contact the Allegheny Trail Alliance, 419 College Avenue, Greensburg, PA 15601 (call 724-853-2453 or e-mail atamail@atatrail.org), or visit its Web site at www.atatrail.org.

9

JOHNSTOWN INCLINED PLANE

I suppose that we have all known terror at one time or another—
perhaps by way of an accident, a near miss, or a tragedy, or by
having endured the events of September 11, 2001. Visitors to
Johnstown can easily conjure up a similar feeling and experience
an emotional connection with the citizens trapped at the bottom
of Yoder Hill during the Johnstown Flood. First, view Johnstown
from the Johnstown Inclined Plane observation deck, take in the
history and circumstances surrounding the flood, and then place
yourself at the bottom of the hill on the banks of the Stonycreek
River around 4:00 P.M. on May 31, 1889. Surely terror is exactly
what the flood victims felt that afternoon as a wall of water 30 to
60 feet high roared toward them from the Little Conemaugh
River Valley. The force was so great that the floodwaters allegedly
rolled halfway up Yoder Hill, the incline's mountain.

Johnstown's topography, like that of Pittsburgh, shaped its
history and industrial development. The city grew on a 2-mile-
wide floodplain where the Little Conemaugh River and
Stonycreek River join to form the Conemaugh River. The narrow
Conemaugh River Gap, which skirts Johnstown to the
northwest, drains the area. Steel mills occupied the flat land
along the riverbanks, but as this industry grew rapidly in the late
1800s, the incline allowed workers to live on the hillsides of
Westmont and commute to their jobs reasonably inexpensively
and quickly. (Westmont, Johnstown's suburb at the top of Yoder
Hill, is said to be one of America's first suburban communities.)

Though Pittsburgh's inclines were built initially for
transportation, the Johnstown Inclined Plane had a quite different and tragic origin. In the late nineteenth century, some 14
miles northwest of Johnstown, South Fork Dam held back the
waters of Lake Conemaugh, which was a remnant of the earlier
canal era and a sportsmen's haven. The lake's elevation was 450
feet higher than that of Johnstown. Heavy spring rains each year
during the late 1880s stirred up talk that sooner or later the
dam—neglected and in disrepair—would fail. On May 31,
1889, hours of heavy rain raised the lake's water level overnight

The observation deck at the Johnstown Inclined Plane.

by 2 feet. At 4:07 in the afternoon, South Fork Dam gave way, sending twenty million tons of water through the narrow Conemaugh Valley toward Johnstown. The wave that crashed onto Johnstown was some 30 to 40 feet high, and at times it rose to 60 feet high. Four square miles of the city were completely washed away. In only a few hours, more than 2,200 people lost their lives—and Johnstown's total population in 1889 was only 10,000. About 280 businesses were destroyed; property damage from the flood totaled some $17 million.

The Johnstown Incline was built the following year to save lives and prevent another disaster like the flood of 1889. The incline opened in June 1891. The lower entrance, an iron bridge with thick girders and stone abutments, crosses the Stonycreek River, and the upper entrance is at the top of Yoder Hill.

The incline runs a little more than 896 feet from top to bottom with a steep runway grade of 70.9 percent. The top of Yoder Hill is about 530 feet above the Stonycreek River. The incline was built with railway rails, train wheels, and other railroad parts. Two sets of tracks built into the hillside transported two cars, which were attached to steel cables and powered by an electric motor. Originally, the cars were specially built to provide a level ride for wagons and horses. Each car weighs 92 tons and is approximately 15 feet wide and nearly 34 feet long. Today, the

The Johnstown Inclined Plane viewed from the lower entrance.

cars move people, passenger cars, and trucks up and down the hillside. (The cars are the same as those used by the Allegheny Portage Railroad, which moved cargo boats over the Allegheny Mountains.)

On March 17, 1936, and on July 20, 1977, floodwaters again devastated the Conemaugh and Stonycreek Valleys. However, during both floods, the incline carried people and families—and even vehicles—to safety. The incline is credited with saving some 4,000 lives during the 1936 flood. In 1977, when flood-waters swept away roads and thwarted rescuers' efforts, the incline allowed workers to fix the damage and helped victims obtain provisions.

The top of Yoder Hill and the observation deck are some 1,693 feet above sea level. The view from the observation deck is easterly, about 0 degrees north to 150 degrees south-southeast. Directly below the incline is the Stonycreek River; visitors looking easterly from the observation deck through the valley will see the Little Conemaugh River. Just to the left below are a stadium and baseball field and a small "point" of land. That area is the confluence of the Stonycreek River and the Little Conemaugh River. (The stadium is where part of the movie *All the Right Moves* [1983], starring Tom Cruise, was filmed.) The stone bridge visible across the Stonycreek River on the far left dammed 30 acres of flood debris and left 4 square miles of Johnstown devastated in 1889. In Johnstown, the First Presbyterian Church—its architecture recalling castle turrets—is visible. Beyond the church is the University of Pittsburgh Medical Center complex. The steel mills in the center of the view and to the left are owned by Bethlehem Steel. To the far right, the first building above the treeline is the Johnstown War Memorial Hockey Arena; the movie *Slap Shot* (1977), with Paul Newman, was filmed there. The area below the incline is called the Conemaugh Valley. The Johnstown Flood Museum, in the former Carnegie Library, stands directly across the view near a green metal bridge over the Little Conemaugh River.

OPPORTUNITIES: Sightseeing, visiting historic sites, and wildlife-watching.

ADMINISTRATION AND AMENITIES: A small fee is required to ride the incline. The incline is open daily from 7:00 A.M. to 8:00 P.M. Call for current operating hours. Services are available at the concessions near the observation deck. The upper level has—along with the observation deck—coin-operated binoculars, benches, a restaurant, an ice cream shop, a visitors center, and an information and souvenir shop. At the observatory and restaurant you can see the motor room, which houses a massive array of gears and the motor that drives the incline. The Johnstown Inclined Plane is listed on the National Register of Historic Places, and in 1994, the American Society of Mechanical Engineers named it a Regional Historic Mechanical Engineering Landmark.

DIRECTIONS: The lower level of the Johnstown Inclined Plane can be reached by following PA Route 56 into Johnstown. The upper level is on Edgehill Drive in Westmont. From PA Route 271 in

Johnstown, follow Menoher Boulevard to Geneva Street. Turn right onto Millcreek Road, and then turn left onto Bucknell Street. Turn right onto Tioga Street, and then left onto Edgehill. The upper level has free street parking. The lower level has a metered parking lot.

FOR MORE INFORMATION: Contact The Johnstown Inclined Plane, Inc., 711 Edgehill Drive, Johnstown, PA 15905 (814-536-1816) or visit its Web site at www.inclinedplane.com.

NEARBY OVERLOOKS: Ohiopyle State Park overlooks (Fayette County); Blue Knob State Park overlooks (Bedford County); and Altoona-area overlooks (Blair County).

OTHER NEARBY OPPORTUNITIES

Keystone State Park (Westmoreland County). Activities include boating (with electric motors only), tent and trailer camping [$], fishing for warm-water species, ice fishing, hiking on 5 trail miles, hunting, picnicking, ice skating, cross-country skiing, sledding, lake swimming, and wildlife-watching. The park also offers boat launching and mooring [$], modern cabin rental [$], environmental education, a food concession, pavilion rental [$], a playfield, and a visitors center.

Laurel Mountain State Park, northwest of Somerset (Westmoreland and Somerset Counties). Activities include cross-country and downhill skiing.

Laurel Ridge State Park (Cambria, Fayette, Westmoreland, and Somerset Counties). Activities include organized group tent camping [$], trout fishing, hiking and backpacking [$] on 94 trail miles with trailhead, hunting, picnicking, and cross-country skiing [$] on 35 trail miles. The park also offers pavilion rental [$].

Laurel Summit State Park (Westmoreland County). Activities include picnicking, snowmobiling with trailhead, and cross-country skiing; the park also offers pavilion rental [$].

Yellow Creek State Park (Indiana County). Activities include boating (with a 10hp limit), ice boating, fishing for warm-water species, ice fishing, hiking on 5 trail miles, hunting, picnicking, ice skating, cross-country skiing, sledding, snowmobiling on 350 acres, lake swimming, and wildlife-watching. The park also offers boat launching and mooring [$], boat rental [$], a food concession, pavilion rental [$], a playfield, a playground, and a visitors center.

The *Johnstown Flood National Memorial* is located about 10 miles northeast of Johnstown. For more information, contact the Johnstown Flood National Memorial, 733 Lake Road, South Fork, PA 15956 (814-495-4643) or visit its Web site at www.nps.gov/jofl.

The *Johnstown Flood Museum's* twenty-six-minute documentary film won a 1989 Academy Award. The museum's multimedia exhibits provide a thorough review of the cause, the experience, and the aftermath of the flood. For details, contact the Johnstown Flood Museum, 304 Washington Street, Johnstown, PA 15901 (1-888-222-1889) or visit its Web site at www.jaha.org.

10

FORBES STATE FOREST

Mt. Davis and High Point Lake Vista

Forbes State Forest includes more than 50,000 acres in Fayette, Somerset, and Westmoreland Counties. The state forest has twenty separate areas, but most of the state forest land is located on Laurel Ridge.

Mt. Davis

Mt. Davis, the highest point in Pennsylvania at 3,213 feet, is located in the state forest's Negro Mountain Administrative Division in Somerset County. Even though Mt. Davis is Pennsylvania's highest point, it is the lowest high point in all the Appalachian Mountain states. (Pennsylvania's actual "highest point" is a U.S. Geological Survey marker placed atop a boulder close to the tower.) The observation tower offers a panoramic view of the surrounding mountaintops. Looking to the northeast from the observation tower, you can see an antenna array sticking up above the trees, about 1 mile away. To the southeast you can see two ridges: Meadow Mountain, about 8 miles away, and beyond and a bit more to the east, Savage Mountain, about 10.5 miles away. In the valley to the southeast you can see Salisbury, Pennsylvania, about 5.5 miles away.

Near the observation tower, wayside exhibits describe "Industry on Negro Mountain" (logging), "Tar Kiln" (a nearby site for pine tar extraction from pitch pine), "The Wild Child" (a local folktale), "Baughman Rocks" (about Henry Baughman), "Pennsylvania's Physiography," "The High Point," "Management of Pennsylvania's State Forest Lands," "Shrubs and Flowers," "Trees of the Area," and "Mt. Davis High Point Area."

The lowest point in the Mt. Davis Natural Area is more than 2,800 feet above sea level, and because of the area's height, it often receives harsh winds, cold temperatures, and ice storms. For this reason, the trees on the mountaintop are short, almost brush-like, and a bit gnarled, as if they were shrugging and crouching from the cold. Nevertheless, viewed from the observation tower, the trees still appear magnificent in the fall.

Pennsylvania's actual highest point is marked on a boulder.

High Point Lake Vista

The High Point Lake Vista was built as an Eagle Scout project in 1989 by Christopher Smith. The overlook is a formal wooden platform that has a picnic table and bench seating, and it is accessible to people with disabilities. It provides a wonderful view of High Point Lake and the surrounding countryside. The overlook is a peaceful, scenic spot for a picnic. The narrow view is westerly,

about 240 degrees west-southwest to about 315 degrees
northwest. To the north of High Point Lake, Glade Mountain is
visible; to the south, you can see Winding Ridge.

OPPORTUNITIES: Mountain biking, primitive camping [$], trout
fishing, hiking on 69 trail miles, horseback riding, hunting, picnicking in two designated areas, cross-country skiing on 40 trail
miles, snowmobiling on 78 trail miles, and wildlife-watching.

Forbes State Forest also boasts several natural areas. Mt. Davis
Natural Area encompasses 581 acres in Somerset County and
features Mt. Davis—Pennsylvania's highest point—as well as
concentric stone rings of geological interest, picnic areas, and
hiking trails. Roaring Run Natural Area covers more than 3,000
forest land acres near PA Route 31 (Westmoreland County).
Spruce Flats Wildlife Management Area, which comprises 305
acres near the Laurel Summit Picnic Area and the border between
Westmoreland and Somerset Counties, includes the 28-acre
Spruce Flats Bog, a wetland area.

ADMINISTRATION AND AMENITIES: Near Mt. Davis on SR 2004,
about 0.5 mile east of its intersection with South Wolf Rock
Road, the Mt. Davis Picnic Area has water and pit toilets.

DIRECTIONS: To reach Mt. Davis: From the west at Listonburg,
take SR 2004 east, following the signs to Mt. Davis (about 10
miles). Along the way, below State Game Lands #271, you will
find excellent southerly views of Winding Ridge, Packhorse
Mountain, and Negro Mountain, all of which straddle the Pennsylvania border with Maryland. In Forbes State Forest, at the sign
for Mt. Davis State Forest Monument and Natural Area and the
Highest Point in Pennsylvania, turn south onto South Wolf Rock
Road, a one-lane road that is paved but rutted. Follow the signs
about 0.7 mile to the Mt. Davis Observation Tower.

From the east and U.S. Business Route 219 in Meyersdale,
follow Broadway Street (which becomes SR 2004) westerly about
10 miles, and then turn south onto South Wolf Rock Road.
Drive 0.7 mile to the observation tower.

The observation tower and exhibits are about a 100-yard walk
from the parking lot on a blacktop road from which traffic is now
blocked.

To reach High Point Lake Vista: From the observation tower
turnoff on South Wolf Rock Road, follow South Wolf Rock Road
south 0.4 mile. The overlook will be on the right, with ample
off-road parking.

FOR MORE INFORMATION: Contact Forbes State Forest, Bureau of Forestry, Forest District #4, PO Box 519, Laughlintown, PA 15655 (call 724-238-1200 or e-mail fd04@dcnr.state.pa.us), or visit its Web site at www.dcnr.state.pa.us/forestry/stateforests/forests/forbes/forbes.htm.

NEARBY OVERLOOKS: Ohiopyle State Park overlooks (Fayette County); Blue Knob State Park overlooks (Bedford County); and Johnstown Incline (Cambria County).

OTHER NEARBY OPPORTUNITIES

Kooser State Park (Somerset County). Activities include tent and trailer camping [$], organized group tent camping [$], fishing for trout, hiking on 1 trail mile, picnicking, cross-country skiing, and creek swimming. The park also offers rustic cabin rental [$], environmental education, a food concession, pavilion rental [$], and playground facilities.

Laurel Hill State Park (Somerset County). Activities include boating (with electric motors only), tent and trailer camping [$], organized group tent camping [$], fishing for trout and other species, ice fishing, hiking on 12 trail miles, hunting, picnicking, ice skating, snowmobiling on 10 trail miles with trailhead, and lake swimming. The park also offers boat launching and mooring, boat rental [$], environmental education, a food concession, pavilion rental [$], and playfield and playground facilities.

Laurel Mountain State Park, northwest of Somerset (Westmoreland and Somerset Counties). Activities include cross-country and downhill skiing.

Laurel Ridge State Park (Cambria, Fayette, Westmoreland, and Somerset Counties). Activities include organized group tent camping [$], trout fishing, hiking and backpacking [$] on 94 trail miles with trailhead, hunting, picnicking, and cross-country skiing [$] on 35 trail miles. The park also offers pavilion rental [$].

Linn Run State Park, south of Ligonier (Westmoreland County). Activities include tent and trailer camping [$], hiking on 5 trail miles, picnicking, and snowmobile trailhead to Forbes State Forest trails. The park also offers rustic cabin rental [$], pavilion rental [$], and playground facilities.

Ohiopyle State Park (Fayette County). (See Chap. 8.)

The *Allegheny Trail Alliance* is part of the Pennsylvania Rails-to-Trails program. It consists of seven trail organizations that have combined their efforts to link Pittsburgh and Washington, D.C., in a motor-free connection. Some 150 miles of this connection will run from Point State Park in Pittsburgh to Cumberland, Maryland. The C&O Canal Towpath extends 185 miles from Cumberland to Washington. For more information, contact the Allegheny Trail Alliance, 419 College Avenue, Greensburg, PA 15601 (call 724-853-2453 or e-mail atamail@atatrail.org), or visit its Web site at www.atatrail.org.

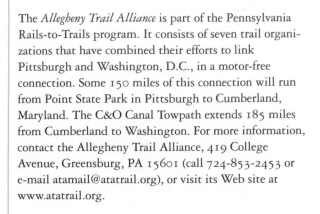

High Point Lake (Somerset County). Activities include boating (with electric motors only) and fishing for warm-water species; boat launching is also available. For details, visit the Pennsylvania Fish and Boat Commission's Web site at www.fish.state.pa.us.

11

ALTOONA-AREA OVERLOOKS

Horseshoe Curve National Historic Landmark and
Chimney Rocks Park

Horseshoe Curve National Historic Landmark

In today's world of computer-assisted design, engineers can build
almost anything digitally, transforming mountains and whole
landscapes with just a few keystrokes and the momentary
whirring of a hard drive. Then they can virtually explore their
creation from all sides—even inside and out. But in 1854, when
the Horseshoe Curve was built, every load of earth, every boulder,
every railroad tie, and every piece of track was either put in place
or carted away by hand. In this pre–Civil War period, no diesel-
powered trucks, tractors, end-loaders, bulldozers, or other earth-
moving equipment existed.

Such facts make this part of America's industrial heritage an
engineering marvel. Practically curving back onto itself, the
Horseshoe Curve was the first successful conquest by rail of the
Allegheny Mountains in America's westward expansion. What
makes the accomplishment even more amazing is that this
Norfolk-Southern main line is still a major east-west railroad
crossing of the steep Allegheny Mountains, with more than
fifty trains each day negotiating the Curve.

Pennsylvania Railroad civil engineer J. Edgar Thompson
designed Horseshoe Curve. He believed that a train could
traverse a mountain by climbing it gradually—and he created
Horseshoe Curve to do just this. The Curve is 1,800 feet across
and 2,375 feet long. The east end elevation is 1,594 feet; the
west end elevation is 1,716 feet. It rises 91 feet per mile.

The best part of Horseshoe Curve is that visitors can stand
only about 30 to 40 feet away from the trains as they thunder
by. Listen to the broadcast of the train operators as they reveal
their approach to the Curve. The UHF working channel is
broadcast over a loudspeaker at the track level so that visitors
can anticipate a train's approach and know the direction from
which it will arrive. A low rumble breaks the area's silence, and
its crescendo confirms the direction from which the train

At the Horseshoe Curve, visitors have a close-up view of the trains.

advances. As the train negotiates the Curve, the engineer blows the whistle. Train passengers and Curve visitors exchange waves, the engine roars, the wheels squeal, and the ground trembles. The train sounds fade. The radio again crackles as engineers and operators confirm their approach and departure from the area, and soon a low rumble once more prepares Curve visitors for the next train's arrival.

A small overlook area at track level offers an easterly view of the Altoona metropolitan area and the Altoona water supply reservoirs. The narrow easterly view is about 75 degrees east-northeast to 150 degrees east-southeast. The building at the Curve is now vacant, but it was a watchman's shanty and toolhouse built after 1900.

OPPORTUNITIES: Train-watching and picnicking. At the track level, there are benches, picnic tables, and four wayside exhibits. The exhibits explore the GP-9, one of the first diesel-electric motors; trackside buildings and wayside buildings; "Watching the Curve" facts and figures; and "Over the Hill: How Railroads Surmounted the Spine of the Alleghenies Between Altoona and Johnstown."

ADMINISTRATION AND AMENITIES: Entrance to the museum and track level requires a small fee. Closed January through March.

Summer hours (April through October) are 10:00 A.M. to 7:00 P.M., seven days a week; winter hours (November and December) are Tuesday through Sunday, 10:00 A.M. to 4:00 P.M. (closed Monday). Call for the latest operating schedule and information about special events. There are several services, including a visitors center, museum store, rest rooms, water, and snack bar. The museum exhibits show how the Curve was built, who built it, the land features the Curve overcame, and construction artifacts.

DIRECTIONS: From southwest Altoona, take Fortieth Street (SR 4008) northwesterly out of Altoona and follow the signs for the Horseshoe Curve National Historic Landmark. The road curves around three small reservoirs (Altoona's water supply). The visitors entrance to the landmark is on the right, about 4 miles from Altoona, just before you reach the one-lane tunnel.

Approaching from the west on U.S. Route 22, take the Gallitzin exit and follow the signs 7 miles to Horseshoe Curve.

FOR MORE INFORMATION: Contact the Horseshoe Curve National Historic Landmark, Railroaders Memorial Museum, 1300 Ninth Avenue, Altoona, PA 16602 (call 814-946-0834 or 1-888-425-8666 [toll-free], or e-mail rrcity@aol.com), or visit its Web site at www.railroadcity.com for details.

Chimney Rocks Park, Hollidaysburg

Chimney Rocks is the name of a sheer cliff just outside of Hollidaysburg (Blair County). On its ridge stand chimneylike limestone pillars. Near these monoliths, visitors can enjoy spectacular views of the borough of Hollidaysburg. The overlooks are in Chimney Rocks Park, which includes some 120 acres. The most prominent overlook is called the Lower Overlook—and in this case, "Lower" refers to a Hollidaysburg attorney, T. Dean Lower, who donated $125,000 to the borough of Hollidaysburg. The donation allowed the borough to match a Community Recreation Grant from the Pennsylvania Department of Conservation and Natural Resources to complete the park's development and construction of the pavilions, picnic areas, trails, and other facilities. The overlook is 1,300 feet above sea level and about 440 feet above Hollidaysburg, and it has a railing at the cliff's edge and a bench. The walk from the park's upper parking lot to the overlook is about 100 yards.

The breathtaking view, which is mainly to the northwest from 270 degrees west to about 15 degrees north-northeast, surveys Hollidaysburg; Altoona is visible to the north. Chimney Rocks also provides a magnificent view of the Allegheny Front—the dividing line between the Ridge and Valley physiographic province and the Appalachian Plateaus province. Blair County landmarks visible from Chimney Rocks include Canal Basin Park, the Blair County courthouse, Altoona Hospital, and the Hollidaysburg municipal building.

The park—the site of a former limestone quarry—has a 0.25-mile level hiking trail as well as another 0.25-mile rugged hiking trail that leads to the top of Chimney Rocks. This trail also leads to two overlooks that survey the main park area and provide views similar to those from the Lower Overlook. The park has a picnic pavilion and picnic tables. On the left side of the park entrance road, just before you reach the lower parking lot, note the remains of a stone furnace that was used as a kiln to convert the limestone to lime. The remains of a building foundation can also be seen: this building served as the main quarry office and weigh station. The borough of Hollidaysburg plans to restore this site.

OPPORTUNITIES: Hiking and picnicking; a playfield is also available.

ADMINISTRATION AND AMENITIES: Rest rooms are located at the upper parking lot. The park is open year-round from dawn to dusk.

DIRECTIONS: From U.S. Route 22 in Hollidaysburg, follow PA Route 36 south out of town. As you cross the railroad bridge, glance at the mountaintop just left of center and you will see the Chimney Rocks. Follow PA Route 36 a few hundred yards to the first left turn. A small blue sign directs you to turn left to Chimney Rocks Park. Follow the signs to the park. The park entrance is 0.2 mile farther on the left.

FOR MORE INFORMATION: Contact the Borough of Hollidaysburg, 401 Blair Street, Hollidaysburg, PA 16648 (814-695-7543) or visit its Web site at www.hollidaysburgpa.org.

NEARBY OVERLOOKS: Johnstown Incline (Cambria County); Ralph's Majestic Vista (Centre County); and Raystown Lake overlooks (Huntingdon County).

A view of Hollidaysburg from Chimney Rocks.

OTHER NEARBY OPPORTUNITIES

Canoe Creek State Park (Blair County). Activities include bicycling, boating (with electric motors only), ice boating, fishing for trout and other species, ice fishing, hiking on 8 trail miles, horseback riding on 5 trail miles, hunting, picnicking, ice skating, cross-country skiing, sledding, lake swimming, and wildlife-watching. The park also offers boat launching and mooring [$], boat rental [$], modern cabin rental [$], environmental education, a food concession, pavilion rental [$], a playfield, a playground, and a visitors center.

Yellow Creek State Park (Indiana County). Activities include boating (with a 10hp limit), ice boating, fishing for warm-water species, ice fishing, hiking on 5 trail miles, hunting, picnicking, ice skating, cross-country skiing, sledding, snowmobiling on 350 acres, lake swimming, and wildlife-watching. The park also offers boat launching and mooring [$], boat rental [$], a food concession, pavilion rental [$], a playfield, a playground, and a visitors center.

The *Lower Trail,* which extends over 11 miles in Blair and Huntingdon Counties, is part of the Pennsylvania Rails-to-Trails program. Trailheads are located at Alexandria, Williamsburg, Canoe Creek State Park, and Flowing Springs. For more information, contact Rails-to-Trails of Blair County, Inc., PO Box 592, Hollidays-burg, PA 16648 (814-695-8521).

State Game Lands #176, also known as The Barrens, is located west of State College (Centre County) and offers mountain biking, hiking, hunting, cross-country skiing, and wildlife-watching.

The *Allegheny Portage Railroad National Historic Site* (Cambria and Blair Counties). This part of America's industrial heritage predates the Horseshoe Curve, representing an earlier attempt to conquer the Allegheny Mountains. For more information, contact the Allegheny Portage Railroad National Historic Site, 110 Federal Park Road, Gallitzin, PA 16641 (call 814-886-6150 or e-mail alpo_visitor_center@nps.gov), or visit its Web site at www.nps.gov/alpo.

12

BLUE KNOB STATE PARK

Blue Knob and Willow Springs Picnic Area

Blue Knob State Park includes some 5,614 woodland acres in northwest Bedford County. The park takes its name from the 3,146-foot quartzite peak, Blue Knob, which is Pennsylvania's second-highest mountain. Mt. Davis, in Somerset County, is only 67 feet higher (see Chap. 10). The mountain occupies a spur of the Allegheny Front, with northerly views of the Allegheny Mountains and easterly views of Pennsylvania's Ridge and Valley province. The park offers year-round activities, from summertime mountain biking, backpacking, and swimming to snowmobiling, cross-country skiing, and downhill skiing.

Blue Knob

Blue Knob is unique among downhill ski areas because the lodge is at the top of the mountain, not at the bottom. For this reason, some people visit Blue Knob not for the skiing but just to enjoy the lodge and take in the views.

The magnificent view at the chairlifts is mainly easterly, o degrees north to about 135 degrees southeast. The chairlift area's elevation is some 1,400 feet above the low spots to the north. Looking due north (beyond the ski slopes), Round Knob, Schaefer Head, Cattle Knob, Ritchey Knob, and Pine Knob are visible. On the horizon, about 17 miles away to the north-northeast, is Brush Mountain. Looking easterly, visitors can also see Bunns Mountain and State Game Lands #67 on the horizon about 21 miles away. In front of Bunns Mountain is Martinsburg (12 miles away), and Curryville is visible just south (to the right) of Martinsburg. Sideling Hill, some 28 miles away, crosses the easterly horizon. Visible to the east-southeast, 6 miles away, are I-99 and Claysburg. Southeasterly, Kimber Mountain stands on the horizon, and just south (to the right) is Harbor Mountain. Both are about 20 miles away.

In clear conditions, the night views are magnificent: you can see the lights from Altoona, Hollidaysburg, Portage (10 miles), Johnstown (19 miles), and Windber (15 miles). To the south-southeast, the lights of Bedford shine from 18 miles away.

Blue Knob is Pennsylvania's second-highest mountain.

To the north and northwest is an excellent view of the Appalachian Plateaus province. The Allegheny Front, of which Blue Knob is a part, is visible to the north-northwest.

Willow Springs Picnic Area

The Willow Springs Picnic Area overlook is best viewed from the top of the loop road that encircles the picnic area. The overlook view is to the south, about 135 degrees southeast to about 225 degrees southwest. The picnic area's elevation is about 1,000 feet above the lowest spots to the south. Southwest on the horizon, about 19 miles away, is Kinton Knob, which looks a bit like a volcano. It is the beginning of Wills Mountain, which leads off to the southwest into Maryland. (Looking due south to the horizon, note the continuation of Wills Mountain.) Bedford is located to the east (left) of Kinton Knob, but the view from the picnic area does not include the city. To the southeast, the first hill—as yet unnamed—in the foreground beyond the picnic area obscures the village of Weyant. Due south, Fishertown is visible in the valley, about 12 miles away, and beyond Fishertown is Dry Ridge, about 21 miles away. To the south-southwest as far as the eye can see on a clear, bright day, the Cumberland Water Gap in Maryland is visible—a distance of about 50 miles.

OPPORTUNITIES: Backpacking on the 17-mile Lost Turkey Trail, mountain biking (on multi-use trails), camping [$], group camping [$], stream fishing for trout, hiking on 17 trail miles with more overlooks, picnicking, cross-country skiing, downhill skiing, snowmobiling (8 miles of roads and trails), pool swimming, and wildlife-watching. Environmental education programs (on summer weekends), pavilion rental [$], and playfield and playground facilities are also available.

Hiking is a major activity at Blue Knob State Park. For more information on hiking in the park and a description of the trails, contact the park office.

Skiing at Blue Knob is challenging. Blue Knob Recreation, Inc., leases the downhill ski area from the park. The vertical drop is Pennsylvania's highest—1,050 feet. Skiing is available day and night with four chairlifts and ample snowmaking equipment.

ADMINISTRATION AND AMENITIES: Some activities are seasonal and end with the summer. Rest rooms and water are available throughout the park. Willow Springs Picnic Area has benches, a pavilion that can be rented, a playfield, rest rooms, and water. Day-use areas are open from 8:00 A.M. to dusk.

DIRECTIONS: From PA Route 164 in the village of Blue Knob, turn south onto Blue Knob Road, following the signs to the state park. The state park entrance is about 4.3 miles farther. To reach Pennsylvania's second-highest point: At the main entrance (marked by the Blue Knob State Park sign), bear left at the fork in the road and follow the signs to the ski area. This road is Tower Road, but it is unmarked at the fork. The ski area entrance is 1 mile farther.

To reach the Willow Springs Picnic Area overlook and southern view: Backtrack from the ski area and turn sharply left at the main park entrance and sign. After about 3 miles, turn left (north) onto Whysong Road, pass the park office, and drive to the Willow Springs Picnic Area. After about 1.8 miles, the paved road becomes a single lane and circles the picnic area.

FOR MORE INFORMATION: Contact Blue Knob State Park, 124 Park Road, Imler, PA 16655-9207 (call 814-276-3576 or e-mail blueknob@dcnr.state.pa.us), or visit its Web site at www.dcnr.state.pa.us/stateparks/parks/b-knob.htm.

NEARBY OVERLOOKS: Raystown Lake overlooks (Huntingdon County); Altoona-area overlooks (Blair County); Johnstown Incline (Cambria County); and Buchanan State Forest overlooks (Fulton and Franklin Counties).

OTHER NEARBY OPPORTUNITIES

Canoe Creek State Park (Blair County). Activities include bicycling, boating (with electric motors only), ice boating, fishing for trout and other species, ice fishing, hiking on 8 trail miles, horseback riding on 5 trail miles, hunting, picnicking, ice skating, cross-country skiing, sledding, lake swimming, and wildlife-watching. The park also offers boat launching and mooring [$], boat rental [$], modern cabin rental [$], environmental education, a food concession, pavilion rental [$], a playfield, a playground, and a visitors center.

Shawnee State Park (Bedford County). Activities include mountain bicycling, boating (with electric motors only), ice boating, tent and trailer camping [$], organized group tent camping [$], fishing for warm-water species, ice fishing, hiking on 12 trail miles, hunting, picnicking, ice skating, cross-country skiing, sledding, snowmobiling on 12 trail miles, lake swimming, and wildlife-watching. The park also offers bicycle rental [$], boat launching and mooring [$], boat rental [$], environmental education, a food concession, pavilion rental [$], and playfield facilities.

Trough Creek State Park (Huntingdon County). Activities include tent and trailer camping [$], fishing for trout and other species, hiking on 6 trail miles, hunting, picnicking, snowmobile trailhead to Rothrock State Forest trails, and wildlife-watching. The park also offers modern cabin rental [$], environmental education, pavilion rental [$], and playfield facilities.

Warriors Path State Park (Bedford County). Activities include fishing for warm-water species, hiking on 3 trail miles, hunting, picnicking, and wildlife-watching. The park also offers boat launching, pavilion rental [$], and a playfield.

ELK STATE FOREST

State Game Lands #311 Elk-Viewing Sites and
Ridge Road Vistas

So, you have seen plenty of deer near your home, but never an
elk? Elk make deer look tiny, and you can view these magnificent
animals at some of the overlooks in Elk State Forest. Like moose
and white-tailed deer, elk belong to the deer family—but they
are considerably larger than the white-tailed deer commonly seen
in Pennsylvania. A bull elk can weigh nearly 1,000 pounds and
measure 5 feet high at the shoulder. Females can weigh up to
about 600 pounds. Everyone interested in wildlife-watching of
any kind should take advantage of an opportunity to view elk.

The eastern elk, from which the state forest takes its name,
was once found nearly everywhere in Pennsylvania. By the mid-
1800s, the eastern elk range included only a portion of Elk
County, and by 1867, elk had been extirpated in Pennsylvania
(the species did live elsewhere, however). The Pennsylvania Game
Commission attempted to restore elk in the state during the early
1900s by bringing in Rocky Mountain elk, a species closely
related to eastern elk, from South Dakota and Yellowstone
National Park. Since then, the Pennsylvania range of this noble
animal has increased. Currently, the elk range includes southeastern Elk County and southwestern Cameron County, and elk have
also been seen in the counties surrounding Elk and Cameron.
These animals are the descendants of the Rocky Mountain elk.

Elk State Forest encompasses some 200,000 acres in Elk and
Cameron Counties. When elk numbers dwindled in the 1800s,
Elk County and portions of Elk State Forest were their final
stronghold; for this reason, the county and state forest were
chosen as ideal places for elk reintroduction.

Visitors can observe today's thriving Pennsylvania elk
population mainly in the Benezette area eastward toward Hicks
Run (a tributary of Sinnemahoning Creek) along PA Route 555.
In addition to the PA Route 555 area, elk can be seen just about
anywhere on Winslow Hill Road at Benezette and in two
overlook elk-viewing areas on Winslow Hill.

Seeing elk "anywhere" means just that. Drive along PA

An elk-viewing area along Winslow Hill Road.

Route 555 and Winslow Hill Road slowly and watch for elk along wood lines, in open fields, along and on the roads, and in yards. Dawn and dusk—the first and last two hours of daylight—are the best times to view elk, especially during the rut, or mating season, which occurs in September and October. You might happen to get a close-up view of an elk, but people most often see them from a distance. If you wish to photograph them, consider using a telephoto lens. Weekdays during September and October offer less-crowded conditions.

State Game Lands #311

State Game Lands #311 includes two formal elk-viewing sites. The first is about 1 mile from Benezette on Winslow Hill Road. The second is 1.3 miles farther on Winslow Hill Road. The first elk-viewing area, a recent Game Commission acquisition, is called the Gilbert Tract, and it consists of a wood-railed 100-yard viewing area in the tract's 197 acres. The view is westerly, about 225 degrees southwest to about 315 degrees northwest, and the area includes a large parking lot.

The second viewing area, Dents Run, also offers an ample parking lot, along with an amphitheater and wayside exhibits on

Logue Run Vista on Ridge Road.

elk habitat and behavior. The observation area, marked with a stone fence about 30 yards long, represents a cooperative venture among the Pennsylvania Game Commission, Rocky Mountain Elk Foundation, Pennsylvania Wildlife Habitat Unlimited, and Pennsylvania Conservation Corps.

Ridge Road Vistas

Three of the best vistas in Elk State Forest are within a few miles of one another on Ridge Road, which follows a north-south ridge. The east slope drainages flow into First Fork Sinnemahoning Creek, and the west slope drainages flow into Driftwood Branch Sinnemahoning Creek. All three of the Ridge Road overlook views include the valleys drained by small creeks running off the ridge.

Norcross Run Vista offers a narrow but delightful easterly view from about 60 degrees east-northeast to about 120 degrees east-southeast. The view includes the Norcross Run Valley. The ridge across the end of the valley marks the site at which Norcross Run meets First Fork Sinnemahoning Creek. The vista is about 2,120 feet above sea level and about 1,000 feet above the bottom of the Norcross Run Valley.

The Logue Run Vista view is easterly, about 60 degrees east-northeast to about 150 degrees south-southeast, and the overlook stands about 2,020 feet above sea level and about 1,000 feet above the valley. It looks straight down the Logue Run Valley to the ridge at which Logue Run meets First Fork Sinnemahoning

Creek. A cleared strip straddling the mountain in the distance is a gas pipeline right-of-way. Logue Run Vista (which has a picnic table) provides a lovely spot for a quiet woodland picnic.

Square Timber Vista is on Ridge Road, about 0.9 mile south of its intersection with Stillhouse Road. (Another Square Timber Vista is about 0.5 mile farther south on Ridge Road, but it is overgrown.) The view is westerly, about 255 degrees west-south-west to about 315 degrees northwest; the overlook stands about 2,060 feet above sea level and about 1,000 feet above Square Timber Run, a tributary of Driftwood Branch Sinnemahoning Creek. The view looks down the Square Timber Run Valley. The mountains on the other side of Driftwood Branch Sinnemahoning Creek—near its confluence with Square Timber Run—appear as a ridge in the distance.

OPPORTUNITIES: Mountain biking, primitive camping [$], fishing for trout and other species, hiking on 100 trail miles, horseback riding, hunting, picnicking in one designated area, cross-country skiing on 23 trail miles, snowmobiling on 98 trail miles, and wildlife-watching.

Elk State Forest also features natural areas. Bucktail State Park Natural Area, a 75-mile scenic drive on PA Route 120 (Emporium to Lock Haven), comprises more than 16,400 acres in Elk and Sproul State Forests. Johnson Run Natural Area, near Driftwood (Cameron County), covers 216 acres, largely with hardwoods and old-growth hemlocks. Lower Jerry Run Natural Area, near Dutchman Road (Cameron and Clinton Counties), is 892 acres, with white pine and old-growth hemlock. Pine Tree Trail Natural Area, near West Hicks Run Road and East Hicks Run Road (Elk County), comprises 276 acres of pine that took over abandoned farmland before the area's virgin forest was harvested. Wykoff Run Natural Area, near Wykoff and New Hoover Roads (Cameron County), encompasses 1,215 acres and boasts large open areas with white birch, hemlock, white pine, oaks, and hardwoods.

ADMINISTRATION AND AMENITIES: The State Game Lands #311 Dents Run elk-viewing area has portable toilets.

Near the northerly Ridge Road overlooks, water and rest rooms are available at Sizerville State Park. Take Crooked Run Road west from Ridge Road. Near the southerly Ridge Road overlooks, water and rest rooms are available at nearby Sinnemahoning State Park, located east of these overlooks on PA Route 872.

DIRECTIONS: Winslow Hill Road north of Benezette has two elk-viewing areas. The first is about 1 mile from Benezette: take Winslow Hill Road north, and follow the blue signs 1.1 miles to the elk-viewing area. (In Benezette, Winslow Hill Road begins opposite a Gulf station on PA Route 555.) The second Winslow Hill elk-viewing area is about 1.3 miles beyond the first.

To reach the Ridge Road overlooks: From PA Route 120, take Stillhouse Road (the sign says "Stillhouse Run Road") about 4.1 miles east. Stillhouse Road is a state forest one-lane improved dirt road that borders a golf course. At the intersection with Ridge Road, turn north to Norcross Run Vista, which appears 0.8 mile farther. Logue Run Vista is about 1.3 miles north of Norcross Run Vista.

To reach Square Timber Vista: Follow Ridge Road south. The vista is on Ridge Road, 0.9 mile from its intersection with Stillhouse Road.

To reach the Ridge Road overlooks from the east: Follow Brooks Run Road west from PA Route 872 about 5 miles to Ridge Road and turn right (north). All three overlooks are between Brooks Run Road and Whitehead Road, a distance of about 5 miles.

FOR MORE INFORMATION: Contact Elk State Forest, Bureau of Forestry, Forest District #13, RR 4, Box 212, Suite 1, Emporium, PA 15834 (call 814-486-3353 or e-mail fd13@dcnr.state.pa.us), or visit its Web site at www.dcnr.state.pa.us/forestry/stateforests/forests/elk/elk.htm.

NEARBY OVERLOOKS: Kinzua Bridge State Park (McKean County); Susquehannock State Forest overlooks (Potter County); Tiadaghton State Forest overlooks (Lycoming County); and Sproul State Forest overlooks (Clinton County).

OTHER NEARBY OPPORTUNITIES

Bendigo State Park, Jones Township (Elk County). Activities include fishing for trout, picnicking, sledding, and pool swimming; the park also offers pavilion rental [$].

Bucktail State Park, Emporium to Lock Haven (Cameron and Clinton Counties). Activities include driving along a 75-mile scenic route, fishing for trout and other species, hiking and backpacking, and wildlife-watching.

Elk State Park, near Rasselas (Elk and McKean Counties). Activities include boating (with unlimited horsepower), ice boating, fishing for trout and other species, ice fishing, hunting, picnicking, ice skating, and water skiing. The park also offers boat launching and environmental education.

Sinnemahoning State Park, east of Emporium (Cameron and Potter Counties). Activities include boating (with electric motors only), camping [$], fishing, hiking, hunting, picnicking, and snowmobiling on 5 trail miles with trailhead. The park also offers boat launching and mooring [$], modern cabin rental [$], environmental education, pavilion rental [$], and playfield and playground facilities.

Sizerville State Park, northeast of Emporium (Cameron and Potter Counties). Activities include tent and trailer camping [$], fishing for trout, hiking and backpacking on 5 trail miles with trailhead, hunting, picnicking, cross-country skiing, snowmobiling on 2 trail miles with trailhead, and pool swimming. The park also offers environmental education, a food concession, pavilion rental [$], playground facilities, and a visitors center.

The U.S. Army Corps of Engineers *Recreation Area* on the East Branch Dam at Wilcox (Elk County), adjacent to Elk State Park, features boating and camping [$].

The *Pennsylvania Lumber Museum* is located on private property surrounded by Susquehannock State Forest at Galeton (Potter County). It focuses on the history and technology of Pennsylvania's lumber industries. Contact the museum (814-435-2652) or visit its Web site at www.lumbermuseum.org for details. The museum is administered by the Pennsylvania Historical and Museum Commission: for more information, visit the Commission's Web site at www.phmc.state.pa.us.

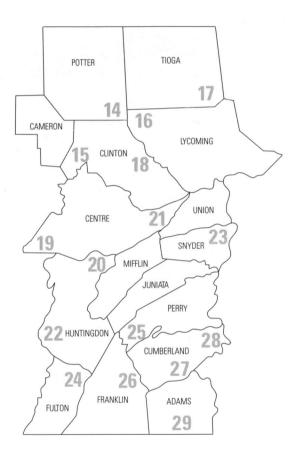

14

SUSQUEHANNOCK STATE FOREST

Jamison Run Vista, Junction Road Vista, and
PA Route 44 Vistas

Susquehannock State Forest includes 265,000 acres in Clinton, Potter, and McKean Counties. From the late 1800s through the 1920s, the Pennsylvania logging industry cut down the original forest in the state forest lands. (Since then, a new forest has grown, consisting mostly of hardwoods such as cherry and ash.)

In the mid-1800s the demand for white pine increased rapidly: bridges, buildings, furniture, barns, spars, mine props, and masts were made mostly of white pine. Lacking access to roads and railroads, lumber companies used the area's waterways to send enormous quantities of timber downriver to sawmills. The Susquehanna River and its many tributaries became "highways" by which the lumber companies moved their products to sawmills for processing and then on to markets. (The acreage of the present-day Susquehannock State Forest is located in the West Branch Susquehanna River Watershed.) The region's tributary waterways were either too shallow or too narrow to move logs, so lumbermen created "splash dams" to swell these waterways periodically to send the logs downstream. In addition to the wood itself, lumbermen removed the bark from cut hemlocks and extracted tannin from it. A solution of tannin and water cured animal hides to make leather, and the Civil War had brought a significant increase in the demand for leather items such as industrial belts, harnesses, and military equipment.

From the 1880s into the 1920s, railroads increased production by allowing loggers to load cut logs onto cars. This work was accomplished first by hand and then by steam-powered log-loaders. After about 1880, band saws were commonly used, allowing large sawmills at Lock Haven and Williamsport to increase their daily production to more than 100,000 feet of lumber.

Forest fires repeatedly incinerated the logging debris, leaving the land scarred during and even after the railroad era. The repeated burning prevented the regeneration of the pine and hemlock forests. Instead of holding the spoiled acres, the lumber

Jamison Run Vista's westerly view.

companies sold much of the land to the state and ventured west-ward, searching for new forests.

Hemlock and virgin pine stumps can still be seen today, and abandoned railroad logging grades remind us of the region's lumber-industry era. Along tributary streams, visitors can still identify remnants of splash dams.

Jamison Run Vista

This vista is a small pull-off from the one-lane improved state forest dirt road. Jamison Run Vista has a westerly view, 225 degrees southwest to about 315 degrees northwest, straight down the Jamison Run Valley. The mountains in the distance mark the point at which Jamison Run meets the First Fork Sinnemahoning Creek. It is difficult to view the lush, green carpetlike landscape of this vista and the others in Susquehannock State Forest and imagine them as they looked only one hundred years ago—sparse and even charred, gray and black, and bare.

Junction Road Vista

Junction Road Vista is also a pull-off from a one-lane improved state forest dirt road. Junction Road Vista's expansive, breathtaking view is southeast from 60 degrees east-northeast to about 195 degrees south-southwest. Visitors will note the Short Run Valley and the southern Potter County topography whose runs and riffles feed Cross Fork. The overlook stands 2,400 feet above sea

Easterly view from Junction Road Vista.

level and more than 600 feet higher than the low terrain to the southeast.

PA Route 44 Vistas

Cherry Springs Vista is a large pull-off with a substantial parking area on the south side of PA Route 44. At the Cherry Springs Vista sign, the view is to the south, 135 degrees southeast to about 225 degrees southwest. Move to the parking area for an even more distant southwest view (trees obscure it at the vista sign). Junction Road is visible to the southwest, and to the south-southeast, the Short Run Valley can be seen. Just behind the first ridge is where Boone Road runs southeast to northwest. Cherry Springs Vista is about 2,400 feet above sea level and some 600 feet above the Short Run Valley.

Water Tank Hollow Vista is located about 3 miles south of Cherry Springs Vista on PA Route 44. The vista is a pull-off from PA Route 44 with ample parking. This view is north-northeast, about 300 degrees west-northwest to about 45 degrees northeast; the overlook stands 2,235 feet above sea level and a bit more than 500 feet above Water Tank Hollow's low points. The wonderful view of the West Branch Pine Creek Valley includes a high ridge in the distance where the West Branch Pine Creek meets Pine Creek.

Pine Mountain Vista is a small pull-off from PA Route 44 with head-in parking. It appears suddenly at the summit of Pine Hill, about 3 miles south of Oleona on PA Route 44. The sign at the summit reads "Pine Hill Summit, Allegheny Mountains, 2,175 feet," but the vista is called Pine Mountain Vista. The summit stands about 475 feet above the Francis Branch Valley to the east; its narrow view is easterly from 45 degrees northeast to 135 degrees southeast. Carefully walk about 20 yards south on PA Route 44 for a more distant northeasterly view (the view is obscured by trees at the parking area). From this overlook you can see portions of eastern Potter County and western Tioga County.

OPPORTUNITIES: ATV riding on 35 trail miles, mountain biking, primitive camping [$], fishing for trout and other species, hiking on 85 trail miles, horseback riding, hunting, cross-country skiing on 30 trail miles, snowmobiling on 224 trail miles, and wildlife-watching.

ADMINISTRATION AND AMENITIES: No services at these overlooks. Pit toilets and water are available at Lyman Run State Park, west of Galeton, and at Ole Bull State Park, located on PA Route 144 southwest of Oleona.

DIRECTIONS: To reach Jamison Run Vista: From Wharton, turn easterly onto East Fork Road (SR 3001) and follow the signs 10 miles to Conrad. Enter the state forest and continue another 0.8 mile. Turn right (south) onto Horton Run Road, a one-lane improved dirt road. Drive about 2 miles to McConnell Road, and turn south on McConnell Road. Drive 1.1 miles to Jamison Run Vista. The Junction Road Vista is on Junction Road, 1 mile from its intersection with PA Route 44 (which occurs about 2 miles south of Cherry Springs).

To reach all of the PA Route 44 vistas: Follow PA Route 44 south from its intersection with Junction Road. These overlooks are all located within about a 25-mile stretch of PA Route 44.

FOR MORE INFORMATION: Contact Susquehannock State Forest, Bureau of Forestry, Forest District #15, PO Box 673, Coudersport, PA 16915-0673 (call 814-274-3600 or e-mail fd15@dcnr.state.pa.us), or visit its Web site at www.dcnr. state.pa.us/forestry/stateforests/forests/susquehannock/ susquehannock.htm.

NEARBY OVERLOOKS: Kinzua Bridge State Park (McKean County); Elk State Forest overlooks and State Game Lands #311 elk-viewing sites (Cameron, Potter, and Elk Counties); Sproul State Forest overlooks (Clinton County); Hyner View State Park (Clinton County); Tiadaghton State Forest overlooks (Lycoming County); Tioga State Forest overlooks (Tioga and Bradford Counties); and Bald Eagle State Forest overlooks (Centre County).

OTHER NEARBY OPPORTUNITIES

Cherry Springs State Park at Cherry Springs on PA Route 44 (Potter County). Activities include tent and trailer camping [$], organized group tent and trailer camping [$], hiking, backpacking with trailhead, hunting, picnicking, snowmobile trailhead to Susquehannock State Forest trails, stargazing, and wildlife-watching; the park also offers a playfield and pavilion rental [$]. Cherry Springs State Park hosts "star parties" from May through October during new-moon periods. These stargazing camp-outs sometimes lure hundreds of amateur astronomers and astrophotographers as well as the simply curious. This site boasts some of the darkest night skies in the eastern United States. For more information on its star parties, contact Cherry Springs State Park c/o Lyman Run State Park, 454 Lyman Run Road, Galeton, PA 16922 (call 814-435-5010 or e-mail lymanrunsp@state.pa.us), or visit its Web site at www.dcnr.state.pa.us/stateparks/parks/cherry.htm.

Denton Hill State Park, west of Walton (Potter County). Activities include fishing for trout, hiking and backpacking on 2 trail miles with trailhead, picnicking, downhill skiing, snowmobiling on 2 trail miles with trailhead, and wildlife-watching; the park also offers modern cabin rental [$].

Lyman Run State Park, west of Galeton (Potter County). Activities include ATV riding, mountain biking, boating (with electric motors only), tent and trailer camping [$], fishing for trout, ice fishing, hiking and backpacking on 2 trail miles with trailhead, hunting, picnicking, ice skating, snowmobiling on 4 trail miles with trailhead, lake swimming, and wildlife-watching. The park also offers boat launching and mooring [$] as well as playfield and playground facilities.

Ole Bull State Park, southwest of Oleona (Potter County). Activities include mountain biking, tent and trailer camping [$], organized group tent and trailer camping [$], fishing for trout and other species, hiking and backpacking on 2 trail miles with trailhead, hunting, picnicking, cross-country skiing, snowmobile trailhead to Susquehannock State Forest trails, snowshoeing, creek swimming, and wildlife-watching. The park also offers modern cabin rental [$], pavilion rental [$], and playfield and playground facilities.

 Patterson State Park, south of Denton Hill (Potter County). Activities include mountain biking, tent and trailer camping [$], hiking and backpacking on 1 trail mile with trailhead, picnicking, and wildlife-watching; the park also offers playfield facilities.

 The *Pennsylvania Lumber Museum* is located on private property surrounded by Susquehannock State Forest at Galeton (Potter County). It focuses on the history and technology of Pennsylvania's lumber industries. Contact the museum (814-435-2652) or visit its Web site at www.lumbermuseum.org for details. The museum is administered by the Pennsylvania Historical and Museum Commission: for more information, visit the Commission's Web site at www.phmc.state.pa.us.

15

SPROUL STATE FOREST

Ridge Road (PA Route 144) Vistas and Kettle Creek Vista

Sproul State Forest, which occupies some 292,000 acres in western Clinton and northern Centre Counties, is located in the Deep
Valleys Section of Pennsylvania's Appalachian Plateaus province
(on the province, see the sidebar in Chap. 2). Look northeasterly
from Kettle Creek Vista, and you will notice that the mountaintops all rise to about the same height—a characteristic of the
Appalachian Plateaus province. The Deep Valleys Section has
steep-sided mountains that rise from deep, narrow valleys. The
streams in the deepest valleys in this section are more than 1,000
feet below the bordering high land. Sproul State Forest and the
rugged land in the Deep Valleys Section comprise some of the
state's most isolated and rough country.

A small tract in Clinton County's Young Womans Creek
watershed was the state's first purchase of forest land, and with this
acquisition in 1898, the state forest system arose. A small monument—"The First Purchase of Forest Land"—marks the area.

Ridge Road Vistas

Near the Fish Dam Run Wild Area on Ridge Road, two
unnamed overlooks on Barneys Ridge provide outstanding views
of the Fish Dam Run Wild Area. The more southerly of the two
has a view to the northwest, straight up the Fish Dam Run Valley, from about 285 degrees west-northwest to about 45 degrees
northeast. This overlook stands about 2,100 feet above sea level
and about 1,000 feet above Fish Dam Run Wild Area's lowest
points. The mountains on the other side of the West Branch
Susquehanna River appear far in the distance.

The second (more northerly) overlook gives an even better
view of the Fish Dam Run Wild Area. This overlook is 2,300 feet
above sea level, some 200 feet higher than the one before, closer
to the summit of Barneys Ridge. You can see the other overlook
below on the left. The view is west-northwest down the Fish
Dam Run Valley from 225 degrees southwest to about 0 degrees
north. Both overlooks offer spectacular views of colorful fall

The lower overlook on Barneys Ridge offers a northwesterly view of the Fish Dam Run Wild Area.

foliage. To the northwest in the distance is the Kettle Creek Gorge, and to the west-northwest, the First Fork Sinnemahoning Creek Valley.

Kettle Creek Vista

Kettle Creek Vista stands 2,080 feet above sea level and 1,240 feet above the surrounding terrain. Its magnificent view runs

A magnificent northeasterly view from Kettle Creek Vista.

northeast from 0 degrees north to about 105 degrees east-south-east. Kettle Creek Lake Dam (also known as Alvin R. Bush Dam) and Kettle Creek Lake, which lies about 840 feet above sea level, are visible. The expansive valley to the north-northeast is the Kettle Creek Valley. Beyond the ridge, by the open field, are Spicewood Run and the Spicewood Run Valley.

OPPORTUNITIES: ATV riding on 32 trail miles, mountain biking, primitive camping [$], fishing for trout and other species, hiking on 257 trail miles, horseback riding, hunting, picnicking in one designated area, cross-country skiing on 14 trail miles, snow-mobiling on 204 trail miles, and wildlife-watching.

ADMINISTRATION AND AMENITIES: No services at these overlooks. Pit toilets and water are available at nearby Kettle Creek State Park.

DIRECTIONS: To reach the Ridge Road vistas: Drive north on PA Route 144 (Ridge Road) from the village of Moshannon. After about 16.1 miles, there are occasional pull-offs for viewing both north and south. After driving a total of about 27.5 miles from

Moshannon, pull off the road at the first Fish Dam Run Wild Area overlook on the left (north) side of the road.

To reach the second overlook: Continue easterly on PA Route 144 for 0.3 mile. At the Chuck Keiper Trail sign, turn left (northwest) to another informal parking area and overlook. The turn is adjacent to Swamp Branch Road on the other side of PA Route 144.

To reach Kettle Creek Vista: From PA Route 120 at Westport, follow the signs north on SR 4001 to Kettle Creek State Park and Alvin R. Bush Dam. After driving 8.7 miles, turn left (west) onto Sugar Camp Road at the sign reading "Kettle Creek Vista, 3.5 miles." This is a one-lane improved dirt road. After driving 1.5 miles, turn left at the intersection and take Crawley Road south, following the brown sign for Kettle Creek Vista. On this road you will pass two overgrown vistas—Sugar Camp Vista and Cooks Run Vista. After 3 more miles, turn east, following the sign to the overlook. The turnaround at this vista appears after another 0.4 mile. You can drive right up to the precipice.

FOR MORE INFORMATION: Contact Sproul State Forest, Bureau of Forestry, Forest District #10, HC 62, Box 90, Renovo, PA 17764 (call 570-923-6011 or e-mail fd10@dcnr.state.pa.us), or visit its Web site at www.dcnr.state.pa.us/forestry/stateforests/forests/sproul/sproul.htm.

NEARBY OVERLOOKS: Elk State Forest overlooks and State Game Lands #311 elk-viewing sites (Cameron, Potter, and Elk Counties); Susquehannock State Forest overlooks (Potter County); Tiadaghton State Forest overlooks (Lycoming County); Hyner View State Park (Clinton County); Rothrock State Forest overlooks (Huntingdon County); and Ralph's Majestic Vista (Centre County).

OTHER NEARBY OPPORTUNITIES

Bucktail State Park, Emporium to Lock Haven (Cameron and Clinton Counties). Activities include driving along a 75-mile scenic route, fishing for trout and other species, hiking and backpacking, and wildlife-watching.

Hyner Run State Park, east of Renovo (Clinton County). Activities include tent and trailer camping [$], fishing, hiking, hunting, picnicking, snowmobiling, pool swimming [$], and wildlife-watching. The park also offers cabin rental [$] and a playground.

Hyner View State Park. (See Chap. 18.)

Kettle Creek State Park, near Westport (Clinton County). Activities include mountain biking, boating, tent and trailer camping [$], fishing, ice fishing, hunting, picnicking, ice skating, cross-country skiing, sledding, snowmobiling, lake swimming, and wildlife-watching.

Bald Eagle State Park, southwest of Lock Haven (Centre County). Activities include boating, primitive and modern camping [$], fishing, ice fishing, hiking, picnicking, ice skating, water-skiing, cross-country skiing, sledding, lake swimming, and wildlife-watching. The park also offers boat rental [$] and environmental education.

The *Pennsylvania Lumber Museum* is located on private property surrounded by Susquehannock State Forest at Galeton (Potter County). It focuses on the history and technology of Pennsylvania's lumber industries. Contact the museum (814-435-2652) or visit its Web site at www.lumbermuseum.org for details. The museum is administered by the Pennsylvania Historical and Museum Commission: for more information, visit the Commission's Web site at www.phmc.state.pa.us.

16

TIADAGHTON STATE FOREST

PA Route 44 Overlook near Elimsport and
U.S. Route 15 Overlook near Williamsport

Tiadaghton State Forest includes more than 215,000 acres, most of which are located in Lycoming County. Smaller state forest areas include portions of Clinton, Potter, Sullivan, Tioga, and Union Counties. Tiadaghton State Forest is divided into three major tracts, or "blocks." The West Block, the largest portion of the state forest, covers much of the Pine Creek Valley. It adjoins Susquehannock and Sproul State Forests. The East Block includes Loyalsock and Lycoming Creeks and borders Wyoming State Forest. The South Block is south of the West Branch Susquehanna River, adjoining Bald Eagle State Forest.

PA Route 44 Overlook

The PA Route 44 overlook is in Tiadaghton State Forest's South Block on North White Deer Ridge (Lycoming County) between Elimsport and Collomsville. It is a large pull-off with ample parking. The view is mainly to the north and northwest, 255 degrees west-southwest to about 45 degrees north-northeast. This overlook stands some 1,900 feet above sea level and 500 feet above the low points to the north. Bald Eagle Mountain spans much of the view. Looking north-northeast, about 10 miles away, you can see the space occupied by the Lycoming Creek Valley between Bald Eagle Mountain and the Allegheny Front. To the northeast, about 14 miles away, lies the Loyalsock Valley. Across the horizon, about 20 miles away, you can see the Allegheny Front and the Appalachian Plateaus province with its characteristically even mountaintops. About 8 miles away to the northwest is a gap where PA Route 44 cuts through Bald Eagle Mountain. Visible to the northwest about 12 miles away is Short Mountain; to the west, an antenna array stands atop a more southerly portion of North White Deer Ridge.

Follow PA Route 44 northwesterly to reach other vistas in Tiadaghton State Forest's West Block; you can reach still others by continuing along PA Route 44 northwesterly into Susquehannock State Forest. (See Chap. 14.)

The U.S. Route 15 overlook near Williamsport has coin-operated binoculars.

U.S. Route 15 Overlook

The U.S. Route 15 overlook on Bald Eagle Mountain—also in
Tiadaghton State Forest's South Block—is about 4 miles east of
Williamsport. The overlook is a fenced area about 100 yards
long with views of the West Branch Susquehanna River Valley,
the Allegheny Front, and the Appalachian Plateaus province.
The overlook land was donated by the citizens of Montoursville.
It stands about 1,800 feet above sea level and some 500 feet
above the West Branch Susquehanna River, with a mainly
northerly view, about 200 degrees north-northwest to about
60 degrees north-northeast. Visible to the north-northwest is
Williamsport. Looking northerly, you will see Loyalsock Township and Loyalsock Creek. To the north in the valley is the
Williamsport-Lycoming County Airport, and beyond the
airport, Montoursville Borough. Below the overlook flows the
West Branch Susquehanna River.

OPPORTUNITIES: ATV riding on 14 trail miles, mountain biking,
primitive camping [$], fishing for trout and other species, hiking
on 200 trail miles, horseback riding, hunting, picnicking, cross-
country skiing on 60 trail miles, snowmobiling on 289 trail
miles, and wildlife-watching.

Tiadaghton State Forest includes several natural and wild
areas, all located in Lycoming County. Algerine Swamp Natural
Area, near Cedar Run, is 84 acres and features black spruce and
balsam fir. Bark Cabin Natural Area, near Little Pine State

Easterly view from the U.S. Route 15 overlook.

Park, comprises 73 acres and includes the Mid-State Trail. The Devils Elbow Natural Area, near Yorktown, encompasses 404 acres, containing wetlands, hemlock, and northern hardwoods. Miller Run Natural Area, near Haneyville, covers more than 4,000 acres and is a roadless area with three streams. Lebo Red Pine Natural Area, east of Lucullus, includes 124 acres as well as First Big Fork and Trout Run, white birch, oaks, and old-growth red pine. Torbert Island Natural Area, near Jersey Shore, features 18-acre Pine Creek Island. Algerine Wild Area, near Slate Run, comprises more than 4,000 acres and contains the Black Forest Trail. The McIntyre Wild Area, near Ralston, is more than 7,000 acres, including four streams, waterfalls, and mining town ruins. Wolf Run Wild Area, near Cammal, also covers some 7,000 acres; this remote area includes the Golden Eagle Trail.

ADMINISTRATION AND AMENITIES: The PA Route 44 overlook has no services. The Route 15 overlook has coin-operated binoculars and picnic tables. Find services on Route 15 as you head into South Williamsport.

DIRECTIONS: The PA Route 44 overlook is located near the top of White Deer Ridge on PA Route 44 between Collomsville and Elimsport. The U.S. Route 15 vista is marked with small blue signs 1 mile from the overlook as you approach from either direction on U.S. Route 15—South Williamsport from the north or Allenwood from the south.

FOR MORE INFORMATION: For the PA Route 44 overlook, contact the Bureau of Forestry, Forest District #12, 423 East Central Avenue, South Williamsport, PA 17702 (call 570-327-3450 or e-mail fd12@dcnr.state.pa.us), or visit Tiadaghton State Forest's Web site at www.dcnr.state.pa.us/forestry/stateforests/forests/tiadaghton/tiadaghton.htm. For the U.S. Route 15 overlook, contact PennDOT District 3-0, 715 Jordan Avenue, Montoursville, PA 17754 (call 1-877-723-6830 or e-mail penndot3@dot.state.pa.us).

NEARBY OVERLOOKS: Susquehannock State Forest overlooks (Potter County); Tioga State Forest overlooks (Tioga and Bradford Counties); and Bald Eagle State Forest overlooks (Centre County).

OTHER NEARBY OPPORTUNITIES

Little Pine State Park, north of Waterville (Lycoming County). Activities include bicycling, boating (with electric motors only), ice boating, tent and trailer camping [$], organized group tent camping [$], fishing for trout and other species, ice fishing, hiking and backpacking on 13 trail miles with trailhead, hunting, picnicking, ice skating, cross-country skiing, sledding, snowmobiling on 6 trail miles with trailhead, lake swimming, and wildlife-watching. The park also offers boat launching and mooring [$], boat rental [$], modern cabin rental [$], environmental education, pavilion rental [$], and playfield and playground facilities.

Ravensburg State Park, near Rauchtown (Clinton County). Activities include tent and trailer camping [$], fishing for trout, hiking and backpacking on 1 trail mile with trailhead, picnicking, and wildlife-watching. The park also offers pavilion rental [$] and playfield and playground facilities.

The *Pennsylvania Lumber Museum* is located on private property surrounded by Susquehannock State Forest at Galeton (Potter County). It focuses on the history and technology of Pennsylvania's lumber industries. Contact the museum (814-435-2652) or visit its Web site at www.lumbermuseum.org for details. The museum is administered by the Pennsylvania Historical and Museum Commission: for more information, visit the Commission's Web site at www.phmc.state.pa.us.

17

TIOGA STATE FOREST

Lambs Vista, West Rim Road Vistas,
Colton Point State Park,
and Leonard Harrison State Park

Tioga State Forest, which includes Colton Point and Leonard
Harrison State Parks, encompasses some 160,000 acres of
mostly forest land in Bradford, Lycoming, and Tioga Counties.
The acreage was largely a timber-producing area that flourished
for some fifty years and includes the sawmill towns of Leetonia
and Ansonia. The first purchase of Tioga State Forest land
occurred in 1900 with the acquisition of 900 acres bordering
Cedar Run in Tioga and Lycoming Counties. The last
acquisition was a tract of nearly 14,000 acres in 1955. Civilian
Conservation Corps (CCC) camps established in 1933 initiated a
period of major state forest development. The CCC workers
built trails, roads, bridges, picnic areas, and scenic vistas. At
Leonard Harrison State Park, a monument and a wayside
exhibit honor the Civilian Conservation Corps: "Tioga County
CCC Workers, 1933–1942."

Tioga State Forest was named after the American Indian
Seneca Tyoga Tribe. The Seneca word "Tyoga" means "meeting
of two rivers."

Lambs Vista

Lambs Vista is just inside the eastern edge of Tioga State Forest,
north of Canton, in southwest Bradford County. The spectacular
view from Lambs Vista is mostly east-southeast from 45 degrees
northeast to 165 degrees south-southeast. The vista elevation
above sea level is 2,310 feet, and it stands a little more than 700
feet above the valley floor. You can see the Towanda Creek watershed and the rolling countryside beyond. To the southeast are the
mountains of State Game Lands #12 and #36 as well as other
mountains in the extreme southeastern portion of Tioga State
Forest. Lambs Vista was the centerpiece of a state forest picnic
area until vandalism caused the picnic area's closing. On some
older topographic maps, the overlook is called "Lambs Hill

Lambs Vista, Tioga State Forest.

Picnic Area." Luckily, the vista is still open to the public. Parking at the overlook is informal; to reach and leave the area, you follow the remnants of a more heavily traversed turnaround. Luckily, you can park almost directly in front of the overlook. The concrete slab that remains in the center of the turnaround is the foundation of a dismantled picnic pavilion. The vista still has two picnic tables.

West Rim Road Vistas

From PA Route 414 about 0.6 mile west of Blackwell, turn north onto West Rim Road to reach several named and unnamed vistas. West Rim Road is a narrow state forest improved dirt road. Elevations above sea level along West Rim Road are about 1,700 to 1,800 feet; Pine Creek's elevation is about 1,000 feet above sea level. About 1.2 miles after turning onto West Rim Road, you reach the impressive West Rim Vista, a 40-yard-wide clearing. This view is mainly easterly, 30 degrees east-northeast to about 135 degrees southeast. (The valley containing Babb Creek and PA Route 414 is visible to the southeast.) Drive about 5.7 miles farther, and you will reach Spinning Wheel Vista. This vista's narrow view is westerly, about 240 degrees south-southwest to about 315 degrees northwest. After another 4.3 miles, you will find Pine Creek Vista, a very narrow slice cut through the trees. The view is to the southeast and includes Pine Creek.

After driving another 4.8 miles, you reach Painter-Leetonia Road. Follow this road northeast: Little Slate Vista will appear after another 1.4 miles. This view looks northeasterly into the Pine Creek Gorge. It, too, is a very narrow slice of a view. After another 6.5 miles, Painter-Leetonia Road meets Colton Road. Turn right (easterly) toward Colton Point State Park. About 3.2 miles farther is an unnamed overlook. After another 1.6 miles, you reach Colton Point State Park. The distance from the intersection of PA Route 414 and West Rim Road to Colton Point State Park is about 21.4 miles.

Colton Point and Leonard Harrison State Parks

Colton Point and Leonard Harrison State Parks straddle the Pine Creek Gorge, also known as "The Grand Canyon of Pennsylvania." Less than twenty thousand years ago, before the last ice age, a high land divide separated the flow of Pine Creek. Some rivers flowed southwest; others flowed northeast from near Ansonia through what is today the drainage areas of Marsh and Crooked Creeks. During the last ice age, ice probably blocked the rivers flowing northeast, and as it melted, the gathering meltwater spilled over the valley rim and forcefully flowed south, creating today's Pine Creek and carving the Pine Creek Gorge.

Today, the Pine Creek Gorge reaches about 50 miles from Ansonia to Waterville. The Gorge is about 4,000 feet wide, rim to rim, and some 600 to 800 feet deep. In 1968, the National Park Service designated Pine Creek Gorge a National Natural Landmark.

COLTON POINT STATE PARK

When you enter Colton Point State Park, you can drive to several west-rim overlooks and pavilions. Take the paved road past the park office and, at the first one-way indication, turn left onto the dirt road: this road is literally right at the rim. If you prefer to visit more formal overlooks, stay on the paved road at the first one-way indication, and follow the signs to the vistas. You will reach another one-way indication. Follow this paved road to the first parking area, from which you can walk to two railed overlooks. Colton Point State Park is about 1,700 feet above sea level and about 700 feet above Pine Creek.

The first overlook view is mainly due east from 30 degrees north-northeast to about 180 degrees south. From here across the Gorge you can see the main Leonard Harrison State Park overlook. Walk north about 100 yards on the trail to another

A vista on Colton Road offers one of Colton Point State Park's best views of the Pine Creek Gorge.

railed overlook. It is a narrower view obscured by some foliage and a large pine tree, but it still provides a wonderful northeasterly picture of the Gorge.

To reach one of the best views of Pine Creek Gorge, leave the park heading north on Colton Road. The next railed formal overlook has parking available on the left (the west side of Colton Road). The main view at this overlook is due south right down the Gorge, 225 degrees southwest to about 45 degrees northeast. Visible from this overlook are Pine Creek and the Gorge, Leonard Harrison State Park, and an old tower moved from Valley Forge. You will find coin-operated binoculars at this overlook.

Travel 0.6 mile north from the park on Colton Road, and on the right (east) you will reach the Barbour Rock Trail parking area. This trail leads to another spectacular view of the Gorge at

In 1968, the National Park Service designated Pine Creek Gorge a National Natural Landmark.

Barbour Rock, which is considered the northern end of the Pine Creek Gorge. The area near Bluestone, south of Cammal, marks the southern end of the Gorge.

LEONARD HARRISON STATE PARK

At the "entrance to views" in Leonard Harrison State Park, there are exhibits on the Endless Mountains, the creation of the Gorge, the white pine in the forests, and the area's wildlife—including bears, raptors, and small game. The main overlooks at Leonard Harrison State Park are formal railed areas along a 75-yard stretch at the rim. Leonard Harrison State Park's elevation above sea level is about 1,833 feet and more than 800 feet above Pine Creek. The breathtaking view is westerly, about 210 degrees south-southwest to nearly 0 degrees north. Several points along the fence have coin-operated binoculars. A small wayside exhibit, "Picture-Taking Tips for a View," has notes on lighting, weather, composition, and getting most elements in focus.

Visible from Leonard Harrison State Park's southernmost vista, looking north, are Harrison View, Colton Ridge, Pine Creek Vista, Snyder Point, Colton View, Bear Run Falls, and Barbour Rock. To the south, from the same vista, visitors can discern Stowell Run, Pine Island, Clear Cut, Slate Run, Big Ridge, Tumbling Run, Horse Run, and Burdick Run. Just below the overlook—look down!—is Stowell Island.

Fall color here can be nothing short of magnificent. The color peaks around the first two weeks of October.

OPPORTUNITIES: Colton Point State Park offers tent and trailer camping [$], organized group tent camping [$], fishing for trout and other species, hiking on 4 trail miles with trailhead, hunting, picnicking, cross-country skiing, snowmobiling on 1 trail mile with trailhead, and wildlife-watching, as well as pavilion rental [$] and playground facilities. Leonard Harrison State Park offers bicycling, tent and trailer camping [$], fishing for trout and other species, hiking on 2 trail miles, hunting, picnicking, and wildlife-watching, as well as environmental education, a food concession, pavilion rental [$], playfield and playground facilities, and a visitors center.

Opportunities in Tioga State Forest include mountain biking, primitive camping [$], fishing for trout and other species, horseback riding, hunting, picnicking in three designated areas, cross-country skiing on 7 trail miles, snowmobiling on 175 trail miles, and wildlife-watching.

Tioga State Forest boasts several natural and wild areas. Black Ash Swamp Natural Area, in the Asaph Wild Area north of Ansonia, includes 308 acres and much second-growth cherry and maple. Pine Creek Gorge Natural Area, from Ansonia to Blackwell, covers more than 12,000 acres—18 miles straddling both shores of Pine Creek—and is a National Natural Landmark. Reynolds Spring Natural Area, at Reynolds Spring Road near the Lycoming County border with Tioga County, covers 1,302 acres and includes an open pine swamp, oaks, aspens, and northern hardwoods. Asaph Wild Area, located northwest of Asaph (Tioga County), encompasses 2,070 acres of rugged forest land, and backpack camping [$] is permitted.

ADMINISTRATION AND AMENITIES: Lambs Vista is open only during daylight hours from Memorial Day to Thanksgiving, and there are no facilities. From Lambs Vista, find services in nearby Canton. Water and pit toilets are available at Colton Point and Leonard Harrison State Parks. The state parks are open from 8:00 A.M. to sundown.

DIRECTIONS: To reach Lambs Vista: From Canton, drive north on PA Route 14 (Troy Street in Canton) and turn left onto Upper Mountain Road. After about 0.8 mile, the road splits. Take the left fork. Just beyond the split, Upper Mountain Road becomes a dirt road. Continue on Upper Mountain Road up the mountain. A mile after the split, turn right onto Lambs Park Road (T516). After about 0.2 mile, turn left onto a dirt road, following a small brown sign with an arrow ("Vista" appears on the sign). This is Lambs Lookout Road, a gated state forest road. The sign for "Lambs Lookout" appears about 0.7 mile farther.

Roads in Colton Point and Leonard Harrison State Parks—and Colton Road all the way to the park from U.S. Route 6—are paved, two-lane roads. Approaching Colton Point State Park from the south, keep in mind that West Rim Road and Painter-Leetonia Road are narrow, one-lane, improved dirt roads. From U.S. Route 6, it is 3.7 miles to Colton Point State Park on Colton Road.

To reach Colton Point State Park: From U.S. Route 6, follow the signs to the Grand Canyon West Rim and turn south onto Colton Road in Ansonia.

To reach Leonard Harrison State Park and the east rim: From U.S. Route 6, turn east onto PA Route 362, following signs to the Grand Canyon East Rim and Leonard Harrison State Park. After about 4 miles, turn right, following the signs to the East Rim. After another 2.5 miles, you will reach the intersection with PA Route 660. Follow PA Route 660 west to the park entrance. Enter the park, drive past the park office, and follow the sign to the Grand Canyon Overlook.

To reach West Rim Road: Follow PA Route 414 west from Blackwell and turn north onto West Rim Road, a one-lane, improved state forest dirt road.

FOR MORE INFORMATION: Contact Tioga State Forest, Bureau of Forestry, Forest District #16, One Nessmuk Lane, Wellsboro, PA 16901 (call 570-724-2868 or e-mail fd16@dcnr.state.pa.us), or visit its Web site at www.dcnr.state.pa.us/forestry/stateforests/forests/tioga/tioga.htm.

Contact Leonard Harrison State Park, RR 6, Box 199, Wellsboro, PA 16901-8970 (call 570-724-3061 or e-mail leonardharrisonsp@state.pa.us), or visit its Web site at www.

dcnr.state.pa.us/stateparks/parks/leon.htm.

Contact Colton Point State Park through Leonard Harrison State Park's address and phone number; its Web address is www.dcnr.state.pa.us/stateparks/parks/colton.htm.

NEARBY OVERLOOKS: Round Top Park (Bradford County); Mt. Pisgah County Park (Bradford County); Wyalusing Rocks and Marie Antoinette Overlook (Bradford County); High Knob Overlook (Sullivan County); Canyon Vista (Wyoming County); Susquehannock State Forest overlooks (Potter County); Hyner View State Park (Clinton County); and Tiadaghton State Forest overlooks (Lycoming County).

OTHER NEARBY OPPORTUNITIES

Hills Creek State Park (Tioga County). Activities include boating (with electric motors only), tent and trailer camping [$], fishing for warm-water species, ice fishing, hiking on 5 trail miles, picnicking, ice skating, and wildlife-watching. The park also offers boat launching and mooring [$], boat rental [$], modern cabin rental [$], environmental education, a food concession, pavilion rental [$], playfield and playground facilities, and a visitors center.

The *Pine Creek Trail,* part of the Pennsylvania Rails-to-Trails program, follows Pine Creek at the base of the east rim with trailheads at Blackwell, Darling Run, Rattlesnake Rock, and Tiadaghton. Some 44 trail miles are planned. For more information, contact Tioga State Forest.

The *Pennsylvania Lumber Museum* is located on private property surrounded by Susquehannock State Forest at Galeton (Potter County). It focuses on the history and technology of Pennsylvania's lumber industries. Contact the museum (814-435-2652) or visit its Web site at www.lumbermuseum.org for details. The museum is administered by the Pennsylvania Historical and Museum Commission: for more information, visit the Commission's Web site at www.phmc.state.pa.us.

18

HYNER VIEW STATE PARK

The overlook at Hyner View State Park—one of Pennsylvania's best overlooks—offers a magnificent view of the West Branch Susquehanna River Valley from Hyner Mountain.

Hyner View's vista is mainly to the northwest, 150 degrees south-southeast to about 0 degrees north. The overlook is 1,940 feet above sea level and fully 1,300 feet above the river. To the northwest at the curve in the river is the town of North Bend. Below are the village of Hyner and PA Route 120, which crosses the West Branch Susquehanna River on the bridge below Hyner View State Park. To the west, beyond Hyner on the north side of the river, is Dry Run Mountain. On the south side of the river opposite Dry Run Mountain is a wide, flat-topped mountain called Boggs Ridge. Renovo and South Renovo, not visible from Hyner View, straddle the West Branch Susquehanna River on the other side of Boggs Ridge. To the southeast is the valley of the West Branch Susquehanna River, which includes the Bucktail State Park Natural Area.

Hang gliding is a popular spectator sport at Hyner View, but conditions have to be just right to attract hang gliders. Ideal conditions include northwest winds of 10 to 15 miles per hour. The bulletin board on the rest room wall has an annual schedule of hang gliding events involving the Hyner Hang Gliding Club. Events often occur on holiday weekends. Check the weather report, and if the conditions are right, you will likely see hang gliders.

A monument at the overlook erected by the Forest Inspectors Association honors Pennsylvania forest fire wardens from 1915 to 1965, recognizing "their faithful service to the Commonwealth during the past 50 years."

When you look northwest from Hyner View, notice that the mountaintops are all about the same height. This feature charac-terizes the Appalachian Plateaus province, one of seven physiographic provinces in Pennsylvania (on the province, see the sidebar in Chap. 2). From Hyner View, the province arcs eastward and southwestward.

The West Branch Susquehanna River from the overlook at Hyner View.

OPPORTUNITIES: Hang gliding (only for the trained and experienced), hunting, picnicking, snowmobiling on 5 trail miles, and wildlife-watching.

ADMINISTRATION AND AMENITIES: The park hours are 8:00 A.M. to sunset. There are pit toilets at the overlook parking lot. Water and pit toilets are also available at nearby Hyner Run State Park, a few miles north on Hyner Run Road.

DIRECTIONS: From PA Route 120, turn north onto Hyner Run Road, following the signs to both state parks. After about 1.8 miles, turn sharply right into Hyner View State Park at the entrance sign. Follow that road up the mountain. The one-lane road is narrow and winding, but it is paved. After about 4 miles, you will reach the one-way loop around the parking area.

FOR MORE INFORMATION: Contact Hyner Run State Park, Box 46, Hyner, PA 17738-9999 (call 570-923-6000, or e-mail littlepine@dcnr.state.pa.us), or visit its Web site at www.dcnr.state.pa.us/stateparks/parks/h-view.htm.

NEARBY OVERLOOKS: Elk State Forest overlooks and State Game Lands #311 elk-viewing sites (Cameron, Potter, and Elk Counties); Susquehannock State Forest overlooks (Potter County); Sproul State Forest overlooks (Clinton County); Tiadaghton State Forest overlooks (Lycoming County); and Bald Eagle State Forest overlooks (Centre County).

OTHER NEARBY OPPORTUNITIES

Bucktail State Park, Emporium to Lock Haven (Cameron and Clinton Counties). Activities include driving along a 75-mile scenic route, fishing for trout and other species, hiking and backpacking, and wildlife-watching.

Hyner Run State Park, east of Renovo (Clinton County). Activities include tent and trailer camping [$], fishing, hiking, hunting, picnicking, snowmobiling, pool swimming [$], and wildlife-watching. The park also offers cabin rental [$] and a playground.

Kettle Creek State Park, near Westport (Clinton County). Activities include mountain biking, boating, tent and trailer camping [$], fishing, ice fishing, hunting, picnicking, ice skating, cross-country skiing, sledding, snowmobiling, lake swimming, and wildlife-watching.

Upper Pine Bottom State Park (Lycoming County). Activities include fishing for trout, picnicking, and wildlife-watching.

Little Pine State Park, north of Waterville (Lycoming County). Activities include bicycling, boating (with electric motors only), ice boating, tent and trailer camping [$], organized group tent camping [$], fishing for trout and other species, ice fishing, hiking and backpacking on 13 trail miles with trailhead, hunting, picnicking, ice skating, cross-country skiing, sledding, snowmobiling on 6 trail miles with trailhead, lake swimming, and wildlife-watching. The park also offers boat launching and mooring [$], boat rental [$], modern cabin rental [$], environmental education, pavilion rental [$], and playfield and playground facilities.

19

MOSHANNON STATE FOREST

Ralph's Majestic Vista

Moshannon State Forest includes more than 183,900 acres in Cameron, Centre, Clearfield, Clinton, and Elk Counties. (The word "Moshannon" comes from the American Indian word "moss-hanne," which means "moose stream.") Before the lumber industry controlled this area in the 1860s, large tracts of pure virgin white pine and white pine–hemlock forests once covered the land. There were also areas of virgin hardwoods, some growing with pine and hemlock species and others in separate pure tracts.

Today, visitors can note the signs of effective stewardship of our forest resources—in sharp contrast to past practices that ignored conservation. By law, the purpose of all Pennsylvania state forests now is "to provide a continuous supply of timber, lumber, wood, and other forest products; to protect the watersheds, conserve the water and regulate the flow of rivers and streams of the state; and to furnish opportunities for healthful recreation to the public." Government agencies, however, are not the only entities providing stewardship of our natural resources; private conservation groups, sporting organizations, and individuals also watch over these resources. The Allegheny Front Trail and Ralph's Majestic Vista in Moshannon State Forest are excellent examples of individual and small-group leadership in conserving our natural resources and engaging in partnerships with government agencies.

Ralph Seeley, for whom Ralph's Majestic Vista was named, has been active in the Keystone Trails Association (KTA) for many years. The retired Penn State University electrical engineer began working with others on building the Mid-State Trail in the 1970s. In the following decade, along with the Penn State Outing Club, he built the Rock Run Trail system for cross-country skiing. In 1985, he became involved in renovating the neglected, deteriorating trails in the Moshannon State Forest's Quehanna Wild Area.

Seeley was one of the first people to envision a trail along the Allegheny Front: in 1995, he and Moshannon State Forester Ken Barnes began scouting the Allegheny Front Trail. Various hiking

Easterly view from Ralph's Majestic Vista—note the sign on the tree—on the Allegheny Front Trail.

club volunteers from the KTA, the Penn State Outing Club, the Quehanna Area Trails Club, and the Ridge and Valley Outings Club—with the cooperation of the Moshannon State Forest—built the trail under Seeley's leadership.

Trails need volunteers to maintain them and keep them open to the public. Advocates for the Allegheny Front Trail and the KTA constantly seek people to help maintain trails. Get involved by contacting Ralph Seeley at 814-355-2933 or at his e-mail address, rsbb219@pennswoods.net. (To learn of another outstanding example of individual, group, and government agency partnership in conserving our natural resources, see the discussion of Rothrock State Forest in Chap. 20.)

Ralph's Majestic Vista is located on the Allegheny Front Trail's Front Vista Section. The narrow view at Ralph's Majestic Vista is mainly to the south-southeast, about 135 degrees southwest to about 180 degrees south. The vista is about 2,100 feet above sea level and 1,000 to 1,300 feet above the valley. Leafless trees allow visitors to see more, but the fall colors make Ralph's Majestic Vista, well, majestic. A bench at the vista lets you sit and admire the view. Below the vista are the foothills of the Allegheny Front and Bald Eagle Valley; the somewhat lumpy ridge across the horizon is Bald Eagle Mountain. Continue hiking the trail easterly to reach a series of more views.

Moshannon State Forest still has a few small scattered areas of virgin timber left. However, they are very difficult to find without directions from a state forester. If you want to see old-growth forests—and you should certainly take this opportunity—try the Jerry Run Natural Area in Elk State Forest or Cook Forest State Park. (See the individual listings for these areas in Chaps. 13 and 4.)

OPPORTUNITIES: Mountain biking, primitive camping [$], fishing for trout and other species, hiking on 244 trail miles, horseback riding, hunting, cross-country skiing on 13 trail miles, and wildlife-watching.

Moshannon State Forest boasts two natural and wild areas. Marion Brooks Natural Area, near Medix Run along Quehanna Highway, encompasses 917 acres and includes white birch, mixed oaks, mountain laurel, and wetlands. Quehanna Wild Area, on the border of Cameron, Clearfield, and Elk Counties, covers 48,186 acres administered by Moshannon and Elk State Forests; the opportunities there include backpacking and hiking.

Also nearby is Shaver's Creek Environmental Center at Penn State's Stone Valley Recreation Area, located 14 miles south of State College. The center offers year-round programs and activities. For details, contact Shaver's Creek (call 814-667-3424 or e-mail shaverscreek@outreach.psu.edu), or visit its Web site at www.shaverscreek.org. Opportunities at Stone Valley include boating, fishing for trout and other species, ice fishing, hiking, and cross-country skiing; boat launching and cabin rental [$] are also available.

ADMINISTRATION AND AMENITIES: No services at these overlooks. Water and flush toilets are available in nearby Black Moshannon State Park.

DIRECTIONS: From U.S. Route 220 at Julian, take Julian Pike (SR 3032), also known as Beaver Road, northwest about 5.1 miles to Underwood Road. Turn right (easterly) onto Underwood Road and drive 1.4 miles to the trail. A small sign at an informal parking area on the north side of Underwood Road identifies the trail. Follow the trail south. At first, the trail moves along an old woods road. You must negotiate a rocky outcrop as you approach the overlook, but the rocks are like steps (a maintainer built them this way), so it is easier than it might first appear. The hike to Ralph's Majestic Vista is about 0.6 mile and takes about fifteen minutes.

FOR MORE INFORMATION: Contact Moshannon State Forest, Bureau of Forestry, Forest District #9, RR 1, Box 184, Penfield, PA 15849 (call 814-765-0821 or e-mail fd09@dcnr.state.pa.us), or visit its Web site at www.dcnr.state.pa.us/forestry/stateforests/forests/moshannon/moshannon.htm. The Allegheny Front Trail Web site is located at www.aft.altoona-pa.com/index.html.

NEARBY OVERLOOKS: Altoona-area overlooks (Blair County); Raystown Lake overlooks (Huntingdon County); Rothrock State Forest overlooks (Huntingdon and Centre Counties); Bald Eagle State Forest overlooks (Centre County); Johnstown Incline (Cambria County); Sproul State Forest overlooks (Clinton County); and Hyner View State Park (Clinton County).

OTHER NEARBY OPPORTUNITIES

Black Moshannon State Park, east of Phillipsburg (Centre County). Activities include bicycling, boating (with electric motors only), ice boating, tent and trailer camping [$], group tent camping [$], fishing for trout and other species, ice fishing, hiking and backpacking on 16 trail miles with trailhead, hunting, picnicking, ice skating, cross-country skiing, lake swimming, and wildlife-watching. The park also offers boat launching and mooring [$], boat rental [$], modern and rustic cabin rental [$], environmental education, a food concession, pavilion rental [$], and playground facilities.

Parker Dam State Park, southeast of Mill Run (Clearfield County). Activities include bicycling, boating (with electric motors only), tent and trailer camping [$], organized group tent and trailer camping [$], fishing for trout, ice fishing, hiking and backpacking on 4 trail miles with trailhead, hunting, picnicking, ice skating, cross-country skiing, sledding, lake swimming, and wildlife-watching. The park also offers boat launching, boat rental [$], rustic cabin rental [$], environmental education, a historical center, pavilion rental [$], playfield and playground facilities, and a visitors center.

S. B. Elliott State Park, northwest of Clearfield (Clearfield County). Activities include tent and trailer camping [$], hiking on 3 trail miles, hunting, picnicking, cross-country skiing, snowmobiling with trailhead to Moshannon State Forest trails, and wildlife-watching. The park also offers rustic cabin rental [$], pavilion rental [$], and playfield and playground facilities.

The *Pennsylvania Lumber Museum* is located on private property surrounded by Susquehannock State Forest at Galeton (Potter County). It focuses on the history and technology of Pennsylvania's lumber industries. Contact the museum (814-435-2652) or visit its Web site at www.lumbermuseum.org for details. The museum is administered by the Pennsylvania Historical and Museum Commission: for more information, visit the Commission's Web site at www.phmc.state.pa.us.

State Game Lands #176, also known as The Barrens, is located west of State College (Centre County) and offers mountain biking, hiking, hunting, cross-country skiing, and wildlife-watching.

The Pennsylvania Fish and Boat Commission's *Fish Culture Stations at Pleasant Gap and Bellefonte* both have visitors centers with exhibits and tours available. Contact the Bellefonte Fish Culture Station at 1150 Spring Creek Road, Bellefonte, PA 16832 (814-355-3371) or the Pleasant Gap Fish Culture Station at 450 Robinson Lane, Pleasant Gap, PA 16823 (814-359-5132).

20

ROTHROCK STATE FOREST

Jo Hays Vista, Pennsylvania Furnace Vista, and
Stone Mountain Hawk Watch

Rothrock State Forest includes more than 94,280 acres in Centre,
Huntingdon, and Mifflin Counties—and more than 200 miles of
roads. In addition to the overlooks described here, a drive on
Wampler and Bear Gap Roads can provide wonderful scenic views.

Jo Hays Vista

The most accessible overlook is Jo Hays Vista, located on PA Route
26 between Pine Grove Mills and Monroe Furnace. The overlook is
on the ridge of Tussey Mountain, on the border between Huntingdon and Centre Counties, and it stands some 2,000 feet above sea
level and 700 feet above the valley to the north. The view is mostly
north and north-northeasterly, about 330 degrees west-northwest
to about 45 degrees northeast. Jo Hays Vista provides impressive
views of State College and the Nittany and Spruce Creek Valleys in
Centre County. Looking north-northeast, you can see Penn State's
Bryce Jordan Center and Beaver Stadium about 6 miles away.
Looking north, the first ridge is Bald Eagle Mountain, about 10
miles away. Beyond Bald Eagle Mountain are the Allegheny Front
and the Appalachian Plateaus province.

The Mid-State Trail crosses PA Route 26 at Jo Hays Vista.
The overlook's wooded surroundings and trails include beech,
birch, gum, maple, oak, and hemlock; the fall color in October
can be stunning. The vista is named for former state senator Jo
Hays, who served from 1955 to 1962 and led the efforts to estab-
lish the site.

There is a gravel pull-off with ample parking on the west side
of the road at the top of the mountain. The overlook is jointly
maintained by PennDOT and Rothrock State Forest personnel.

Pennsylvania Furnace Vista

Like the Jo Hays Vista, the Pennsylvania Furnace Vista is on
Tussey Mountain, about 2,200 feet above sea level and some 400

Southerly view from Pennsylvania Furnace Vista.

feet above the low points to the south. Its southerly view, about 105 degrees east-southeast to 225 degrees southwest, includes Leading Ridge, the nearest ridge across the view. To the south, the secondary ridge about 6 miles away (beyond the farms and woodlots) is Warrior Ridge, and it spans most of the view. The ridge along the horizon to the south and southeast is Stone Mountain, about 10 miles away. Beyond Stone Mountain you can see parts of Jacks Mountain, about 15 miles away. Also to the south, the mountain ends at a gap where the Juniata River passes through Jacks Mountain in the Mt. Union vicinity. To the southwest, the mountains on the horizon are those that flank Raystown Lake; just a bit farther west, Tussey Mountain's ridge curves southward. Though you cannot see it, Huntingdon is beyond Warrior Ridge to the southwest.

The light-colored rocks deposited on the mountain above and below this overlook are called talus slopes, which result from water seeping into cracks in the mountain's exposed rock portions. As the water freezes and thaws in cracks in the rock, it breaks the rock into pieces that fall off and accumulate, forming slopes. Talus slopes are commonly seen on the mountains of Pennsylvania's Ridge and Valley physiographic province. (On the province, see the sidebar in Chap. 21.)

Stone Mountain Hawk Watch

The magnificent views at the Stone Mountain Hawk Watch are to the southeast and northwest. Except for the ridge top, the view

A magnificent view from the Stone Mountain Hawk Watch platform.

is fully 360 degrees. The hawk watch is about 2,170 feet above sea level and more than 1,000 feet above the valley floor to the southeast. The observation deck raises you above the ridge top even more and enhances the view. To the northwest, the long ridge on the horizon is Tussey Mountain, about 11 miles away, and the ridge in the middle of the valley is Warrior Ridge, some 5 miles away. To the north-northwest is a power-line cut, and Jo Hays Vista is just to the right of that. The hawk watch site and the Pennsylvania Furnace Vista are actually right across the valley from each other. The bare spots you see on Tussey Mountain are talus slopes, similar to those at the Pennsylvania Furnace Vista.

Looking west-northwest, a larger gap in the mountains reveals where the Little Juniata River flows through Tussey Mountain. A smaller gap in front of the larger one is where the Frankstown Branch Juniata River passes through Tussey Mountain. To the northwest is Stone Valley. On a clear day, looking northwest, you can see the Allegheny Front and the Appalachian Plateaus province.

Looking to the east and southeast, the first ridge is Jacks Mountain. The ridges beyond Jacks Mountain are Blacklog Mountain and then Shade Mountain. The gap off to the east-northeast is where U.S. Route 322 cuts through Jacks Mountain near Reedsville. To the east, the town in the valley is Belleville, about 6 miles away. Spanning the view, the Kishacoquillas Valley lies below the overlook.

This is an outstanding site for spotting migrating raptors. Stone Mountain Hawk Watch is active from September 1 into

North-northeasterly view from Jo Hays Vista, with State College and Penn State University visible.

late November; activity peaks in October. In 2000, 4,500 hawks were counted, and 5,500 were tallied in 1999. These figures reflect only part-time observation. Also included in the totals for 2000 were 30 bald eagles and about 70 golden eagles.

The hawk watch site's observation deck is a monument to resource stewardship and conservation and the partnership that supports both. The hawk watch began in 1991, and for four years was located at the now-overgrown Allensville Vista. Penn State University instructor and avid bird-watcher Greg Grove, along with several colleagues (including David Kyler, the designer of the observation deck), sought a better site from which to count migrating raptors. After locating the current hawk watch site, they enlisted the help of Rothrock State Forest, and with permission, they built the observation deck. The deck is a reminder that government agencies and private organizations are not the only effective stewards of our natural resources. Individuals such as Greg Grove, David Kyler, and the other hawk watch counters prove that getting involved can reap great benefits.

Greg Grove tallies the hawk watch counts each year and shares that information with Hawk Mountain Sanctuary (see Chap. 37), Cornell University, and the Hawk Migration Association of North America (HMANA). The information helps scientists better understand bird migration, their protection, and their conservation. To get involved with the Stone Mountain Hawk Watch, contact Greg Grove, RD 1, Box 483, Petersburg, PA 16669 (call 814-667-2305 [evenings] or e-mail gwg2@psu.edu).

OPPORTUNITIES: Mountain biking, primitive camping [$], fishing for trout and other species, hiking on 47 trail miles, horseback riding, hunting, picnicking in three designated areas, cross-country skiing on 38 trail miles, snowmobiling on 207 trail miles, and wildlife-watching.

ADMINISTRATION AND AMENITIES: No services at these overlooks.

DIRECTIONS: The Jo Hays Vista is on PA Route 26 between Pine Grove Mills and Monroe Furnace.

To reach the Pennsylvania Furnace Vista: From Jo Hays Vista, continue south on PA Route 26 for about 1.1 miles and turn southwest (right) onto Harrys Valley Road, a one-lane improved state forest dirt road. After 5.2 miles, turn right (west) onto Tram Road. After 0.5 mile, turn right (northeast) onto the gated Pennsylvania Furnace Road. (Pennsylvania Furnace Road is unmarked at this intersection.) Continue about 1.5 miles to the overlook. Drive 0.1 mile farther to pull off the road for parking. The parking area is where the Mid-State Trail crosses Pennsylvania Furnace Road.

To reach the hawk watch site: From PA Route 655 (Main Street) in Allensville, turn northwest onto Water Street. After about 1 mile, Water Street becomes Allensville Road, a one-lane improved state forest dirt road. Drive a total of about 3.1 miles to the hawk watch site parking area at the border marker for Mifflin and Huntingdon Counties.

FOR MORE INFORMATION: Contact Rothrock State Forest, Bureau of Forestry, Forest District #5, PO Box 403, Rothrock Lane, Huntingdon, PA 16652 (call 814-643-2340 or e-mail fd05@dcnr.state.pa.us), or visit its Web site at www.dcnr.state.pa.us/forestry/stateforests/forests/rothrock/rothrock.htm.

NEARBY OVERLOOKS: Bald Eagle State Forest overlooks (Centre County); Tuscarora State Forest overlooks (Perry County); Raystown Lake overlooks (Huntingdon County); Altoona-area overlooks (Blair County); Moshannon State Forest overlooks (Centre County); Blue Knob State Park overlooks (Bedford County); and Buchanan State Forest overlooks (Fulton County).

OTHER NEARBY OPPORTUNITIES

 Greenwood Furnace State Park, northwest of Belleville (Huntingdon County). Activities include tent and trailer camping [$], fishing for trout, ice fishing, hiking and backpacking on 6 trail miles with trailhead, hunting, picnicking, ice skating, cross-country skiing, snowmobiling on 5 trail miles with trailhead, lake swimming, and wildlife-watching. The park also offers environmental education, a food concession, a historical center, pavilion rental [$], and playfield and playground facilities.

Penn Roosevelt State Park, southeast of Boalsburg (Centre and Huntingdon Counties). Activities include tent and trailer camping [$], organized group tent camping [$], fishing for trout, ice fishing, hiking and backpacking on 1 trail mile with trailhead, picnicking, ice skating, cross-country skiing, snowmobiling on 1 trail mile, and wildlife-watching; pavilion rental [$] is also available.

Trough Creek State Park (Huntingdon County). Activities include tent and trailer camping [$], fishing for trout and other species, hiking on 6 trail miles, hunting, picnicking, snowmobile trailhead to Rothrock State Forest trails, and wildlife-watching. The park also offers modern cabin rental [$], environmental education, pavilion rental [$], and playfield facilities.

Rothrock State Forest boasts two natural and six wild areas. Alan Seeger Natural Area, near Greenwood Furnace State Park (Huntingdon County), occupies 390 acres and features Standing Stone Creek, trails, yellow birch, eastern hemlock, white pine, and rhododendron. Bear Meadows Natural Area, near Boalsburg (Centre County), is a National Natural Landmark that covers 890 acres and features trails and an observation platform for wildlife-watching. Big Flat Laurel Natural Area, near Boalsburg (Centre and Huntingdon Counties), occupies 184 acres and features mountain laurel. Detweiler Run Natural Area, near Boalsburg (Huntingdon County), occupies 463 acres in which eastern hemlock, white pine, and rhododendron appear. Little Juniata Natural Area, near Barree (Huntingdon County), encompasses 624 acres as well as a Tussey Mountain water gap and talus slopes. Rocky Ridge Natural Area, near Martin Gap (Huntingdon County), covers 150 acres and features woodlands and wildflowers. Thickhead Mountain Wild Area, near State College

(Centre and Huntingdon Counties), occupies 4,886 acres with a mixed-oak forest. And Trough Creek Wild Area, near Raystown Lake (Huntingdon County), comprises 1,703 acres, with hiking and wildlife-watching possible on Terrace Mountain.

Also nearby is *Shaver's Creek Environmental Center* at Penn State's Stone Valley Recreation Area, located 14 miles south of State College. The center offers year-round programs and activities. For details, contact Shaver's Creek (call 814-667-3424 or e-mail shaverscreek@outreach. psu.edu), or visit its Web site at www.shaverscreek.org. Opportunities at Stone Valley include boating, fishing for trout and other species, ice fishing, hiking, and cross-country skiing; boat launching and cabin rental [$] are also available.

The Pennsylvania Fish and Boat Commission's *fish culture stations at Pleasant Gap and Bellefonte* both have visitors centers with exhibits and tours available. Contact the Bellefonte Fish Culture Station at 1150 Spring Creek Road, Bellefonte, PA 16832 (814-355-3371) or the Pleasant Gap Fish Culture Station at 450 Robinson Lane, Pleasant Gap, PA 16823 (814-359-5132).

21

BALD EAGLE STATE FOREST

Penns View, Bells Majestic View, Winkelblech Mountain
Overlook, and McCall Dam Overlook (R. B. Winter State Park)

Bald Eagle State Forest includes more than 195,620 acres in
Centre, Clinton, Mifflin, Snyder, and Union Counties, and it
possesses a wealth of spectacular overlooks. The state forest is in
Pennsylvania's Ridge and Valley province, one of seven physiographic provinces in Pennsylvania. The varied patterns and
shapes of the ridges and valleys provide Bald Eagle State Forest
with diverse panoramic overlooks.

Penns View

Penns View is a 50-yard clearing on the summit of Poe Mountain.
The site is 1,700 feet above sea level and about 1,000 feet above
the valley below; its vista is northerly from about 315 degrees
northwest to about 90 degrees east, providing a spectacular view
of Penns Valley. To the north, up the river valley, Coburn is
visible. Across the valley to the northeast is Woodward Mountain.
Farther to the right is Sand Mountain, and to the north, Brush
Mountain and Nittany Mountain. Millheim and Aaronsburg are
also visible. To the east, you can see the north end of Elk Gap as
well as Korman Gap.

   You can continue driving east from Penns View on Poe
Paddy Drive to reach other overlooks, but the road becomes
unimproved.

Bells Majestic View

Bells Majestic View's vista is north-northwest, about 285 degrees
west-northwest to about 30 degrees north-northeast. The vista
stands about 1,800 feet above sea level and some 700 feet above
the low spots to the north. To the northwest are First Mountain
and Zerby Gap. Penns Valley lies beyond First Mountain. To the
north is Millheim, and a little to the right, Aaronsburg. You can
see the traffic on PA Route 45 to the north. Beyond First Mountain is Egg Hill; beyond Penns Valley is Brush Mountain; farther

Penns View is about 1,000 feet above Penns Valley.

north is Shriner Mountain. Beyond Brush and Shriner Mountains is Nittany Mountain.

Winkelblech Mountain Overlook

Winkelblech Mountain Overlook is about 1,970 feet above sea level and 370 feet above the low spots to the south. Its view is to the south, about 105 degrees east-southeast to about 240 degrees south-southwest. Visible from Winkelblech Mountain Overlook to the southeast are Bear Mountain, Stitzer Mountain, and Bear Gap (through which runs PA Route 45). Beyond the gap is Paddy Mountain, and beyond Paddy Mountain is Penns Creek Mountain to the southeast. Just north of the overlook, about 50 yards away, the blue-blazed Winkelblech Trail crosses the road.

McCall Dam Overlook (R. B. Winter State Park)

McCall Dam Overlook borders Bald Eagle State Forest and R. B. Winter State Park. It is a pull-off with ample parking and a formal wood-railed area. The overlook is about 1,840 feet above sea level and about 340 feet above Halfway Lake. The view at McCall

McCall Dam Overlook is a pull-off with ample parking and a formal railed area.

Dam Overlook is southerly, about 135 degrees southeast to about 225 degrees southwest. Visible below is Halfway Lake in R. B. Winter State Park and the Rapid Run Water Gap, through which PA Route 192 winds. Beyond the gap is Shriner Mountain, which rises before the Hook Natural Area.

OPPORTUNITIES: ATV riding on 7 trail miles, mountain biking, primitive camping [$], fishing for trout and other species, hiking on 58 trail miles, horseback riding, hunting, picnicking in 5 designated areas, cross-country skiing on 24 trail miles, snowmobiling on 466 trail miles, and wildlife-watching.

ADMINISTRATION AND AMENITIES: McCall Dam State Park has water and pit toilets. The Sand Bridge and Hairy Johns picnic areas have pit toilets. R. B. Winter State Park has water and pit toilets.

DIRECTIONS: To reach Penns View: From Georges Valley Road, turn south onto Synagogue Gap Road (a single-lane improved dirt road) and follow it 0.9 mile to Decker Valley Road. Turn left (east) onto Decker Valley Road, and follow it 2.2 miles to Mount Church Road. Follow Mount Church Road 0.3 mile to its end. Then turn left (north) around a curve onto Millheim Pike. Follow Millheim Pike 1.1 miles, and turn right (east) onto Pine Swamp Road, following the signs to Penns View.

To reach Bells Majestic View: From Penns View, retrace your steps to Pine Swamp Road, and turn south off Pine Swamp Road onto Siglerville-Millheim Pike (SR 2012). Follow it a few hundred yards to the overlook.

To reach the Winkelblech Mountain Overlook: From PA Route 45 east of Woodward, turn left (north) into the Hairy Johns State Forest Picnic Area. Continue through the picnic area about 50 yards until you reach Winkelblech Road. Wind around the picnic area, and at the ski trail sign, continue north, staying on Winkelblech Road. Follow Winkelblech Road north 3 miles to the overlook. The overlook is a clearing with a pull-off.

To reach the McCall Dam Overlook: From PA Route 192, enter R. B. Winter State Park and turn north off of PA Route 192 onto McCall Dam Road. As soon as you make the turn, the road forks. Take the left fork up the mountain 0.5 mile to the overlook—it is a pull-off on the right (south) side of the road.

FOR MORE INFORMATION: Contact Bald Eagle State Forest, Bureau of Forestry, Forest District #7, Box 147, Laurelton, PA 17835 (call 570-922-3344 or e-mail fd07@dcnr.state.pa.us), or visit its Web site at www.dcnr.state.pa.us/forestry/stateforests/forests/baldeagle/baldeagle.htm.

NEARBY OVERLOOKS: Hyner View State Park (Clinton County); Rothrock State Forest overlooks (Huntingdon, Centre, and Mifflin Counties); Shikellamy State Park overlooks (Union County); Ralph's Majestic Vista (Centre County); and Altoona-area overlooks (Blair County).

OTHER NEARBY OPPORTUNITIES

Poe Valley State Park, near Millheim (Centre County). Activities include boating, tent and trailer camping [$], fishing for trout and other species, picnicking, lake swimming, and wildlife-watching. The park also offers boat launching and mooring [$], boat rental [$], a food concession, pavilion rental [$], playground and playfield facilities, and a visitors center.

R. B. Winter State Park, near Lewisburg (Union County). Activities include tent and trailer camping [$], fishing for trout, ice fishing, hiking and backpacking on 6 trail miles with trailhead, hunting, picnicking, snowmobiling on 2 trail miles with trailhead, lake swimming, and wildlife-watching. The park also offers modern cabin rental [$], a food concession, pavilion rental [$], and playfield and playground facilities.

Reeds Gap State Park, near Reedsville (Mifflin County). Activities include tent and trailer camping [$], trout fishing, hiking and backpacking on 5 trail miles with trailhead, picnicking, pool swimming [$], and wildlife-watching; playground facilities are also available.

Snyder-Middleswarth State Park, near Troxelville (Snyder County). The park features a 425-acre area of original-growth timber, the largest in all of Pennsylvania's state forests.

Bald Eagle State Forest boasts a number of natural and wild areas. The Hook Natural Area, near Hartleton (Union County), covers more than 5,100 acres, and foot trails provide access to the complete Buffalo Creek Watershed. Joyce Kilmer Natural Area, also near Hartleton, includes 77 acres and features hemlock and virgin white pine. Mt. Logan Natural Area, near Castanea (Clinton County), encompasses 512 acres, on which visitors will find a Tuscarora sandstone outcrop and old-growth hemlock. Rosencrans Bog Natural Area, near Loganton (Clinton County), covers 152 acres and features high-mountain wetlands. Snyder-Middleswarth Natural Area, near Troxelville (Snyder County), has 500 acres with foot trails and access to areas of pitch pine, virgin white pine, and hemlock. Tall Timbers Natural Area, near Snyder-Middleswarth Natural Area, comprises 660 acres, and its forest land includes second-growth hemlock, hard pine, oak, and white pine. And White Mountain Wild Area, just southwest of Weikert (Mifflin and Union Counties), encompasses more than 3,500 acres; it is accessible only by trail, and visitors can observe the talus slopes of White Mountain.

Also nearby is *Shaver's Creek Environmental Center* at Penn State's Stone Valley Recreation Area, located 14 miles south of State College. The center offers year-round programs and activities. For details, contact Shaver's Creek (call 814-667-3424 or e-mail shaverscreek@outreach.psu.edu), or visit its Web site at www.shaverscreek.org. Opportunities at Stone Valley include boating, fishing for trout and other species, ice fishing, hiking, and cross-country skiing; boat launching and cabin rental [$] are also available.

The Pennsylvania Fish and Boat Commission's *fish culture stations at Pleasant Gap and Bellefonte* both have visitors centers with exhibits and tours available. Contact the Bellefonte Fish Culture Station at 1150 Spring Creek Road, Bellefonte, PA 16832 (814-355-3371) or the Pleasant Gap Fish Culture Station at 450 Robinson Lane, Pleasant Gap, PA 16823 (814-359-5132).

The *Northeast Fisheries Center and Lamar Fish Health Unit* of the U.S. Fish and Wildlife Service engage in research on salmonid species and Atlantic sturgeon. Contact the center in Lamar (call 570-726-4247 or e-mail fw5ffa_lftc@fws.gov), or visit its Web site at http://northeast.fws.gov/pa/nefclnfh.htm.

RIDGE AND VALLEY PROVINCE

The Ridge and Valley physiographic province, like the Appalachian Plateaus province, is one of seven areas of common geologic activity in Pennsylvania. The province's main features are high, long, nearly parallel sandstone ridges that rise sharply from wide valleys to heights of 2,300 feet above sea level. Between these ridges, the valleys are composed of softer rock more susceptible to erosion, such as shale or limestone. The alternating ridges and valleys of this province begin in the area of Bedford and Fulton Counties and reach northeastward.

The ridges of the Ridge and Valley province hindered westward expansion by English colonial settlers in the 1700s and prevented easy commercial links between eastern and western settlers in Pennsylvania. The French reached western Pennsylvania more readily by way of the Great Lakes and the Allegheny River. Settlers from what is now West Virginia reached western Pennsylvania by following river routes. Only in the mid-1800s did the Pennsylvania Railroad begin to conquer the province's mountains. The Pennsylvania Turnpike's tunnels through these ridges forged a modern east-west route in the state—but not until 1940.

22

RAYSTOWN LAKE

Raystown Dam Overlook and Ridenour Overlook

In western Huntingdon County, Raystown Lake snakes along a narrow, 28-mile path with 118 shoreline miles and some 8,300 water acres for recreation. The U.S. Army Corps of Engineers built the lake in the late 1960s and 1970s, damming the Raystown Branch of the Juniata River as a flood-control measure. Raystown Lake is the largest lake that lies wholly within Pennsylvania's borders, and it is one of the state's most popular boating and fishing spots.

Raystown Lake is surrounded on the west by several ridges and on the east by Terrace Mountain. This rugged terrain encourages a wealth of outdoor activities. Enthusiasts visit the area for its excellent fishing, hunting, camping, and boating. You can find overnight accommodations in Huntingdon and in cottages and campgrounds around the lake. (Contact the Raystown Country Visitors Bureau for these details.)

Raystown Lake is principally known for its fishing. The lake's steep sides and mountainous surroundings beckon anglers, and the lake is indeed "fishy"—largemouth bass, smallmouth bass, muskellunge, walleyes, panfish, trout, and lake trout are the main attractions. In addition, Raystown Lake offers some of the East Coast's best landlocked striped bass fishing. Stripers weighing more than 50 pounds have been caught. The Raystown Country Visitors Bureau can help you enlist the services of a fishing guide, who will quickly familiarize you with the lake's features.

The lake has several noteworthy overlooks. The Raystown Dam Overlook is at the dam itself. Ridenour Overlook and Hawn Overlook are on the west side of the lake.

Raystown Dam Overlook

The Raystown Dam Overlook view is to the southwest over the lake, 165 degrees south-southwest to about 300 degrees north-northwest. The overlook is not particularly high: it stands only

View of Raystown Lake from Ridenour Overlook.

about 50 feet above the lake. A small pavilion and wayside exhibits, however, provide information on the 21-megawatt William F. Matson Generating Station, which began commercial operation in 1988. The triangular pavilion has bench seating for lectures, classes, and presentations. Other exhibits explore the rural electric cooperatives in Pennsylvania and New Jersey that formed the Allegheny Electric Cooperative, which provides electricity for some 8,500 customers.

Ridenour Overlook

Ridenour Overlook's view is mainly to the southeast down the lake, from 45 degrees northeast to about 180 degrees south. The overlook stands 1,214 feet above sea level and 428 feet above the lake level. Terrace Mountain, on the other side of the lake, domi-nates the view.

A sign at Ridenour Overlook directs you to Hawn Overlook, 300 yards south down a path, which provides another view of the lake and Terrace Mountain. Hawn Overlook is near the location of the former Raystown Dam and the old Hawn's Bridge.

OPPORTUNITIES: Boating, tent and trailer camping [$], fishing, ice fishing, hiking, hunting, water skiing, lake swimming, and wildlife-watching; boat launching, boat rental [$], concessions, playground facilities, and restaurants are also available.

ADMINISTRATION AND AMENITIES: The Raystown Dam overlook closes at sundown. Rest rooms and water are available. The Ridenour Overlook has no services.

DIRECTIONS: Signs for Ridenour Overlook appear on U.S. Route 22 in Huntingdon approaching Snyders Run Road from either direction. From U.S. Route 22 in Huntingdon, just east of the Burger King, take Snyders Run Road easterly (nearly paralleling U.S. Route 22) for about 0.3 mile. When Snyders Run Road turns to the right, continue straight on Henderson Hollow Road. Follow the signs to the overlook. From U.S. Route 22 at Snyders Run Road, the Ridenour Overlook parking lot is about a 3.8-mile drive.

To reach the Raystown Dam Overlook: Leave the Ridenour Overlook parking lot and retrace your route about 0.9 mile to Stonebridge Road, a two-lane dirt road. Follow Stonebridge Road to the dam.

FOR MORE INFORMATION: Contact the U.S. Army Corps of Engineers, Baltimore District, Raystown Lake, RD 1, Box 222, Hesston, PA 16647 (call 814-658-3405 or send e-mail through the Web site at www.nab.usace.army.mil). In addition, the Raystown Country Visitors Bureau (1-800-269-4684) can provide useful information for sightseers. Visit the Bureau's Web site at www.raystown.org.

NEARBY OVERLOOKS: Blue Knob State Park overlooks (Bedford County); Altoona-area overlooks (Blair County); Buchanan State Forest overlooks (Fulton County); Rothrock State Forest overlooks (Huntingdon and Centre Counties); Ralph's Majestic Vista (Centre County); Tuscarora State Forest overlooks (Perry County); and Michaux State Forest overlooks (Franklin County).

OTHER NEARBY OPPORTUNITIES

 Canoe Creek State Park (Blair County). Activities include bicycling, boating (with electric motors only), ice boating, fishing for trout and other species, ice fishing, hiking on 8 trail miles, horseback riding on 5 trail miles, hunting, picnicking, ice skating, cross-country skiing, sledding, lake swimming, and wildlife-watching. The park also offers boat launching and mooring [$], boat rental [$], modern cabin rental [$], environmental education, a food concession, pavilion rental [$], a playfield, a playground, and a visitors center.

 Trough Creek State Park (Huntingdon County). Activities include tent and trailer camping [$], fishing for trout and other species, hiking on 6 trail miles, hunting, picnicking, snowmobile trailhead to Rothrock State Forest trails, and wildlife-watching. The park also offers modern cabin rental [$], environmental education, pavilion rental [$], and playfield facilities.

 Warriors Path State Park (Bedford County). Activities include fishing for warm-water species, hiking on 3 trail miles, hunting, picnicking, and wildlife-watching. The park also offers boat launching, pavilion rental [$], and a playfield.

 Also nearby is *Shaver's Creek Environmental Center* at Penn State's Stone Valley Recreation Area, located 14 miles south of State College. The center offers year-round programs and activities. For details, contact Shaver's Creek (call 814-667-3424 or e-mail shaverscreek@outreach.psu.edu), or visit its Web site at www.shaverscreek.org. Opportunities at Stone Valley include boating, fishing for trout and other species, ice fishing, hiking, and cross-country skiing; boat launching and cabin rental [$] are also available.

 The *Lower Trail,* which extends over 11 miles in Blair and Huntingdon Counties, is part of the Pennsylvania Rails-to-Trails program. Trailheads are located at Alexandria, Williamsburg, Canoe Creek State Park, and Flowing Springs. For more information, contact Rails-to-Trails of Blair County, Inc., PO Box 592, Hollidaysburg, PA 16648 (814-695-8521).

WATER QUANTITY

Pollution laws protect the quality of our water and the animals and plants living in and around our waterways. But water quantity is an equally significant aspect of conservation.

Pennsylvania's natural resources are held for all of us in the public trust, according to the Pennsylvania Constitution, and those natural resources include water. Water use and withdrawal rights, however, belong to the riparian (shoreline) owners. Gigantic Raystown Lake, for instance, is created by a dam; the dam and lake exist primarily to control flooding. The U.S. Army Corps of Engineers owns Raystown Lake and regulates water releases from the dam. (Alvin R. Bush Dam on Kettle Creek Lake {see Chap. 15} and Kinzua Dam {see Chap. 2} were also created largely for flood control.)

In Pennsylvania, two federal agencies regulate water withdrawals from their respective watersheds: the Susquehanna River Basin Commission and the Delaware River Basin Commission. Each agency requires permits for water withdrawals of more than one hundred thousand gallons per day. The U.S. Geological Survey and the U.S. Fish and Wildlife Service work with the river basin commissions and with state agencies, such as the Pennsylvania Department of Environmental Protection (DEP) and the Pennsylvania Fish and Boat Commission, to ensure that water withdrawals meet human needs and do not harm the animals and plants that depend on the waterways.

From overlooks, we admire the natural beauty of moving and still waters. Those waters do not maintain their levels and flows only through rain, runoff, and other natural processes, however. They also rely on human intervention—on state and federal laws.

23

SHIKELLAMY STATE PARK

Shikellamy State Park includes about 130 acres in Union and Northumberland Counties. The park was named after Iroquois Chief Shikellamy, who played a leading role in Pennsylvania's frontier development in the 1700s. Two main overlooks are in the Union County portion of the park, on the southwest side of the confluence of the North Branch Susquehanna River and the West Branch Susquehanna River. This confluence creates the Susquehanna River's main stem, which flows some 100 miles to the head of the Chesapeake Bay in Maryland.

The Shikellamy State Park overlooks stand approximately 400 feet above the river on a cliff at the end of Blue Hill's ridge. The most easterly overlook, the first one you see when arriving from U.S. Route 11, is a dramatic northeast view up the North Branch Susquehanna River and a northwest view of the West Branch Susquehanna River. The precipice is almost directly above the U.S. Route 11 bridge. A picnic table only 6 feet or so from the fenced cliff makes for a spectacular picnic setting. This spot has a nearly 180-degree view of the river, the cities of Northumberland and Sunbury, and the woods, farms, and countryside beyond. From this spot you can see Packers Island reaching up the North Branch. (The south end of Packers Island includes a boat access, picnic area, and the Basse A. Beck Environmental Education Center.)

The second overlook view is located about 100 yards west of the first. It is equally impressive: its northeast view up the North Branch Susquehanna River, 315 degrees northwest to about 135 degrees southeast, offers close to a 180-degree panorama. The overlook also provides a dramatic northwest view up the West Branch Susquehanna River—and a playfield, a sandbox, and swings, as well as a large parking lot. From the second overlook, you can follow a narrow path along a chain-link fence to reach other vistas, including the first one. (From late spring through fall, however, most of the view is hidden by tree foliage.)

Northeast view of the confluence of the north and west branches of the Susquehanna River. Below is the U.S. Route 11 bridge over the North Branch Susquehanna River.

OPPORTUNITIES: Bicycling, boating (with unlimited horsepower), fishing for trout and other species, hiking on 2 trail miles, picnicking, cross-country skiing, and wildlife-watching. Boat launching and mooring [$], boat rental [$], environmental education, a food concession, pavilion rental [$], and playfield and playground facilities are also available.

ADMINISTRATION AND AMENITIES: Water and pit toilets are available in the park near both overlooks. The park is open from 8:00 A.M. to sunset.

DIRECTIONS: From U.S. Route 11 in Sunbury and from points south, follow the signs to Shikellamy State Park. Turn westerly onto a small, unmarked, two-lane paved road leading uphill. Drive about 0.1 mile and turn right for the state park (follow the sign). Drive another 0.5 mile to the first overlook's parking area.

To reach the second overlook: Turn right after leaving the first overlook's parking lot and continue another 0.2 mile to the second overlook's parking lot.

You can also reach Shikellamy State Park from U.S. Route 15. Turn easterly onto County Line Road at the sign for "Shikellamy State Park Scenic Overlook."

FOR MORE INFORMATION: Contact Shikellamy State Park, Bridge Avenue, Sunbury, PA 17801-1005 (call 570-988-5557 or e-mail shikellamy@dcnr.state.pa.us), or visit its Web site at www.dcnr.state.pa.us/stateparks/parks/shilk.htm.

NEARBY OVERLOOKS: Hyner View State Park (Clinton County); Sproul State Forest overlooks (Clinton County); Bald Eagle State Forest overlooks (Centre County); Hawk Mountain Sanctuary overlooks (Berks County); Council Cup Scenic Overlook (Luzerne County); High Knob Overlook (Sullivan County); and Canyon Vista (Sullivan County).

OTHER NEARBY OPPORTUNITIES

Milton State Park (Northumberland County). Bicycling, fishing for trout and other species, hiking on 1 trail mile, and picnicking; the park also offers boat launching, a playfield, and a playground.

R. B. Winter State Park, near Lewisburg (Union County). Activities include tent and trailer camping [$], fishing for trout, ice fishing, hiking and backpacking on 6 trail miles with trailhead, hunting, picnicking, snowmobiling on 2 trail miles with trailhead, lake swimming, and wildlife-watching. The park also offers modern cabin rental [$], a food concession, pavilion rental [$], and playfield and playground facilities.

Sand Bridge State Park (Union County). Activities include fishing for trout, picnicking, snowmobiling with trailhead to Bald Eagle State Forest trails, and wildlife-watching.

Montour Preserve (Montour County), owned by the PPL Corporation. Activities include boating (with electric motors only), fishing for warm-water species, ice fishing, hiking on 12 trail miles, picnicking in two designated areas, cross-country skiing on 12 trail miles, and wildlife-watching. The preserve also offers environmental education and has a visitors center (717-437-3131).

24

BUCHANAN STATE FOREST

Cliff Vista and Tuscarora Vista

Buchanan State Forest encompasses some 75,000 acres in
Bedford, Franklin, and Fulton Counties, and it is divided into
five main sections. The park is named after the fifteenth president
of the United States, James Buchanan. His birthplace is located
in the state forest some 5 miles southwest of Fort Loudon,
Franklin County.

Cliff Vista

Cliff Vista is on Sideling Hill. It stands about 2,210 feet above sea
level and juts out about 1,000 feet above the valley floor to the
east. The view is mainly northeast from 45 degrees southeast to
nearly 225 degrees southwest—a spectacular, nearly 180-degree
panorama. Cliff Vista was probably named for the steep drop at its
edge; nearby Cliff Trail was probably named after the vista.
    Visible from Cliff Vista is Scrub Ridge to the east and
Tuscarora Mountain far across the valley. To the south-southeast
are the Potomac River Valley and Maryland.

Tuscarora Vista

Tuscarora Vista's view is easterly, almost 180 degrees north to
south. The overlook is about 2,450 feet above sea level and some
1,000 feet above the Path Valley and West Branch Conoco-
cheague Creek, which it surveys to the east. Visible to the southeast are the ends of Kittatinny Mountain and, beyond the
Kittatinny, Broad Mountain. The view to the southeast also
includes the Great Valley (on the Great Valley, see the sidebar in
Chap. 26). With a more southerly view on a clear day, you can see
into Maryland and glimpse Hagerstown at a distance of about 22
miles. In the valley between Kittatinny Mountain and Broad
Mountain are the headwaters of Conodoguinet Creek, which
flows along a snakelike northeasterly course to the Susquehanna
River at Harrisburg. To the east-northeast stands Blue Mountain.
    Each of the ridges in Buchanan State Forest belongs to Penn-

Cliff Vista is on Sideling Hill, about 1,000 feet above the valley floor.

sylvania's Ridge and Valley physiographic province, as does the Great Valley. Cliff Vista and Tuscarora Vista are on separate ridges about 16 miles apart. (For more information on the Ridge and Valley physiographic province, see the sidebar in Chap. 21.)

OPPORTUNITIES: ATV riding on 26 trail miles, mountain biking, primitive camping [$], fishing for trout and other species, hiking on 87 trail miles, horseback riding, hunting, picnicking in four designated areas, cross-country skiing on 5 trail miles, snowmobiling on 78 trail miles, and wildlife-watching.

Buchanan State Forest includes several natural and wild areas. Pine Ridge Natural Area, near Chaneysville (Bedford County), covers 568 acres; it features abandoned farms of the 1930s reforested by the natural regrowth of Virginia pine and pine plantings with hickory and oak, as well as hiking trails and horseback riding. Sweet Root Natural Area, also near Chaneysville, comprises 1,400 acres of virgin timber, second-growth oak, and areas of pine. Martin Hill Wild Area (southern Bedford County) includes some 11,500 acres as well as two small ponds providing watering areas for deer, turkey, bear, and rattlesnake populations.

Tuscarora Vista provides a dramatic, mainly easterly panorama spanning 180 degrees.

ADMINISTRATION AND AMENITIES: Near Cliff Vista, Sideling Hill Picnic Area has water pumps (which may not operate in cold weather) and pit toilets. Near Tuscarora Vista, Cowans Gap State Park has flush toilets and water fountains.

DIRECTIONS: To reach Cliff Vista: From U.S. Route 30 at the Sideling Hill Picnic Area, turn right onto Bark Road. This road is adjacent to the elevation sign that reads "Sideling Hill Summit,

Blue Ridge Mountain, elevation 2,195 feet." Cliff Vista is about 3 miles down Bark Road on the left. The overlook is about 0.1 mile beyond a sign on the right for Cliff Trail. There is informal parking at the side of the unpaved improved state forest road. The walk to the precipice is about 30 yards over a cleared flat area.

To reach Tuscarora Vista: Travel about 16 miles east of Cliff Vista along U.S. Route 30. On U.S. Route 30, at the top of Tuscarora Mountain, a sign records the elevation of "Tuscarora Summit, Cove Mountains" as 2,123 feet. At this sign, turn north from U.S. Route 30 onto Augwick Road (SR 1005). At the summit you will also find the Mountain House Bar and Grill on the south side of U.S. Route 30. After driving about 0.5 mile on Augwick Road, a sign for Buchanan State Forest will appear. About 0.4 mile farther, you will see a small sign for Tower Road and the scenic view. Turn right onto that road, which becomes a one-lane, improved state forest dirt road. In about 1.7 miles, the road circles the site of an old fire tower. Drive halfway around the old fire tower site and park on the side of the road. Walk 30 yards to the cliff's edge.

FOR MORE INFORMATION: Contact Buchanan State Forest, Bureau of Forestry, Forest District #2, RD 2, Box 3, McConnellsburg, PA 17233 (call 717-485-3148 or e-mail fd02@dcnr.state.pa.us), or visit its Web site at www.dcnr.state.pa.us/forestry/stateforests/forests/buchanan/buchanan.htm.

NEARBY OVERLOOKS: Blue Knob State Park overlooks (Bedford County); Raystown Lake overlooks (Huntingdon County); Rothrock State Forest overlooks (Huntingdon County); Tuscarora State Forest overlooks (Perry County); and Altoona-area overlooks (Blair County).

OTHER NEARBY OPPORTUNITIES

Cowans Gap State Park, near McConnellsburg (Fulton and Franklin Counties). Activities include boating, tent and trailer camping [$], organized group tent camping [$], fishing for trout and other species, ice fishing, hiking and backpacking on 10 trail miles with trailhead, hunting, picnicking, ice skating, cross-country skiing, sledding, lake swimming, and wildlife-watching. The park also offers boat launching and mooring [$], boat rental [$], rustic cabin rental [$], environmental education, and playfield facilities.

25

TUSCARORA STATE FOREST

Three Square Hollow Vista and Henry's Valley Vista

Tuscarora State Forest encompasses more than 91,100 acres in five tracts in Cumberland, Franklin, Huntingdon, Juniata, Mifflin, and Perry Counties. Three Square Hollow Vista and Henry's Valley Vista are located in the state forest's largest section, near the intersection of Cumberland, Perry, and Franklin Counties.

Tuscarora State Forest takes its name from Tuscarora Mountain and the Tuscarora American Indians. The logging industry engulfed this state forest (as it did other state forests) from the late 1800s to about 1930. The original acquisition of land for Tuscarora State Forest occurred in 1902 with the purchase of some 7,600 acres—at a cost of $1.72 per acre!

Three Square Hollow Vista

Three Square Hollow Vista, on Blue Mountain's ridge, stands about 1,800 feet above sea level and about 1,200 feet above the Cumberland Valley's low spots. The view is mainly to the southeast from about 90 degrees east to 210 degrees south-southwest. Visible to the southeast are the nearby valley villages and the farmland of the expansive Cumberland Valley. Looking southeasterly, you can see Newville some 8.5 miles away. While looking southeast toward South Mountain beyond Newville, if you catch a low, late-afternoon sun angle on a bright, clear day, you can see the sun's reflection off the quartzite walls of the mansion at Kings Gap Environmental Education and Training Center, which lies at a distance of about 17 miles. Visible to the south-southeast, about 11 miles away, are Shippensburg and the buildings and grounds of Shippensburg University. With binoculars or a spotting scope, look for Heiges Field House's white domed roof. Directly southeast across the valley—spanning nearly the entire view—is Michaux State Forest and South Mountain, about 17 miles away.

The vista surveys the Cumberland Valley, which is actually part of the Great Valley. The alternating ridges and valleys visible from Three Square Hollow Vista belong to the Ridge and

Three Square Hollow Vista offers a mainly southeasterly view of the Great Valley. Shippensburg and Shippensburg University are visible some 11 miles away.

Valley physiographic province. (For more information on this geological feature and the Great Valley, see the sidebars in Chaps. 21 and 26.)

Henry's Valley Vista

Henry's Valley Vista, on Sherman Mountain, provides a narrow easterly view from about 45 degrees northeast to 120 degrees south-southeast. This overlook stands about 1,900 feet above sea level and about 400 feet above the low spots to the east. The view of Henry's Valley includes the headwaters of Laurel Run and the Frank E. Masland Jr. Natural Area. To the south-southeast is the north face of Blue Mountain; to the northeast is Bower Mountain. Visible nearly 8 miles in the distance is the part of Blue Mountain that creates Doubling Gap, located near the border of Perry and Cumberland Counties.

A small wooden post at Henry's Valley Vista reads "10." The post marks the tenth stop on the Tuscarora State Forest Auto Tour, a 26-mile self-guided drive through the state forest. The tour's twelve stops explain the area's history and natural features and include a few more overlooks. (Contact the state forest office for a copy of the Auto Tour guide.)

OPPORTUNITIES: In Tuscarora State Forest, activities include mountain biking, boating, primitive camping [$], fishing, hiking,

From Henry's Valley Vista, visitors can see the part of Blue Mountain that creates Doubling Gap.

horseback riding, hunting (deer, grouse, squirrel, and turkey), picnicking in the Karl B. Guss State Forest Picnic Area (much of which is accessible by wheelchair), sightseeing (150 road miles and twenty-six bridges), cross-country skiing on 12 trail miles, snowmobiling on 120 trail miles, and wildlife-watching.

Fishing opportunities in the state forest include stream fishing for wild and stocked trout as well as fishing in the Juniata River for smallmouth bass, muskellunge, and panfish. Hikers will enjoy the 23 miles of the Tuscarora Trail, the 1-mile Tunnel Trail, and the 10-mile loop Iron Horse Trail, along with more than 160 miles of shorter trails.

ADMINISTRATION AND AMENITIES: No services at either overlook. Pit toilets and water are available at nearby Big Spring State Park on PA Route 274.

DIRECTIONS: To reach Three Square Hollow Vista: From Exit 201 of the Pennsylvania Turnpike, take PA Route 997 north a few miles to Three Square Hollow Road. Follow Three Square Hollow Road north. About 2 miles farther, the paved road becomes a state forest improved dirt road. Continue on Three Square Hollow Road up the mountain another 2.4 miles to the overlook—a clearing on the ridge.

To reach Henry's Valley Vista: From Three Square Hollow Vista, continue another 0.2 mile northeast up the mountain on Three Square Hollow Road to its intersection with Cowpens Road.

Turn left, following Three Square Hollow Road about 2 miles to its intersection with Laurel Run Road. Turn left onto Laurel Run Road and drive up the mountain about 0.2 mile to the vista.

FOR MORE INFORMATION: Contact Tuscarora State Forest, Forest District Headquarters, RD 1, Box 42-A, Blain, PA 17006 (call 717-536-3191 or e-mail fd03@dcnr.state.pa.us), or visit its Web site at www.dcnr.state.pa.us.tuscarora/tuscarora.htm.

NEARBY OVERLOOKS: Rothrock State Forest overlooks (Centre and Huntingdon Counties); Raystown Lake overlooks (Huntingdon County); Buchanan State Forest overlooks (Fulton County); Kings Gap Environmental Education and Training Center (Cumberland County); and Michaux State Forest overlooks (Franklin County).

OTHER NEARBY OPPORTUNITIES

Big Spring State Park, near New Germantown (Perry County). Activities include hiking and backpacking on 1 trail mile with trailhead, picnicking, cross-country skiing, snowmobile trailhead to Tuscarora State Forest trails, and wildlife-watching; the park also offers pavilion rental [$].

Colonel Denning State Park, near Doubling Gap (Cumberland and Perry Counties). Activities include tent and trailer camping [$], fishing for trout, hiking and backpacking on 18 trail miles with trailhead, hunting, picnicking, ice skating, cross-country skiing, lake swimming, and wildlife-watching. The park also offers environmental education, a food concession, pavilion rental [$], playfield and playground facilities, and a visitors center.

Fowlers Hollow State Park, Tuscarora State Forest, near Blain (Perry County). Activities include tent and trailer camping [$], fishing for trout, hiking and backpacking on 6 trail miles with trailhead, horseback riding on 1 trail mile with trailhead, hunting, picnicking, cross-country skiing, snowmobiling on 1 trail mile with trailhead, and wildlife-watching; pavilion rental [$] and playfield facilities are also available.

Little Buffalo State Park, Tuscarora State Forest, southwest of Newport (Perry County). Activities include boating (with electric motors only), fishing for trout and other species, ice fishing, hiking on 7 trail miles, hunting, picnicking, ice skating, cross-country skiing, sledding, pool swimming [$], and wildlife-watching. The park also offers boat launching and mooring [$], boat rental [$], environmental education, a food concession, a historical center, pavilion rental [$], playfield and playground facilities, and a visitors center.

Tuscarora State Forest boasts three natural areas and one wild area. Hoverter and Sholl Box Huckleberry Natural Area, near New Bloomfield (Perry County), covers 10 acres and features rare box huckleberry and an interpretive trail. The Frank E. Masland Jr. Natural Area, 12 miles southwest of Landisburg (Perry County), encompasses 1,270 acres with second-growth forest. The Hemlocks Natural Area, near Blain (Perry County), includes 131 acres with trails, a narrow ravine, and virgin hemlock. And Tuscarora Wild Area, on Tuscarora Mountain near Millerstown (Perry and Juniata Counties), covers 5,363 acres, featuring primitive backpack camping [$] and the remains of a logging railroad.

The 10-mile *Iron Horse Trail* is part of the Pennsylvania Rails-to-Trails program. It is located in Tuscarora State Forest with trailheads at Big Spring State Park and New Germantown. Contact Tuscarora State Forest for more information.

The *Cumberland Valley Trail* is part of the Pennsylvania Rails-to-Trails program. Its 9 miles extend from Shippensburg to Newville. For more information, contact Jerry Angulo, PO Box 531, Shippensburg, PA 17257 (717-860-0444).

The Pennsylvania Fish and Boat Commission's *fish culture station and visitors center at Huntsdale* (717-486-3419) is open to the public with tours available.

26

MICHAUX STATE FOREST

Buzzard's Rocks Vista and Valley View Vista

Michaux State Forest includes more than 85,000 acres in Adams, Cumberland, and Franklin Counties. Large iron-producing companies owned this land from the mid-1700s to the early 1900s. Iron ore dug from nearby open mines was used to make pig iron, which was forged into equipment such as kettles and other cooking items, tools, and stoves. The iron furnaces of this area also produced cannonballs used in the Revolutionary War.

Caledonia Furnace, located at the intersection of U.S. Route 30 and PA Route 233 at Caledonia State Park, was one enterprise in this early industrial activity. Competition from companies using newer methods and the discovery of richer ore deposits in the western United States, however, caused the demise of ironwork in Pennsylvania.

Michaux State Forest is named after the French botanist André Michaux. In 1785, the king and queen of France sent Michaux here to collect plants for the French royal gardens. Michaux and his son, François André, catalogued and named many area flowers, trees, and shrubs.

Buzzard's Rocks Vista

Buzzard's Rocks Vista stands 1,630 feet above sea level. The view, mostly to the southwest, offers a near southerly view 180 degrees south to 255 degrees northwest. This spot overlooks a wavy sea of forested lands and is wonderful for viewing fall foliage, especially in October. Across the landscape dip is Big Flat Tower on top of South Mountain.

Valley View Vista

Valley View Vista stands 1,400 feet above sea level and 600 feet above the valley below. Its breathtaking panoramic view is mainly westerly from 225 degrees southwest to 0 degrees north. Whitetail Resort's ski area, some 20 miles away, is visible off to

From Valley View Vista, views of more than 22 miles are possible.

the southwest. Looking farther to the southwest, parts of Maryland are visible. Cove Mountain, about 22 miles due west, is also visible. The lower ends of Broad Mountain and Kittatinny Mountain can be seen to the northwest. About 50 yards south of this vista, a wide pipeline right-of-way provides a similar view.

The Cumberland Valley, the expansive area visible from Valley View Vista, is a unique feature in Pennsylvania's Ridge and Valley province. To view the valley from different places, see the separate listings for Tuscarora State Forest, Kings Gap Environmental Education and Training Center, Hawk Mountain Sanctuary, and the Delaware Water Gap (Chaps. 25, 27, 37, and 40).

OPPORTUNITIES: ATV riding on 33 trail miles, mountain biking, primitive camping [$], fishing for trout and other species, hiking on 65 trail miles, horseback riding, hunting, picnicking in one designated area, cross-country skiing on 4 trail miles, snowmobiling on 131 trail miles, visiting historic sites, and wildlife-watching.

ADMINISTRATION AND AMENITIES: Water and flush toilets are located at the state forest district office on U.S. Route 30. Near

A sea of forestland waves below Buzzard's Rocks Vista.

Buzzard's Rocks Vista, Pine Grove Furnace State Park has pit toilets. Near Valley View Vista, Mont Alto State Park has pit toilets.

DIRECTIONS: To reach Buzzard's Rocks Vista: Take Exit 37 from I-81 and follow PA Route 233 south for about 6 miles. Turn right onto Ridge Road, a state forest improved dirt road. After about 2 miles, Ridge Road comes to a T intersection. Bear right, continuing on Ridge Road. (At this intersection you temporarily leave state forest lands.) Stay on Ridge Road about 2 more miles and turn right onto Hogshead Road. The overlook is about 1.8 miles farther: it has a large gravel parking lot with an old stone border that is falling apart and marked with much graffiti.

To reach Valley View Vista: From U.S. Route 30, turn south onto PA Route 233. On PA Route 233, between the Mont Alto State Park entrance and the Penn State Mont Alto campus, turn south onto Oak Road. There is a small sign for Valley View Vista there. Bear left onto the single-lane dirt road about 30 yards after turning onto Oak Road. Follow Oak Road up the mountainside about 1.6 miles to the overlook.

FOR MORE INFORMATION: Contact Michaux State Forest, Bureau of Forestry, Forest District #1, 10099 Lincoln Way East, Fayetteville, PA 17222 (call 717-352-2211 or e-mail fdo1@dcnr.state.pa.us); or visit its Web site at www.dcnr.state.pa.us/forestry/stateforests/forests/michaux/michaux.htm.

NEARBY OVERLOOKS: Buchanan State Forest overlooks (Fulton County); Tuscarora State Forest overlooks (Perry County); Kings Gap Environmental Education and Training Center (Cumberland County); Little Round Top (Adams County); Blue Knob State Park overlooks (Bedford County); and Raystown Lake overlooks (Huntingdon County).

OTHER NEARBY OPPORTUNITIES

Caledonia State Park, east of Chambersburg (Franklin and Adams Counties). Activities include bicycling, tent and trailer camping [$], organized group tent camping [$], fishing for trout, golfing, hiking and backpacking on 10 trail miles with trailhead, hunting, picnicking, cross-country skiing, snowmobiling on 10 trail miles with trailhead, pool swimming [$], and wildlife-watching. The park also offers modern cabin rental [$], environmental education, a food concession, a historical center, pavilion rental [$], and playfield and playground facilities.

Pine Grove Furnace State Park, southwest of Mount Holly Springs (Cumberland County). Activities include bicycling, boating (with electric motors only), tent and trailer camping [$], organized group tent camping [$], fishing for trout and other species, ice fishing, hiking on 2 trail miles, hunting, picnicking, ice skating, cross-country skiing, lake swimming, and wildlife-watching. The park also offers bicycle rental [$], boat launching and mooring [$], boat rental [$], environmental education, a food concession, a historical center, pavilion rental [$], playfield facilities, and a visitors center.

Mont Alto State Park, north of Waynesboro (Franklin County). Activities include fishing for trout, picnicking, snowmobile trailhead to Michaux State Forest trails, and wildlife-watching; pavilion rental [$], a playfield, and a playground are also available.

The *Cumberland County Biker/Hiker Trail* is part of the Pennsylvania Rails-to-Trails program. The 5.5-mile trail has trailheads at Pine Grove Furnace State Park and the Mountain Creek Campground. For more information, contact Pine Grove Furnace State Park (717-486-7174)

or visit its Web site at www.dcnr.state.pa.us/stateparks/parks/pine.htm.

The *Cumberland Valley Trail* is part of the Pennsylvania Rails-to-Trails program. Its 9 miles extend from Shippensburg to Newville. For more information, contact Jerry Angulo, PO Box 531, Shippensburg, PA 17257 (717-860-0444).

The Pennsylvania Fish and Boat Commission's *Fish Culture Station and visitors center at Huntsdale* (717-486-3419) is open to the public with tours available.

THE GREAT VALLEY

The Great Valley is a continuous valley that begins in Georgia, continues northward and arcs northeast through Pennsylvania, and ultimately reaches into New York State and Canada. The Pennsylvania portion of the Great Valley extends more than 150 miles. In southern Pennsylvania, the valley is called the Cumberland Valley (and, in places, the Susquehanna Valley), and it stretches northward and then northeastward toward Harrisburg. Farther northeast, it becomes the Lebanon Valley; still farther northeast, the Lehigh Valley. In Maryland, it is called the Hagerstown Valley. And farther south, it becomes the famed Shenandoah Valley.

27

KINGS GAP ENVIRONMENTAL
EDUCATION AND TRAINING CENTER

Kings Gap Environmental Education and Training Center occupies some 1,450 forest land acres on South Mountain, Cumberland County, about 45 miles southwest of Harrisburg. The Bureau of State Parks—part of the Pennsylvania Department of Conservation and Natural Resources—operates the facility.

The center is housed in the William C. Forrey Training Center mansion, a thirty-two-room stone mansion originally built by James McCormick Cameron (a member of the prominent Harrisburg Cameron family). Cameron's grandfather, Simon Cameron, was a U.S. senator from Pennsylvania who served as Abraham Lincoln's Secretary of War. The Cameron family accumulated great wealth in various enterprises, including railroading, printing, and banking. James McCormick Cameron built the mansion around 1908 as a summer residence.

After Cameron died in 1949, the C. H. Masland and Son Carpet Company bought the mansion, including the surrounding woodland acres; in 1973, the Commonwealth of Pennsylvania acquired the mansion and land through The Nature Conservancy. During the 1970s and 1980s, the environmental education center and training center opened. The training center's name honors William C. Forrey, director of the Pennsylvania Bureau of State Parks from 1973 through 1991. Forrey championed the efforts to acquire the property.

The overlook from the mansion's flagstone terrace is 1,300 feet above sea level and about 650 feet above the valley floor. Outstanding views of some 25 miles are possible from the mansion in the clearest, brightest conditions. The view of the Cumberland Valley is mostly northerly and nearly 180 degrees west to east. In the foreground is Antietam Ridge. On the western horizon is South Mountain. Looking westerly, you can see McAlisters Gap at Roxbury some 22 miles away. Visible closer to the west is Clark's Knob, and just east of that is Kings Gap Hollow. To the north, about 16 miles across the Cumberland Valley, stands Blue Mountain. Doubling Gap, a part of Blue Mountain, is visible to the north-northeast across the valley, and just east of

Views of more than 25 miles are possible from the mansion's terrace at Kings Gap Environmental Education and Training Center.

that is McClures Gap. Blue Mountain is the southernmost ridge in the Ridge and Valley physiographic province. (See the sidebars in Chaps. 21 and 26 for more information on the Ridge and Valley province and the Great Valley, of which the Cumberland Valley is a part.) Pastoral, panoramic wintry scenes, blooming mountain laurel, and fall foliage make this overlook pleasing throughout the year.

OPPORTUNITIES: Hiking (16 miles on thirteen trails, with additional overlooks along the more challenging trails), hunting, orienteering, picnicking, and wildlife-watching; year-round environmental education programs and activities are also available.

ADMINISTRATION AND AMENITIES: Kings Gap is open from 8:00 A.M. to sunset and has some wheelchair-accessible facilities. Water and pit toilets are available near the mansion.

DIRECTIONS: From Pine Road west of Mount Holly Springs, turn south on the road to the Kings Gap mansion at the sign for Kings Gap. This road is shared by horses, hikers, and bikers. The distance from Pine Road to the mansion is about 4 miles along a one-lane winding road through a thickly wooded area. Hiking trails crisscross the road. Follow the signs to the mansion's visitor parking.

FOR MORE INFORMATION: Contact Kings Gap Environmental Education and Training Center, 500 Kings Gap Road, Carlisle, PA 17013 (call 717-486-5031 or e-mail kingsgap@dcnr.state.pa.us), or visit the center's Web site at www.dcnr.state.pa.us/stateparks/parks/k-gap.htm.

NEARBY OVERLOOKS: Michaux State Forest overlooks (Franklin County); Buchanan State Forest overlooks (Fulton County); Tuscarora State Forest overlooks (Perry County); Little Round Top (Adams County); Negley Park (Cumberland County) and Reservoir Park, Harrisburg (Dauphin County); Rocky Ridge County Park (York County); Samuel S. Lewis State Park (York County); Chickies Rock County Park overlooks (Lancaster County); Holtwood Environmental Preserve overlooks (Lancaster County); and Susquehannock State Park overlooks (Lancaster County).

OTHER NEARBY OPPORTUNITIES

Gifford Pinchot State Park (York County). Activities include boating (with electric motors only), ice boating, tent and trailer camping [$], organized group tent and trailer camping [$], fishing for warm-water species, ice fishing, hiking on 18 trail miles, horseback riding on 4 trail miles, hunting, picnicking, ice skating, cross-country skiing, sledding, lake swimming, and wildlife-watching. The park also offers boat launching and mooring [$], boat rental [$], modern cabin rental [$], environmental education, a food concession, pavilion rental [$], a playfield, a playground, and a visitors center.

Pine Grove Furnace State Park, southwest of Mount Holly Springs (Cumberland County). Activities include bicycling, boating (with electric motors only), tent and trailer camping [$], organized group tent camping [$], fishing for trout and other species, ice fishing, hiking on 2 trail miles, hunting, picnicking, ice skating, cross-country skiing, lake swimming, and wildlife-watching. The park also offers bicycle rental [$], boat launching and mooring [$], boat rental [$], environmental education, a food concession, a historical center, pavilion rental [$], playfield facilities, and a visitors center.

The *Cumberland Valley Trail* is part of the Pennsylvania Rails-to-Trails program. Its 9 miles extend from Shippensburg to Newville. For more information, contact Jerry Angulo, PO Box 531, Shippensburg, PA 17257 (717-860-0444).

The *Cumberland County Biker/Hiker Trail* is part of the Pennsylvania Rails-to-Trails program. The 5.5-mile trail has trailheads at Pine Grove Furnace State Park and the Mountain Creek Campground. For more information, contact Pine Grove Furnace State Park (717-486-7174) or visit www.dcnr.state.pa.us/stateparks/parks/pine.htm.

The Pennsylvania Fish and Boat Commission's *Fish Culture Station and visitors center at Huntsdale* (717-486-3419) is open to the public with tours available.

How Water Gaps Form

Several water gaps make an appearance in this book. As you view such gaps from the perspective of an overlook, the idea of a stream dividing a mountain may seem odd. You might think that the waterways in these gaps should flow around *mountains. But water gaps result from waterways flowing* through *mountains and ridges—and you will see this phenomenon again and again in Pennsylvania. The state's water gaps range from the grand Delaware Water Gap to much smaller ones, such as those at Kings Gap and Tussey Mountain. A water gap between Lee and Penobscot Mountains is visible from Council Cup Scenic Overlook (see Chap. 34). The Susquehanna Water Gap at Harrisburg slices through five ridges, three of which are visible from Harrisburg: Peters Mountain, Second Mountain, and Blue Mountain. Visitors can observe this gap clearly from Negley Park (Cumberland County) and from Reservoir Park in Harrisburg (Dauphin County). (See Chap. 28 for these overlooks.)*

Since the 1800s, geologists have debated how gaps form. These processes occurred over millions of years; most of the history of these waterways and the mountains they have conquered has simply been lost in time. Today, geologists subscribe to two general theories on the formation of water gaps. The first holds that the waterway is antecedent: that is, the river existed before the mountain arose. If the mountain rose slowly enough, the river could still maintain its course and continue to cut through the rising ridge.

The second theory suggests that a stream flows through a mountain by a process called headward erosion. If two streams flow in opposite directions on either side of a ridge, the stream on the mountain's steeper slope erodes the mountain faster than the stream on the more gradual slope. When the streams meet, "stream piracy" occurs: the stream on the higher slope begins to flow in the opposite direction, running into the stream at the lower elevation.

28

HARRISBURG-AREA OVERLOOKS

Negley Park and Reservoir Park

Negley Park

Negley Park is a 17-acre community park in the borough of
Lemoyne (Cumberland County). Its rocky ledge along the river-
front is the only public place that provides a wonderful view of
the Susquehanna River, the city of Harrisburg's skyline, City
Island, and the borough of Wormleysburg. The overlook stands
about 140 feet above the Susquehanna River. Its view is mainly
northeasterly, about 0 degrees due north to about 135 degrees
southeast. Looking north, you can see the Harvey Taylor and
George Wade (I-81) bridges, Blue Mountain, Second Mountain,
and Peters Mountain. Northeasterly, beyond the city, you can
see Harrisburg's suburban communities along the slope of Blue
Mountain. To the southeast are the Market Street, Walnut
Street, and South (I-83) Bridges, and beyond, more suburbs,
including Chambers Hill. Looking east over the city you can
see Reservoir Park.

   In the 1800s, the area was called "Hummel's Hill," after the
owner who farmed the land. In the summer of 1863, area citizens
built two forts at the summit in anticipation of Confederate
troops advancing into the Cumberland Valley from the
Chambersburg area. Fort Washington was built on the summit,
across the street from Negley Park to the southwest, on the
slightly higher ground where houses now stand. From the fort,
one could view the Cumberland Valley to the southwest. Fort
Couch was built 0.5 mile west of the park (where the water tower
is today).

   Near this area was the most northerly advance of Confederate
troops during the Civil War. General Robert E. Lee intended to
capture Harrisburg, Pennsylvania's state capital, and destroy the
railroad bridge crossing the Susquehanna River. Two days before
the Battle of Gettysburg began—June 29, 1863—Union troops
from Fort Couch briefly exchanged fire with Confederate cavalry
who were undoubtedly scouting the Harrisburg area. Both sides
sustained casualties.

Southwesterly view of Harrisburg at night from Negley Park.

To see the remains of the Fort Couch breastwork near the water tower, drive westerly from Negley Park along Cumberland Road. It becomes Indiana Avenue at North Fifth Street. Continue straight on Indiana Avenue to North Eighth Street—a total distance of about 0.4 mile from Negley Park. Historic markers have been placed on the north and south sides of the fort's remnants.

Except for this one incident, Fort Couch and Fort Washington were never needed: the Battle of Gettysburg ended General Lee's attempt to bring the Civil War to the North. One wonders what role Fort Washington and Fort Couch would have played if the outcome on the Gettysburg battlefield had been different (see the description of Gettysburg National Military Park in Chap. 29) and if a large Confederate force had advanced on Harrisburg. Perhaps if General Lee and his Army of Northern Virginia had been successful at Gettysburg, Lee might have viewed Harrisburg from what is today Negley Park. From Negley Park he might also have shelled the city or terrified its residents into submission.

In the early 1940s, children used the land (then called Frazier Field) as a baseball field, and in 1942 the Lemoyne Borough Council bought the tract. Lemoyne Borough Council President Paul L. Negley was instrumental in the purchase. In 1945,

The National Civil War Museum is located in Reservoir Park. The museum's flagpole area provides spectacular northerly views.

Frazier Field was renamed Negley Park to honor Paul Negley and commemorate his efforts to secure the area as a park.

Reservoir Park

In the northeast part of Harrisburg (Dauphin County), a hill offers nice views of the Susquehanna Water Gap, the city, and the surrounding terrain. The bump in the landscape that forms the park is about 610 feet above sea level and some 200 to 250 feet above the area. The hill consists of hard conglomerate and sandstone—rocks that resist erosion more than the surrounding softer rock.

Many spots in Reservoir Park provide fine views, but two places are particularly notable. The view from the flagpole at the National Civil War Museum in the park is mainly to the north, about 270 degrees west to 90 degrees east. To the north-northeast is one of the best views of the Susquehanna Water Gap. This panorama also clearly shows three sets of mountains—first, Blue Mountain, followed by Second Mountain, and then by Peters Mountain. Across the north and northeast, against the base of Blue Mountain, is Linglestown. And to the west, between the trees, Blue Mountain stretches as far as the eye can see.

The Mansion Art Gallery parking lot and porch also provide extraordinary views. From the parking lot, look north for another clear view of the Susquehanna Water Gap. Looking north from the Mansion Art Gallery porch, you can also see I-81 and parts of

Enola, West Fairview, and the communities along the west shore of the Susquehanna River in northern Cumberland County. From the west side of the porch, Blue Mountain is visible to the west-northwest, the city of Harrisburg and the state capitol are visible, and to the south-southwest stand the mountains of northern York County, South Mountain, and the South Bridge (I-83). Walk just south of the Mansion Art Gallery and, looking westward, you will see Negley Park.

OPPORTUNITIES: Negley Park has several benches placed along the precipice. There are two roofed pavilions that are available for rent only by borough residents; the largest has benches facing the overlook. On the west side of the large pavilion, several loveseat swings face the overlook. The park also has tennis courts, a ball field, and playground facilities. In warm weather, a small, level grassy area at the overlook beckons visitors, who lounge on blankets and enjoy the view.

Reservoir Park's bandshell hosts a series of outdoor concerts with a variety of musical styles. Reservoir Park is also home to the National Civil War Museum [$], which opened in 2001. (For more information, contact the museum at 1-800-BLU-GRAY, or visit its Web site at www.nationalcivilwarmuseum.com.) The park also has expansive lawns, basketball courts, and playground facilities.

ADMINISTRATION AND AMENITIES: At Negley Park, there are no services. The park closes at 10:00 P.M. Rest rooms and water fountains are located throughout Reservoir Park. The park hours are 6:00 A.M. to 10:00 P.M.

DIRECTIONS: To reach Negley Park: From Market Street in Lemoyne, turn north onto North Third Street (at the Hardee's restaurant). The next turn is only about 100 yards ahead: turn right onto Walnut Street. Follow Walnut Street around—it becomes Cumberland Road—until Negley Park appears on your right. From the turn onto Walnut Street, the drive to the park is about 0.4 mile. Park on the street. A short but steep paved path leads to the overlook; farther on Cumberland Road, a series of steps will also guide you to the overlook. Depending on where you park, the walk from your car to the precipice will be about 40 to 80 yards.

To reach Reservoir Park: Follow Walnut Street in Harrisburg, and at Seventeenth Street, turn south into the park.

FOR MORE INFORMATION: Contact Negley Park, Lemoyne Borough, 665 Market Street, Lemoyne, PA 17043 (717-737-6843). For Reservoir Park, contact the City of Harrisburg, Department of Parks and Recreation, King City Government Center, 10 North Second Street, Suite 401, Harrisburg, PA 17101 (717-255-3020) or visit www.harrisburgevents.com.

NEARBY OVERLOOKS: Kings Gap Environmental Education and Training Center (Cumberland County); Little Round Top (Adams County); Michaux State Forest overlooks (Franklin County); Rocky Ridge County Park overlooks (York County); Mt. Pisgah (York County); Chickies Rock County Park overlooks (Lancaster County); Holtwood Environmental Preserve overlooks (Lancaster County); Tuscarora State Forest overlooks (Perry and Cumberland Counties); and Susquehannock State Park overlooks (Lancaster County).

OTHER NEARBY OPPORTUNITIES

Gifford Pinchot State Park (York County). Activities include boating (with electric motors only), ice boating, tent and trailer camping [$], organized group tent and trailer camping [$], fishing for warm-water species, ice fishing, hiking on 18 trail miles, horseback riding on 4 trail miles, hunting, picnicking, ice skating, cross-country skiing, sledding, lake swimming, and wildlife-watching. The park also offers boat launching and mooring [$], boat rental [$], modern cabin rental [$], environmental education, a food concession, pavilion rental [$], a playfield, a playground, and a visitors center.

City Island is very close to Negley Park and Reservoir Park. Park your car on City Island and walk around the island. For more information, call 717-255-3020 or visit www.harrisburgevents.com/cityisland/index.htm.

Wildwood Lake Sanctuary and the *Olewine Nature Center* in Harrisburg feature year-round exhibits and indoor and outdoor programs. For more information, call 717-221-0292 or visit www.wildwoodlake.org.

The *Holtwood Environmental Preserve* includes the Lock 12 Historic Area, Kelly's Run Natural Area, and Shenk's Ferry Wildflower Preserve. For more information, contact the Holtwood Environmental Preserve, owned by the PPL Corporation. (See Chap. 44 for details.)

State Game Lands #211 (Dauphin and Lebanon Counties) offers fishing for trout, hiking, hunting, rock climbing (only for the trained and experienced), and wildlife-watching.

29

GETTYSBURG NATIONAL MILITARY PARK

Little Round Top

On May 3, 1863, General Robert E. Lee won a decisive victory at the Battle of Chancellorsville in Virginia. He first ordered his Army of Northern Virginia to march westward into the Shenandoah Valley to hide its movements, and he then moved the army northeasterly toward Chambersburg, Pennsylvania, reaching Chambersburg by the end of June. Lee sent two brigades to survey the approach to Gettysburg, which the Confederate troops intended to occupy. They advanced on Gettysburg from the northwest, along Chambersburg Pike (U.S. Route 30), and did not know that Union troops were nearby. On July 1, 1863, the Battle of Gettysburg began northwest of Gettysburg.

On July 2, the second day of the battle, the fighting moved just south of Gettysburg. Union positions extended in a hooklike line from the Round Tops northeasterly to Cemetery Hill and then southeasterly to Culp's Hill. The Confederate lines mirrored those of the Union. Early on July 2, General Lee considered Meade's strong position. He decided that the Union flanks were that army's weakest spots, so he ordered troops to attack the Union's left and right flanks simultaneously. Lee believed that this move would allow him to shrink the Union line toward Cemetery Hill.

Brigadier General Gouverneur K. Warren's swift action allowed the Union to place troops at Little Round Top, a previously undefended key position on the Union left flank, only minutes before Confederate troops attacked from Big Round Top's tree-covered slopes. Fighting was fierce around Little Round Top.

On the third day of the battle, July 3, even after repeated attacks and Pickett's Charge—in which twelve thousand Confederate soldiers attacked the center of the Union ranks—the Confederate forces still could not break Union lines. Devastated by heavy casualties, Lee withdrew his Army of Northern Virginia southward to Virginia on July 4.

The Battle of Gettysburg was the turning point of the American Civil War. The Confederate forces, demoralized and exhausted, retreated to Virginia. General Lee never again tried to bring the war to the North. Estimates vary on the number of both Confederate and Union casualties (killed, wounded, captured, and missing) at the Battle of Gettysburg. Still, estimates of casualties on both sides total some 51,000 men. More than 75,000 Confederate troops and 82,000 Union troops were engaged during the Battle of Gettysburg, the bloodiest battle ever fought in North America.

The best way to place yourself in the midst of July 1–3, 1863, and in the events that made the Little Round Top overlook so important in the battle, is first to tour the park's visitors center. Obtain the official map and guide there. (You can also print the guide from the park's Web site.) Then view the wealth of artifacts in the magnificent Gettysburg Museum of the Civil War, located at the visitors center (free admission). The official map and guide includes a self-guided auto tour, which takes two to three hours. For a fee, you can also arrange a battlefield tour with a licensed guide. Three trails of varying lengths let you walk the battlefield as the soldiers did. Plan on spending at least a morning or an afternoon touring the battlefield; to learn the most about the Battle of Gettysburg, plan to visit at least for an entire day.

Gettysburg National Military Park gets some 1.6 million visitors annually. Nevertheless, the well-organized park and facilities can handle great numbers of visitors and still maintain the dignity of this hallowed place.

The view from Little Round Top is mostly westerly and northwesterly, 210 degrees south-southwest to 0 degrees north. Wayside exhibits describe the "Keen Eye and Decisive Judgment" of Brigadier General Gouverneur K. Warren, the "Union Fishhook," and "The Valley of Death." Another wayside exhibit identifies key battlefield spots. The view surveys the battlefield, and once you visit Little Round Top, the strategic importance of the hill is obvious. Little Round Top is only about 100 to 120 feet higher than the surrounding terrain, but most of the battlefield is visible from this spot. Tree-covered Big Round Top looms to the south. Visible to the west in the distance is South Mountain, about 10 miles away. (The ski area to the southwest is Ski Liberty, about 8 miles away.)

The boulder-strewn look of the entire battlefield, including Little Round Top and its slopes and especially Devil's Den, is the result of igneous volcanic rock. This rock resists erosion and weathering, and it occurs in a long, narrow expanse from southern Adams County northward through the battlefield and into

Westerly view from Little Round Top. On the horizon, about 10 miles away, is South Mountain.

southern Dauphin and Lebanon Counties. Igneous volcanic rock is also present to the east in Montgomery and Bucks Counties.

Both Devil's Den and Little Round Top look much as they did during the battle. Around 1862, Little Round Top's trees were felled; many trees have now grown in the area where there was open ground, however. The National Park Service, which administers Gettysburg National Military Park, plans a long-term project to restore missing features that affected the battle, including fences, orchards, farm lanes, and open fields. The project will require some fifteen to twenty years, but early maps, photographs, sketches, and soldiers' personal accounts provide excellent documentation on the battlefield's appearance in 1863.

OPPORTUNITIES: Auto touring, hiking, and wildlife-watching; a museum and a visitors center are also available.

ADMINISTRATION AND AMENITIES: Park admission is free. The park grounds and roads are open daily from 6:00 A.M. to 10:00 P.M.; the visitors center is open daily from 8:00 A.M. to 5:00 P.M. Summer hours are 8:00 A.M. to 6:00 P.M. daily. There are rest rooms throughout the park, but many are open only seasonally. Full services are available in Gettysburg.

DIRECTIONS: From U.S. Route 15, follow Hanover Street (PA Route 116) westbound about 1.4 miles into Gettysburg, where Hanover Street meets U.S. Route 30. Follow U.S. Route 30 west to the traffic circle in town. Then follow U.S. Business Route 15 South (Baltimore Street) southward, following signs to the park. Bear right at the fork and follow the signs on Steinwehr Avenue to the park. Turn left into the parking lot for the visitors center.

To reach Little Round Top: From the east entrance of the visitors center, turn right (south) onto Taneytown Road (PA Route 134). Turn right onto Wheatfield Road. In 0.1 mile, Little Round Top appears on the left, and one-way traffic begins, circling Little Round Top. Continue straight to Crawford Avenue. Turn left onto Crawford Avenue, then left onto Warren Avenue, and left again onto Sykes Avenue, following the road to Little Round Top's crest.

FOR MORE INFORMATION: Contact Gettysburg National Military Park, 97 Taneytown Road, Gettysburg, PA 17325-2804 (717-334-1124) or visit its Web site at www.nps.gov/gett.

NEARBY OVERLOOKS: Kings Gap Environmental Education and Training Center (Cumberland County); Michaux State Forest overlooks (Franklin County); Tuscarora State Forest overlooks (Perry and Cumberland Counties); Rocky Ridge County Park overlooks (York County); Mt. Pisgah (York County); Chickies Rock County Park overlooks (Lancaster County); the Susquehanna River overlooks owned by the PPL Corporation (Lancaster County); and Susquehannock State Park overlooks (Lancaster County).

OTHER NEARBY OPPORTUNITIES

Caledonia State Park, east of Chambersburg (Franklin and Adams Counties). Activities include bicycling, tent and trailer camping [$], organized group tent camping [$], fishing for trout, golfing, hiking and backpacking on 10 trail miles with trailhead, hunting, picnicking, cross-country skiing, snowmobiling on 10 trail miles with trailhead, pool swimming [$], and wildlife-watching. The park also offers modern cabin rental [$], environmental education, a food concession, a historical center, pavilion rental [$], and playfield and playground facilities.

Codorus State Park (York County). Activities include boating (with a 10hp limit), ice boating, tent and trailer camping [$], organized group tent camping [$], fishing for trout and other species, ice fishing, hiking on 5 trail miles, horseback riding on 7 trail miles, hunting, picnicking, ice skating, cross-country skiing, sledding, snowmobiling on 100 trail miles, pool swimming [$], and wildlife-watching. The park also offers boat launching and mooring [$], boat rental [$], environmental education, a food concession, pavilion rental [$], a playfield, and a visitors center.

Mont Alto State Park, north of Waynesboro (Franklin County). Activities include fishing for trout, picnicking, snowmobile trailhead to Michaux State Forest trails, and wildlife-watching; pavilion rental [$], a playfield, and a playground are also available.

Pine Grove Furnace State Park, southwest of Mount Holly Springs (Cumberland County). Activities include bicycling, boating (with electric motors only), tent and trailer camping [$], organized group tent camping [$], fishing for trout and other species, ice fishing, hiking on 2 trail miles, hunting, picnicking, ice skating, cross-country skiing, lake swimming, and wildlife-watching. The park also offers bicycle rental [$], boat launching and mooring [$], boat rental [$], environmental education, a food concession, a historical center, pavilion rental [$], playfield facilities, and a visitors center.

Adjacent to the battlefield is the *Eisenhower National Historic Site,* President Eisenhower's farm and home, with tours, exhibits, self-guided walks, and special events. Contact the Eisenhower National Historic Site, 250 Eisenhower Farm Lane, Gettysburg, PA 17325 (717-338-9114) or visit its Web site at www.nps.gov/eise.

 The Pennsylvania Fish and Boat Commission's *Fish Culture Station and visitors center at Huntsdale* (717-486-3419) is open to the public with tours available.

 The Pennsylvania Game Commission's *Middle Creek Wildlife Management Area* near Klinefeltersville (Lebanon and Lancaster Counties) features a waterfowl museum and programs on wildlife; for information, call 717-733-1512.

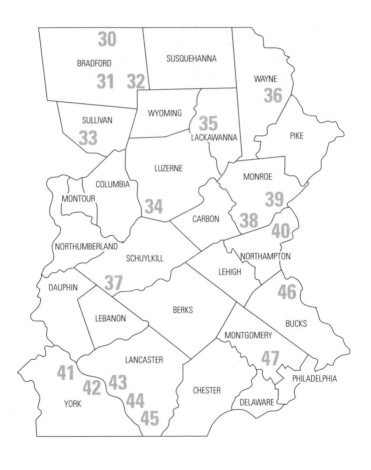

30

ROUND TOP PARK

On the bright September day we visited, Round Top Park had a festive atmosphere. The pavilions buzzed with the activities of reunions, birthday parties, and anniversary celebrations. Families played ball in the field, couples gazed over the vistas' panoramas while swaying arm in arm in the park's unique loveseats, and grills hissed and smoked with all sorts of food. A steady stream of overlook enthusiasts also arrived, crowding the parking lot.

The wonderfully friendly Round Top Park encompasses more than 500 acres in three sections. The top of the mountain is round and level—hence its name. A lower section in the park has a pond, a ball field, and three pavilions. Another isolated section is a field used for flying remote-controlled airplanes, and it also has an overlook view. The upper level, with its magnificent views, has eight pavilions, a children's play area, and a ball field.

At the top of the drive there is a narrower easterly overlook, but the main views can be found near the satellite dishes, in an area about 1,440 feet above sea level and about 700 feet above the North Branch Susquehanna and Chemung Rivers below. The view is mainly north-northeast, 330 degrees west-northwest to about 45 degrees northeast. This spot has benches and four swinglike loveseats, and it features excellent views of the northern part of Athens Township, Sayre, South Waverly, and the city of Athens. Visible farther north are the village of Waverly, New York, and the town of Barton, New York. On the North Branch Susquehanna River's eastern shore, north of East Athens, is Sayre Hill, a moundlike ridge.

In Sayre, the twelve-story brick building is Packer Hospital. In Waverly, New York, the brick building at the foot of the far hills is Tioga General Hospital, and the shiny metallic structures are feed mills. The North Branch Susquehanna River and the Chemung River are visible, and beyond them, New York State. (During the clearest evenings, you may see the lights of television antennas in Binghamton, New York—a distance of some 50 miles.) Enjoy a warm-weather view here with a picnic lunch, or, on a crisp day, make a special trip to see the fall foliage.

Loveseats adorn Round Top Park, which boasts a spectacular northerly view.

OPPORTUNITIES: Fishing, hiking, hunting (when the park closes seasonally), model-airplane flying, picnicking, cross-country skiing, sledding, playing volleyball, and wildlife-watching. Horseshoe pits, pavilion rental [$], playfield and playground facilities, and a softball field are also available.

ADMINISTRATION AND AMENITIES: Park hours are 6:00 A.M. to sunset from mid-May to mid-November. The park is closed mid-November through mid-December for hunting season; it is then open in winter only when snow is on the ground. Rest rooms and water are seasonally available. Pavilions can be reserved by calling or stopping by the Athens Township Municipal Building (570-888-2325) between 8:00 A.M. and 5:00 P.M. weekdays. Pavilions are reserved as much as a year in advance for the birthdays, graduations, weddings, reunions, and other celebrations that take place here.

DIRECTIONS: From U.S. Route 220 at Greens Landing, turn west onto Wolcott Hollow Road (at the Sunoco Station). On the east side of U.S. Route 220 at Wolcott Hollow Road, there is a small, green directional sign for the park. From here, you can reach the park by following the signs. After about 0.5 mile on Wolcott Hollow Road, turn right onto Round Top Road. Follow Round Top Road for about 1.2 miles. Turn right onto Murray Creek Road. Follow this road for about 0.2 mile, and turn right again onto Sutliff Hill Road. The Round Top Park entrance is 0.3 mile farther.

FOR MORE INFORMATION: Contact Athens Township, 184 Herrick Avenue, Sayre, PA 18840 (570-888-2325).

NEARBY OVERLOOKS: Mt. Pisgah County Park (Bradford County); Wyalusing Rocks and Marie Antoinette Overlook (Bradford County); Tioga State Forest overlooks (Tioga and Bradford Counties); and Pine Hill Vista (Lackawanna County).

OTHER NEARBY OPPORTUNITIES

Mt. Pisgah State Park (Bradford County). Activities include boating (with electric motors only), ice boating, fishing for warm-water species, ice fishing, hiking on 10 trail miles, hunting, picnicking, ice skating, cross-country skiing, sledding, snowmobiling on 8 trail miles, pool swimming [$], and wildlife-watching. The park also offers boat launching and mooring [$], boat rental [$], environmental education, a food concession, pavilion rental [$], playfield and playground facilities, and a visitors center.

Salt Spring State Park (Susquehanna County). Activities include fishing for trout, hiking on 2 trail miles, hunting, picnicking, and wildlife-watching.

31

MT. PISGAH COUNTY PARK

At Mt. Pisgah County Park, in Bradford County, you can walk to a number of vistas: several look easterly and northerly, and one at the summit looks westerly. The vistas' varying orientations allow for lovely views of both sunrise and sunset. There are also great views here of fall foliage, and the scenery includes a patchwork of farm hedgerows and forest. Mt. Pisgah's summit is 2,260 feet above sea level and some 1,100 feet higher than the surrounding lower spots.

The first overlook campsite is about 0.6 mile from the park entrance. Its narrow view is mainly north-northeast from 45 degrees northeast to about 105 degrees east-southeast. The second overlook campsite is 0.2 mile beyond the first, with a view that is mainly 45 degrees northeasterly. The restricted view through downed trees is about 15 degrees north-northeast to 60 degrees east-northeast. The third overlook campsite is about 50 yards beyond the second. Its view runs northeast from about 15 degrees north-northeast to 90 degrees east. From all of these campsite overlooks, you can see the fields and tree lots below. And from a spot near the first site, looking easterly, you can see Stephen Foster Lake in Mt. Pisgah State Park, which lies about 3 miles away.

The summit overlook at the antenna array offers a mainly westerly view, 225 degrees southwest to 315 degrees northwest. The overlook view on the west side has a platform. Visible to the west-northwest, about 4 miles away, you can see U.S. Route 6 as an east-west line in the wooded landscape north of Armenia Mountain. Far in the distance, about 17 miles to the northwest, are the mountains north of Mansfield in Tioga County. About 8 miles away, to the west and southwest, are mountains in the easternmost portion of Tioga State Forest.

In the late 1800s, a hotel at the summit of Mt. Pisgah offered affluent tourists fresh air, spring water, and breathtaking views from an observation tower nearly 100 feet high. No signs remain, however, of the hotel or its observation tower.

OPPORTUNITIES: Picnicking, sightseeing, tent and trailer camping [$], and wildlife-watching; playground and playfield facilities are also available.

The view from Mt. Pisgah's summit is westerly. To the west and southwest, about 8 miles away, are the mountains of the easternmost portion of Tioga State Forest.

ADMINISTRATION AND AMENITIES: The summit area has a roofed pavilion with picnic tables, grills, and rest rooms. Other picnic areas are near the pavilion, as is an open area for throwing Frisbees or playing ball. A play area for children features a wooden climbing structure, swings, and slides. The park is open from mid-May to mid-December.

DIRECTIONS: From U.S. Route 6 in East Troy, turn north at the sign for the Leona Meat Plant, and follow the signs to Mt. Pisgah State Park. Pass the school and ball field on the left and turn right (east), still following the signs to Mt. Pisgah County Park and Mt. Pisgah State Park. This right turn is only about 0.2 mile from U.S. Route 6. After about 1.2 miles, turn left (north) at the sign for the county park. (A sign for the state park will tell you to proceed straight ahead.) You will see the county park entrance after another 1.4 miles.

FOR MORE INFORMATION: Contact the Bradford County government (570-265-1707) or visit its Web site at www.bradford-pa.com.

NEARBY OVERLOOKS: Round Top Park (Bradford County); Wyalusing Rocks and Marie Antoinette Overlook (Bradford County); High Knob Overlook (Wyoming County); Canyon Vista, World's End State Park (Wyoming County); Tioga State Forest overlooks (Tioga and Bradford Counties); and Pine Hill Vista (Lackawanna County).

OTHER NEARBY OPPORTUNITIES

Hills Creek State Park (Tioga County). Activities include boating (with electric motors only), tent and trailer camping [$], fishing for warm-water species, ice fishing, hiking on 5 trail miles, picnicking, ice skating, and wildlife-watching. The park also offers boat launching and mooring [$], boat rental [$], modern cabin rental [$], environmental education, a food concession, pavilion rental [$], playfield and playground facilities, and a visitors center.

Mt. Pisgah State Park (Bradford County). Activities include boating (with electric motors only), ice boating, fishing for warm-water species, ice fishing, hiking on 10 trail miles, hunting, picnicking, ice skating, cross-country skiing, sledding, snowmobiling on 8 trail miles, pool swimming [$], and wildlife-watching. The park also offers boat launching and mooring [$], boat rental [$], environmental education, a food concession, pavilion rental [$], playfield and playground facilities, and a visitors center.

U.S. Army Corps of Engineers *Tioga–Hammond Lakes Project.* Activities include boating (with unlimited horsepower), tent and trailer camping [$], organized group tent camping [$], fishing for warm-water species, hiking, hunting, picnicking, and wildlife-watching. Boat launching [$], pavilion rental [$], and playfield facilities are also available. For details, contact the Lakes Project (call 570-835-5281 or e-mail Tioga-Hammond-LakeWEB@nab02.usace.army.mil), or visit its Web site at www.nab.usace.army.mil/recreation/tioga.htm.

32

WYALUSING ROCKS AND
MARIE ANTOINETTE OVERLOOK

Wyalusing Rocks

Wyalusing Rocks, in Bradford County, was a signaling point of the Iroquois. It was a part of the Warrior Path, an old American Indian highway that connected New York tribes with those in the Carolinas.

Wyalusing Rocks is a magnificent vista about 400 feet above the North Branch Susquehanna River. The view is mostly westerly from 225 degrees southwest to about 345 degrees north-northwest. To the west, beyond the hills of Terry Township, stand Robwood Mountain and the mountains of State Game Lands #36 and Tioga State Forest. Kellogg Mountain is also visible. You can walk up the path to the south for more views of the river. The area is marked with long slate outcroppings, but stick to the path—do not venture onto the outcroppings.

Migrating raptors traverse the area in the fall, and the changing leaves at that time provide a terrific scene. The precipice is only a few feet from the pull-off, so set up a lawn chair and take in the scenery with binoculars. This spot is also convenient for photographers who want to set up tripods and shoot views of the river and distant hills. Sunset shots here have the best chance of success because of the expansive, unrestricted westerly panorama.

Marie Antoinette Overlook

The Marie Antoinette Overlook, located about 3 miles north of Wyalusing Rocks, is about 500 feet above the North Branch Susquehanna River. The fantastic view is mostly westerly, 210 degrees south-southwest to 0 degrees north. Visible to the southeast, beyond the river bend, are Rowland Mountain and the mountains of State Game Lands #36 and Tioga State Forest. The overlook's length is marked on each side with two green-shingled turrets, each a few yards in diameter and about 12 feet high. The benches can seat several people.

At the site is a bronze marker that explains French Azilum (or "Asylum"), which is visible on the other side of the river. This

Wyalusing Rocks stands 400 feet above the North Branch Susquehanna River.

historic site was settled in 1793 by French aristocrats fleeing their country's Reign of Terror and the French Revolution. Sympathizers had hoped that Marie Antoinette would find safety here, and one special residence was built for her. But history tells us, of course, that the queen met her fate in France. For more information on French Azilum, which is managed by the Pennsylvania Historical and Museum Commission, call the site at 717-265-3376. (A small sign at the Marie Antoinette Overlook explains how to reach French Azilum.)

OPPORTUNITIES: Picnicking, sightseeing, visiting a historic site, and wildlife-watching.

ADMINISTRATION AND AMENITIES: No services at either overlook. These overlooks are pull-offs with ample off-road parking. Find

Visitors looking southwest from Marie Antoinette Overlook can see French Azilum.

services at Wyalusing to the south on U.S. Route 6 and at Towanda to the north.

DIRECTIONS: To reach the Marie Antoinette Overlook: From the north, follow U.S. Route 6 south of Wysox about 6 miles. As soon as you enter Wyalusing Township, watch for a blue sign that marks the overlook. To reach the overlook from the south, follow U.S. Route 6 north from Wyalusing. There is no sign, but the overlook is on the left, 0.2 mile past the intersection with PA Route 409. Look closely at the overlook site and you will see that it is a piece of old U.S. Route 6, before the four-lane highway was built.

To reach Wyalusing Rocks: From the north, follow U.S. Route 6 and drive 3 miles past the Marie Antoinette Overlook. Watch for a blue scenic overlook sign just before you reach the parking lot, which is on the right. To reach Wyalusing Rocks from the south, follow U.S. Route 6 north from Wyalusing. About 1 mile west of Wyalusing Township (just west of Wyalusing Borough), you will see a sign at the site that says "Scenic Overlook." Turn left into the parking area.

FOR MORE INFORMATION: For Wyalusing Rocks, contact PennDOT District 3-0, 715 Jordan Avenue, Montoursville, PA 17754 (call 1-877-723-6830 or e-mail penndot3@dot.state.pa.us). The Marie Antoinette Overlook is owned by PennDOT (see above for contact information), the Pennsylvania Historical and Museum Commission, and a private entity.

NEARBY OVERLOOKS: Round Top Park (Bradford County); Mt. Pisgah County Park (Bradford County); High Knob Overlook (Wyoming County); Canyon Vista (Wyoming County); Tioga State Forest overlooks (Tioga and Bradford Counties); and Pine Hill Vista (Lackawanna County).

OTHER NEARBY OPPORTUNITIES

Mt. Pisgah State Park (Bradford County). Activities include boating (with electric motors only), ice boating, fishing for warm-water species, ice fishing, hiking on 10 trail miles, hunting, picnicking, ice skating, cross-country skiing, sledding, snowmobiling on 8 trail miles, pool swimming [$], and wildlife-watching. The park also offers boat launching and mooring [$], boat rental [$], environmental education, a food concession, pavilion rental [$], playfield and playground facilities, and a visitors center.

Ricketts Glen State Park (Luzerne County). Activities include boating (with electric motors only), tent and trailer camping [$], organized group tent camping [$], fishing for trout and other species, ice fishing, hiking on 26 trail miles, horseback riding on 13 trail miles, hunting, picnicking, cross-country skiing, snowmobiling on 18 trail miles with trailhead, lake swimming, and wildlife-watching. The park also offers boat launching and mooring [$], boat rental [$], modern cabin rental [$], environmental education, a food concession, and pavilion rental [$].

The *Pocono Environmental Education Center* at Dingmans Ferry offers year-round indoor and outdoor programs and activities. For details, contact the center (call 570-828-2319 or e-mail peec@peec.org), or visit its Web site at www.peec.org.

33

WYOMING STATE FOREST AND
WORLD'S END STATE PARK

High Knob Overlook and Canyon Vista

Wyoming State Forest encompasses several tracts in some 43,570 acres in Lycoming and Sullivan Counties. In the 1930s, the Central Pennsylvania Lumber Company sold the land to the state. For many years—during a time when the lumber industry flourished—trains transported flatcars of lumber to nearby sawmills. The sawmill towns of the region, however, were abandoned as quickly as they had been established. These nearly forgotten towns included Laquinn, Masten, and Sonesville. After the state acquired the land, able-bodied men based in area CCC camps built many facilities in Wyoming State Forest and in nearby World's End State Park.

Most visitors to the state park and the state forest seek outdoor recreation. Some, though, come to Wyoming State Forest in search of their family histories at the locations of the CCC camps, logging camps, lumber towns, and railroads.

Two magnificent vistas in Wyoming State Forest and World's End State Park—High Knob Overlook and Canyon Vista—are separated only by a few miles.

High Knob Overlook

High Knob Overlook is at the end of a northwest-pointing ridge in Wyoming State Forest's high country. The commanding view from High Knob Overlook's parking area is mainly westerly, 180 degrees south to 330 degrees north-northwest. High Knob's elevation is about 2,000 feet above sea level and some 300 feet above the terrain to the west. From this vantage point, the ridges and valleys of seven counties undulate as far as the eye can see. In June, visitors can enjoy the spectacular bloom of mountain laurel; from late September into the middle of October, the reds, oranges, and yellows of fall foliage are equally breathtaking.

At the overlook, a memorial plaque honors Sumner Francis McCarty, the first forest ranger in Wyoming State Forest, Sullivan County, from 1930 to 1950. In addition to the

From High Knob Overlook, visitors survey a blanket of forest land extending over seven counties.

panorama from High Knob Overlook, other views of the valley appear as the road circles the knob and the end of the mountain. Vehicle occupants (except the driver!) will certainly appreciate these scenes.

Canyon Vista

World's End State Park surrounds a winding portion of Loyalsock Creek near Forksville (Sullivan County). Like the state forest land, the park's 780 acres were acquired by the state in the 1930s from the Central Pennsylvania Lumber Company. From the mid-1930s to the early 1940s, CCC crews built most of the park's trails, roads, pavilions, and buildings.

Canyon Vista's elevation is 1,750 feet above sea level, and it stands about 530 feet above the Loyalsock Creek. The breathtaking view is mainly northwesterly and northerly from about 270 degrees west to 45 degrees northeast. The vista looks northerly into the Loyalsock Creek Valley.

The state forest and the park are located in the Endless Mountains region, whose high mountains and steep slopes made journeys dangerous for early travelers. People passing through on the

Canyon Vista is some 530 feet above the Loyalsock Creek.

region's first road thought that they had reached the "end of the world"—and understandably so, on the narrow, steep-sided, precarious route. The park's name, conferred officially in 1943, is derived from this historical reference.

Looking from either High Knob Overlook or Canyon Vista, notice that the ridges in the distance all rise to about the same height—a feature that characterizes the Appalachian Plateaus province. (On the province, see the sidebar in Chap. 2.) From this area, the Appalachian Plateaus province reaches mostly westerly and then southwesterly through Pennsylvania. Conglomerates—rocks that resist erosion more than the surrounding softer rock—form the overlooks.

OPPORTUNITIES: In Wyoming State Forest, opportunities include mountain biking, primitive camping [$], fishing for trout and other species, hiking on 90 trail miles, horseback riding, hunting, picnicking, cross-country skiing on 15 trail miles, snowmobiling on 58 trail miles, and wildlife-watching.

Opportunities in World's End State Park include boating, tent and trailer camping [$], group tent camping [$], fishing for trout and other species, hiking and backpacking on 128 trail miles, horseback riding on 4 trail miles, hunting, picnicking, cross-country skiing, snowmobiling on 3 trail miles, creek swimming, and wildlife-watching. Cabin rental [$], environmental education, a food concession, pavilion rental [$], playfield facilities, and a visitors center are also available.

ADMINISTRATION AND AMENITIES: Water and pit toilets are available in World's End State Park near the park office. State park day-use areas are open from 8:00 A.M. to dusk.

DIRECTIONS: To reach Canyon Vista: From U.S. Route 220, turn northwest onto PA Route 154. Follow PA Route 154 for about 5.3 miles to the park entrance. After another 1.1 miles, you will see a sign that reads "Loyalsock Canyon Vista 2 miles." Here, turn right onto a narrow, steep-sided dirt road. Drive slowly: the road hosts hikers, bikers, and other vehicles. Follow the signs to the vista. From the Canyon Vista parking area, the railing at the overlook is about a 40-yard walk.

To reach High Knob Overlook: From Canyon Vista Overlook, drive back down the road and follow the signs to High Knob. Cross Shannenburg Road and follow High Knob Road, a narrow but paved two-lane road. Stop your vehicle and check out the map at the entrance to High Knob Road. (The sign says that the overlook is 4 miles farther.) About 2.3 miles farther on High Knob Road is a sign for a right turn to the overlook. Turn right. The overlook is about a 2-mile drive from this sign.

FOR MORE INFORMATION: For details about High Knob Overlook, contact Wyoming State Forest, 274 Arbutus Park Road, Bloomsburg, PA 17815 (call 570-387-4255 or e-mail fd20@dcnr. state.pa.us), or visit its Web site at www.dcnr.state.pa.us/forestry/stateforests/forests/wyoming/wyoming.htm. Contact World's End

State Park at PO Box 62, Forksville, PA 18616-0062 (call
570-924-3287 or e-mail worldsend@dcnr.state.pa.us), or visit its
Web site at www.dcnr.state.pa.us/stateparks/parks/worlds.htm.

NEARBY OVERLOOKS: Round Top Park (Bradford County); Mt. Pis-
gah County Park (Bradford County); Wyalusing Rocks and Marie
Antoinette Overlook (Bradford County); Lambs Vista (Bradford
County); and Council Cup Scenic Overlook (Luzerne County).

OTHER NEARBY OPPORTUNITIES

Mt. Pisgah State Park (Bradford County). Activities
include boating (with electric motors only), ice boating,
fishing for warm-water species, ice fishing, hiking on
10 trail miles, hunting, picnicking, ice skating, cross-
country skiing, sledding, snowmobiling on 8 trail
miles, pool swimming [$], and wildlife-watching. The
park also offers boat launching and mooring [$], boat
rental [$], environmental education, a food concession,
pavilion rental [$], playfield and playground facilities,
and a visitors center.

Ricketts Glen State Park (Luzerne County). Activities
include boating (with electric motors only), tent and
trailer camping [$], organized group tent camping [$],
fishing for trout and other species, ice fishing, hiking on
26 trail miles, horseback riding on 13 trail miles, hunting, picnicking, cross-country skiing, snowmobiling on
18 trail miles with trailhead, lake swimming, and
wildlife-watching. The park also offers boat launching
and mooring [$], boat rental [$], modern cabin rental
[$], environmental education, a food concession, and
pavilion rental [$].

Wyoming State Forest boasts three natural areas. Jakey
Hollow Natural Area, on PA Route 42 north of Bloomsburg (Columbia County), covers 59 acres and features
northern hardwoods, hemlock, old-growth white pine,
and a small stream. Kettle Creek Gorge Natural Area,
near Hillsgrove (Sullivan County), comprises 774 acres
with aspen, northern hardwoods, and oak. Tamarack
Run Natural Area in eastern Sullivan County has 234
acres of northern hardwoods, hemlock, and wetlands.

34

COUNCIL CUP SCENIC OVERLOOK

Council Cup Scenic Overlook is part of the Susquehanna Riverlands, one of four recreation areas provided by the PPL Corporation (formerly Pennsylvania Power and Light). It is located on the Susquehanna River at Wapwallopen, Luzerne County. Council Cup stands about 1,220 feet above sea level and is a sheer drop of 720 feet above the Susquehanna River. Native Americans used the site as a lookout and meeting place. The overlook has also been known as Pulpit Rock, Council Bluff, and Council Rock. At the overlook's wayside exhibit and bench, the view runs northerly up the Susquehanna River, 225 degrees southwest to 45 degrees northeast along the perimeter of the fence. The exhibit identifies seven sites visible from the overlook.

Gould Island and Lee, Penobscot, Huntington, and Shickshinny Mountains are visible to the north, as is the water gap between Lee and Penobscot Mountains. Across the river is the PPL Steam Electric Generating Station, a nuclear power plant. Council Cup's view is deceptively expansive. Walk along the chain-link fence to the southwest for more views, especially downriver. To the west across the river is Salem Township. To the southwest, you can get a great view of the North Branch Susquehanna River, and in clear conditions, Berwick is visible. You can also see the PA Route 93 bridge and the I-80 bridge crossing the North Branch Susquehanna River. Mid-October is the height of the autumn leaf color spectacle, and Council Cup is a wonderful spot for viewing fall foliage.

At Council Cup and in the recreation area, bird-watchers scan for migrating raptors and songbirds, including hawks, ospreys, eagles, and warblers. An annual hawk migration count is performed at Council Cup in the fall. Hawk watches are counts of raptors and other birds taken by volunteers, who then pass the information along to educational and conservation institutions. (For more information on hawk watches and their research and conservation purposes, see the individual listings for Hawk Mountain Sanctuary in Chap. 37, Bradys Bend Scenic Overlook in Chap. 3, Rothrock State Forest in Chap. 20, and

A northerly view up the North Branch Susquehanna River from Council Cup Scenic Overlook. Visible to the north is the water gap between Lee and Penobscot Mountains.

Fort Washington State Park in Chap. 47.) During the last twenty years, more than 230 bird species have been sighted at the Riverlands.

OPPORTUNITIES: At Council Cup, activities include hiking and wildlife-watching. In the Riverlands recreation area, biking, boating, fishing for warm-water species, hunting, hiking, cross-country skiing, and wildlife-watching are available, as is boat launching (for boats without motors only).

ADMINISTRATION AND AMENITIES: No services at Council Cup. The Susquehanna Energy Information Center, located on the west side of the river, has rest rooms, water, exhibits, nature programs, and maps. The center is open from 8:00 A.M. until dusk.

DIRECTIONS: From PA Route 239 in Wapwallopen, follow the small brown-and-white signs to the overlook. From the parking lot, the blue-blazed trail to the overlook is at first rocky and interrupted by tree roots. After that, the trail becomes smooth but moderately steep. Reaching the overlook requires a ten-minute leisurely walk on the trail. A map is visible about 40 yards up the trail from the parking lot, and several interpretive signs and maps guide visitors along the way.

FOR MORE INFORMATION: Contact Susquehanna Riverlands, Susquehanna Energy Information Center, RR 1, Box 1797, Berwick, PA 18603 (717-542-2306).

NEARBY OVERLOOKS: High Knob Overlook (Sullivan County); Canyon Vista (Sullivan County); and Pine Hill Vista (Lackawanna County).

OTHER NEARBY OPPORTUNITIES

Nescopeck State Park (Luzerne County). Activities include fishing for trout and other species, hiking, hunting, cross-country skiing, and wildlife-watching.

Ricketts Glen State Park (Luzerne County). Activities include boating (with electric motors only), tent and trailer camping [$], organized group tent camping [$], fishing for trout and other species, ice fishing, hiking on 26 trail miles, horseback riding on 13 trail miles, hunting, picnicking, cross-country skiing, snowmobiling on 18 trail miles with trailhead, lake swimming, and wildlife-watching. The park also offers boat launching and mooring [$], boat rental [$], modern cabin rental [$], environmental education, a food concession, and pavilion rental [$].

Mauch Chunk Lake Park, southwest of Jim Thorpe (Carbon County). Activities on its 2,300 acres include mountain biking, boating, tent camping [$], fishing for warm-water species, ice fishing, hiking on 12 trail miles, hunting, picnicking, cross-country skiing on 11 trail miles, lake swimming, and wildlife-watching. The park also offers boat launching and mooring [$], boat rental [$], family rustic cottage rental [$], environmental education, a fishing pier accessible to people with disabilities, a food concession, and cross-country ski rental [$]. For details, contact the Carbon County Parks and Recreation Commission (570-325-3669).

35

LACKAWANNA STATE FOREST

Pine Hill Vista

The Lackawanna State Forest encompasses more than 8,110 acres in two tracts in Lackawanna and Luzerne Counties. "Lackawanna" is the English phonetic spelling of an American Indian word that means "place where the river forks."

The state forest's Pine Hill Vista is unique: on this hilltop, an observation deck stands about 25 feet above the ground, so the view is a wonderful panorama of the surrounding countryside. The hilltop elevation is about 2,265 feet above sea level. On the clearest days, you can see landmarks more than 25 miles away. The Delaware Water Gap is visible to the east some 35 miles away. To the north, Elk Mountain, in southeast Susquehanna County, is also visible from about 35 miles away. Jack Frost Mountain can be seen 8 miles to the south. Bear Lake, also to the south, is visible 2 miles away.

Pine Hill traces a curvy, invisible dividing line between the Susquehanna River Watershed to the north and west and the Delaware River Watershed to the south and east. Theoretically, a drop of water that falls on any spot within the Delaware River Watershed will eventually flow to the Delaware River. Drip a drop of water only inches away, though, and sooner or later it will end up in the Chesapeake Bay.

A watershed is an area of land drained by a system of streams and rivers. Rivulets, trickles of runoff, and runs become streams, which become mightier and mightier rivers until they finally drain into the Atlantic Ocean. In Pennsylvania, water takes six main avenues to the Atlantic Ocean. These major watersheds are the Delaware River, the Susquehanna River, the Potomac River, the Ohio River, the Genesee River, and Lake Erie. (Surprisingly, one of Pennsylvania's major drainages is not a river but a lake!)

The Delaware River Watershed covers about a third of the eastern part of the state, from Wayne County south to most of Chester County. The Susquehanna River Watershed covers about half the state, from about the middle of Potter County through Susquehanna County across the north, to York, Lancaster, and much of Adams County in the south. The

Pine Hill Vista's observation deck provides panoramic views.

Susquehanna River Watershed includes huge tributaries, which in their own right are also considered watersheds—the North Branch Susquehanna River, the West Branch Susquehanna River, and the Juniata River.

The woodlands in the state forest surrounding Pine Hill support plentiful populations of deer, turkeys, rabbits, grouse, and squirrels. Bears have also been sighted. The abundant plant life and wildlife—and Pine Hill's marvelous vista—make Lackawanna State Park a good spot for all kinds of photography and wildlife study.

OPPORTUNITIES: Mountain biking, primitive camping [$], fishing for trout, hiking on 23 trail miles, horseback riding, hunting, picnicking in one designated area, cross-country skiing on 14 trail miles, snowmobiling on 24 trail miles, and wildlife-watching. Lackawanna State Forest also includes the Spruce Swamp Natural Area, near Thornhurst (Lackawanna County), which covers 87 acres and features a glacial bog surrounded by hardwood forest. The Howley Orienteering Area, northwest of Thornhurst, provides land navigation challenges.

ADMINISTRATION AND AMENITIES: No services at Pine Hill Vista. Water and pit toilets are available at the nearby Manny Gordon Recreation Site on Bear Lake Road.

DIRECTIONS: From Exit 13 on I-380, take PA Route 435 north. After about 1.5 miles, turn left at a blinking light onto River Road. Follow River Road about 7.2 miles to Bear Lake Road, and turn right onto Bear Lake Road. After about 3.9 miles, turn right onto Pittston Road, a gated, one-lane improved dirt road. As you make the turn, you will see two stone pillars and a brown sign that reads "Pittston Road." Follow Pittston Road about 1.5 miles to Pine Hill Road. Turn left onto Pine Hill Road, another one-lane improved dirt road. About 0.4 mile up Pine Hill Road, the road splits. Follow the left fork to the vista parking area and observation deck.

FOR MORE INFORMATION: Contact Lackawanna State Forest, Bureau of Forestry, Forest District #11, 401 Samters Building, 101 Penn Avenue, Scranton, PA 18503 (call 570-963-4561 or e-mail fd11@dcnr.state.pa.us), or visit its Web site at www.dcnr.state. pa.us/forestry/stateforests/forests/lackawanna/lackawanna.htm.

NEARBY OVERLOOKS: Irving Cliff (Wayne County); Mt. Pisgah County Park (Bradford County); Wyalusing Rocks and Marie Antoinette Overlook (Bradford County); Council Cup Scenic Overlook (Luzerne County); Camelback Mountain (Monroe County); and Delaware River National Recreation Area over-looks (Monroe and Northampton Counties).

OTHER NEARBY OPPORTUNITIES

Hickory Run State Park, east of White Haven (Carbon County). Activities include tent and trailer camping [$], organized group tent and trailer camping [$], fishing for

trout, ice fishing, hiking on 45 trail miles, hunting, picnicking, ice skating, cross-country skiing, sledding,
snowmobiling on 20 trail miles with trailhead, creek
swimming, and wildlife-watching. The park also
features the Boulder Field (a National Natural
Landmark) and offers environmental education, a food
concession, pavilion rental [$], playfield and playground
facilities, and a visitors center.

36

GIBBONS MEMORIAL PARK

Irving Cliff

Honesdale, in Wayne County, was an industrial center in the
1800s. Coal mined near Scranton arrived in Honesdale by train,
and from there, canal boats took the coal to Kingston, New York,
a 108-mile trip along the Delaware and Hudson Canal.
Honesdale was named in honor of the Delaware and Hudson
Canal's first president, Phillip Hone. In 1841, Washington
Irving, whose works include "Rip Van Winkle" and "The Legend
of Sleepy Hollow," visited Honesdale and traveled the canal with
Hone. Washington Irving admired the countryside, and because
of his passing interest in the area, Hone insisted that the cliff be
named after the author. Now, more than 160 years later, the
name remains. (In 1955, Frances Haag Gibbons gave the land to
the city of Honesdale in memory of her husband and his parents.)

Irving Cliff is about 1,300 feet above sea level and about 300
feet above Honesdale. The spectacular view from the cliff is westerly, with a near 180-degree view from south to north. In
addition to a wonderful view of the city of Honesdale, you can see
the countryside beyond and the Lackawaxen River meandering
due east (toward you) through the city. Flowing from the north
and meeting the Lackawaxen practically beneath Irving Cliff is
Dyberry Creek.

A large steel star was erected on the cliff, and it is visible from
Honesdale and beyond. (The star is lit from the Tuesday after
Thanksgiving through mid-January, and the cliff is the site of a
fireworks display on the Fourth of July.) Between the steel star's
frame and the cliff's edge, you can set up a lawn chair and admire
the view. Photography here is easy and inviting. Bring a tripod
and use a wide-angle lens to capture unobstructed views in
several directions and in every season. Between sunset and dark,
try time exposures of the city—or the traffic—lighting up the
night.

Irving Cliff is a great place for a picnic, even though the site
has only one picnic table. Bring lawn chairs to observe the view
comfortably. The walk from the parking lot to the overlook is
only about 30 yards.

Gibbons Memorial Park provides outstanding views of Honesdale.

OPPORTUNITIES: Picnicking and sightseeing.

ADMINISTRATION AND AMENITIES: There are no services in the park or at the overlook, but services are available in Honesdale.

DIRECTIONS: From the south side of Honesdale on U.S. Route 6, turn north onto Cliff Street. At this intersection you will find a blinking red light with a small, old-fashioned street sign on the south side of Cliff Street. Follow Cliff Street for about 0.8 mile. Turn left onto Gibbons Park Road. This road narrows to a steep, cliff-sided, one-lane paved road. From the turn onto Gibbons Park Road, the gravel parking lot and small park monument are about 0.3 mile. From the parking lot, walk up the clearing about 30 yards to the open field, the precipice, and the giant steel star.

FOR MORE INFORMATION: Contact Honesdale Borough, 958 Main Street, Honesdale, PA 18431 (717-253-3240).

NEARBY OVERLOOKS: Pine Hill Vista (Lackawanna County); Wyalusing Rocks and Marie Antoinette Overlook (Bradford County); Camelback Mountain (Monroe County); and Delaware Water Gap National Recreation Area overlooks (Monroe and Northampton Counties).

OTHER NEARBY OPPORTUNITIES

Archbald Pothole State Park (Lackawanna County). Activities include hiking on 2 trail miles, hunting, and picnicking.

Promised Land State Park, south of Tafton (Pike County). Activities include boating (with electric motors only), tent and trailer camping [$], fishing for warm-water species, ice fishing, hiking on 29 trail miles, hunting, picnicking, ice skating, cross-country skiing, snow-mobiling on 17 trail miles with trailhead, snowshoeing, lake swimming, and wildlife-watching. The park also offers boat launching and mooring [$], boat rental [$], rustic cabin rental [$], environmental education, a food concession, and a historical center.

Mauch Chunk Lake Park, southwest of Jim Thorpe (Carbon County). Activities on its 2,300 acres include mountain biking, boating, tent camping [$], fishing for warm-water species, ice fishing, hiking on 12 trail miles, hunting, picnicking, cross-country skiing on 11 trail miles, lake swimming, and wildlife-watching. The park also offers boat launching and mooring [$], boat rental [$], family rustic cottage rental [$], environmental education, a fishing pier accessible to people with disabilities, a food concession, and cross-country ski rental [$]. For details, contact the Carbon County Parks and Recreation Commission (570-325-3669).

State Game Lands #180 (Pike County), including Shohola Falls. Activities include boating (canoes, kayaks, and electric-powered motorboats only), fishing, ice fishing, hiking, hunting, picnicking, and wildlife-watching; boat launching is also available.

37

HAWK MOUNTAIN SANCTUARY

If you are new to bird-watching—or would like to introduce someone else to the activity—visit Hawk Mountain Sanctuary.

In 1934, conservationist Rosalie Edge founded Hawk Mountain to end the shooting of migrating raptors. Because Hawk Mountain occupies the eastern edge of the Appalachians, it is a main flyway for the birds that migrate up and down the North American continent. Hawk Mountain was the world's first sanctuary for migrating raptors The sanctuary's mission is to foster the conservation of raptors and educate people on the natural environment, especially the environment in the central Appalachian Mountains. Hawk Mountain Sanctuary includes a staff of fifteen, along with interns and volunteers. A nonprofit organization also supports Hawk Mountain Sanctuary's work. (For details about membership, contact the sanctuary; see the contact information below.)

Today, magnificent landscape views provide a breathtaking background to the soaring raptors and other migratory birds. Spectators have counted a total of some 18,000 raptors—16 species of hawks, eagles, and falcons—annually between mid-August and mid-December. Hummingbirds, swifts, swallows, and warblers also migrate through the area each fall. In fact, every year, more than 240 bird species are observed at Hawk Mountain.

The South Lookout is accessible to people with disabilities and can be reached by way of a short walk on a groomed trail. Wayside exhibits explore a number of subjects, including forest and fauna, and provide a guide to identifying hawks in flight. The South Lookout view is easterly from 0 degrees north to about 150 degrees south-southeast. The overlook's elevation is 1,340 feet above sea level and more than 700 feet above the valley's low points to the east.

Looking south-southeast, you can see two prominent ridges. The farthest ridge is called The Pinnacle; the closer ridge is Owl's Head. The ridge across the north and northeast is Blue Mountain. About 3 miles to the northeast is Dans Pulpit, a point on Blue Mountain. The South Overlook surveys the lowland in a wrinkle in Blue Mountain. In this valley is a light-colored area

Hawk Mountain Sanctuary's South Lookout provides breathtaking easterly views.

known as the River of Rocks, a boulder field about 1 mile long and, in places, a few hundred feet wide. During the last glacial period, the freezing and thawing of water among the rocks on the ridge top fractured large rock pieces and sent them falling to the valley below. Some of the River of Rocks boulders exceed 20 feet in diameter. You can inspect the River of Rocks more closely on one of the trails that crisscross Hawk Mountain Sanctuary.

The North Overlook requires a longer hike over more rugged terrain, but the views are worth the effort. Still, do not attempt this hike without proper footwear and an appropriate level of physical fitness. The North Overlook offers a magnificent 200-degree panorama of the Kittatinny Ridge (Blue Mountain), and on the clearest, brightest days, views of more than 50 miles are possible. The overlook is about 1,520 feet above sea level and nearly 900 feet above the valley floor to the southeast.

Hawk Mountain attracts migratory birds for two main reasons. First, hawks, eagles, ospreys, and other raptors are diurnal—in other words, they are active in daylight hours. They use Blue Mountain and the entire Kittatinny Ridge as landmarks on their migration route. The shores of the Great Lakes and the Atlantic coastline serve a similar function for birds following migration routes. Second, winds that blow frequently from the north and northwest hit Blue Mountain and are pushed upward, creating updrafts. Migratory birds favor these conditions for soaring (which requires less energy than constant flapping). Updrafts from brisk winds also help migrating birds fly faster. In excellent conditions, birds may fly 40 to 80 miles per hour over Hawk Mountain, and they may stay aloft for some six hours.

OPPORTUNITIES: Hiking and wildlife-watching as well as environmental education.

ADMINISTRATION AND AMENITIES: A small fee is required to reach Hawk Mountain overlooks. The visitors center has rest rooms, water, a museum, and a bookstore. Trails are open from dawn to dusk. The visitors center is open from 9:00 A.M. to 5:00 P.M. year-round (and from 8:00 A.M. to 5:00 P.M. between Labor Day and Thanksgiving).

DIRECTIONS: From I-78, take Exit 29B to PA Route 61 northbound. On PA Route 61, drive about 4.4 miles to PA Route 895 and turn right (east). Drive another 2.5 miles to a right turn with a blue-and-white sign indicating the Hawk Mountain Sanctuary. This two-lane paved road crosses railroad tracks and the Little Schuylkill River and then winds through the woods up the mountain. The sanctuary's parking lot is on the right about 2 miles from the blue-and-white sign.

FOR MORE INFORMATION: Contact Hawk Mountain Sanctuary, 1700 Hawk Mountain Road, Kempton, PA 19529 (call the Info Line at 610-756-6000 or the offices at 610-756-6961), or visit its Web site at www.hawkmountain.org.

NEARBY OVERLOOKS: Shikellamy State Park overlooks (Snyder County) and Council Cup Scenic Overlook (Luzerne County).

OTHER NEARBY OPPORTUNITIES

Locust Lake State Park (Schuylkill County). Activities include bicycling, boating (with electric motors only), tent and trailer camping [$], fishing for trout and other species, ice fishing, hiking on 30 trail miles, hunting, and ice skating. The park also offers boat launching, boat rental [$], environmental education, and a playground.

Tuscarora State Park (Schuylkill County). Activities include boating (with electric motors only), fishing for trout and other species, ice fishing, hiking on 3 trail miles, hunting, picnicking, ice skating, lake swimming, and wildlife-watching. The park also offers boat launching and mooring [$], boat rental [$], and a food concession.

Nolde Forest Environmental Education Center, in Reading (Berks County), is operated by the Pennsylvania Department of Conservation and Natural Resources Bureau of State Parks. It offers programs and activities year-round. For information, contact the center (call 610-775-1411 or e-mail noldeforest@dcnr.state.pa.us).

U.S. Army Corps of Engineers Philadelphia District's *Blue Marsh Lake* (Berks County). Activities include mountain biking, boating (with unlimited horsepower), ice boating, fishing, ice fishing, hiking on 35 trail miles, hunting, picnicking, ice skating, cross-country skiing, sledding, lake swimming, and wildlife-watching; boat launching is also available. Call Blue Marsh Lake (610-376-6337) for details.

The Pennsylvania Game Commission's *Middle Creek Wildlife Management Area* near Klinefeltersville (Lebanon and Lancaster Counties) features a waterfowl museum and programs on wildlife; for information, call 717-733-1512.

38

DELAWARE STATE FOREST

Pimple Hill

Pimple Hill is located in an isolated tract in the southwest corner
of Delaware State Forest. Its elevation is 2,212 feet above sea
level—the highest accessible point in Monroe County—and it
stands about 375 feet above the lower ground to the east. The
view is primarily east-southeast, 45 degrees northeast to 180 degrees south. Visible to the east is the small Grass Lake and parts
of State Game Lands #38. Beyond the lake to the east, about 8
miles away, are Camelback Mountain and its antenna array. From
Pimple Hill you can see how Camelback Mountain got its name:
the two humps along the ridge top resemble a camel's back. Farther in the distance to the southeast, across the horizon, is
Kittatinny Mountain at a straight southeast distance of about 13
miles. Pimple Hill's overlook direction makes it perfect for a sunrise view. The break in Kittatinny Mountain to the southeast is
Wind Gap, about 16 miles away. The antennas on Pimple Hill
include those of the Monroe County Control Center, Pennsylvania State Police, and other communications interests.

The 80-foot-high Pohopoco Fire Tower was erected in 1934.
Beyond the fire tower, near the overlook, you will see the foundation and remains of another tower that collapsed during an ice
storm many Aprils ago.

OPPORTUNITIES: ATV riding on 21 trail miles, mountain biking,
primitive camping [$], fishing for trout and other species, hiking
on 150 trail miles, horseback riding, hunting, picnicking in two
designated areas, cross-country skiing on 4 trail miles, snowmobiling on 128 trail miles, and wildlife-watching.

Delaware State Forest boasts six natural areas. Bruce Lake
Natural Area, south of Tafton (Pike County), covers 2,845 acres
and features two lakes—one glacial and one man-made.
Buckhorn Natural Area, north of Milford (Pike County), encom-
passes 535 acres with oak forest and adjoins State Game Lands
#209. Little Mud Pond Swamp Natural Area, southeast of
Germantown (Pike County), comprises 182 acres adjoining State
Game Lands #180 and includes wetlands and rare plants. Pennel

Pimple Hill offers a view of Camelback Mountain, about 8 miles away.

Run Natural Area, east of Canadensis in the extreme southwest of Pike County, is 936 acres, with aspens, birches, and oaks. Pine Lake Natural Area, northeast of Greentown (Pike County), is 67 acres and includes wetlands. Stillwater Natural Area, southwest of Edgemere (Pike County), covers 1,931 acres with wetlands, spruce, fir, and mixed hardwoods.

ADMINISTRATION AND AMENITIES: Area closes at sunset. No services at this overlook.

DIRECTIONS: From I-80, take Exit 284 and follow PA Route 115 south about 5 miles. Watch for a brown sign on the right for the entrance to Delaware State Forest Recreation Area Pohopoco Tract, and turn right onto the dirt road into the state forest. Continue through the yellow gate if it is open. At the antennas, follow the signs to the "scenic view." Elevation signs on the road will confirm that you are climbing. You will pass the state forest fire warden's small home and the 80-foot Pohopoco Fire Tower. Continue on the road around the fire tower to the vista, following the signs to the "ground level lookout." You can drive right to this vista.

FOR MORE INFORMATION: Contact Delaware State Forest, Bureau of Forestry, Forest District #19, HC 1, Box 95A, Swiftwater, PA 18370-9723 (call 570-895-4000 or e-mail fd19@dcnr. state.pa.us), or visit its Web site at www.dcnr.state.pa.us/forestry/stateforests/forests/delaware/delaware.htm.

NEARBY OVERLOOKS: Camelback Mountain (Monroe County) and Delaware Water Gap National Recreation Area overlooks (Monroe and Northampton Counties).

OTHER NEARBY OPPORTUNITIES

Gouldsboro State Park, northwest of Tobyhanna (Pike and Monroe Counties). Activities include boating (with electric motors only), fishing for warm-water species, hiking on 10 trail miles, hunting, picnicking, cross-country skiing, lake swimming, and wildlife-watching. The park also offers boat launching and mooring [$] as well as boat rental [$]. It adjoins Tobyhanna State Park and State Game Lands #127.

Promised Land State Park, south of Tafton (Pike County). Activities include boating (with electric motors only), tent and trailer camping [$], fishing for warm-water species, ice fishing, hiking on 29 trail miles, hunting, picnicking, ice skating, cross-country skiing, snowmobiling on 17 trail miles with trailhead, snowshoeing, lake swimming, and wildlife-watching. The park also offers boat launching and mooring [$], boat rental [$], rustic cabin rental [$], environmental education, a food concession, and a historical center.

Tobyhanna State Park, north of Tobyhanna (Pike and Monroe Counties). Activities include bicycling, boating (with electric motors only), tent and trailer camping [$], organized group tent camping [$], fishing for trout and other species, ice fishing, hiking on 12 trail miles, hunting, picnicking, ice skating, cross-country skiing, snowmobiling on 5 trail miles with trailhead, lake swimming, and wildlife-watching. The park also offers boat launching and mooring [$], boat rental [$], pavilion rental [$], a playfield, and a playground. It adjoins Gouldsboro State Park and State Game Lands #127 and #312.

The *Jacobsburg Environmental Center* near Belfast (Northampton County) offers indoor and outdoor programs and activities throughout the year, including mountain biking, fishing for trout, hiking on 7.5 trail miles, horseback riding on 12 trail miles, hunting, cross-country skiing, and wildlife-watching. It also features a historical center.

The *Messing Nature Center* (Monroe County) also offers programs. It is operated by the Monroe County Conservation District and other agencies.

The *Tarkill Forest Demonstration Area*—82 acres west of Pecks Pond in Pike County—has a guided nature trail demonstrating the results of different forest management practices.

Mauch Chunk Lake Park, southwest of Jim Thorpe (Carbon County). Activities on its 2,300 acres include mountain biking, boating, tent camping [$], fishing for warm-water species, ice fishing, hiking on 12 trail miles, hunting, picnicking, cross-country skiing on 11 trail miles, lake swimming, and wildlife-watching. The park also offers boat launching and mooring [$], boat rental [$], family rustic cottage rental [$], environmental education, a fishing pier accessible to people with disabilities, a food concession, and cross-country ski rental [$]. For details, contact the Carbon County Parks and Recreation Commission (570-325-3669).

The *Pocono International Raceway* is only a few miles north on PA Route 115. For information, contact the Raceway (call 717-646-2300 [administration] or 1-800-RACEWAY [tickets]), or visit its Web site at www.na-motorsports.com/Tracks/Pocono.html.

A few miles northwest of Pimple Hill are the *Big Boulder, Split Rock, and Jack Frost Mountain resorts.* Jack Frost Mountain and Big Boulder offer skiing, snowtubing, snowboarding, and other activities; contact both resorts at 1-800-468-2442 or visit their Web site at www.jackfrostbigboulder.com. Split Rock Resort also offers golf and skiing. Contact Split Rock at 570-722-9111 or visit its Web site at www.splitrockresort.com.

39

BIG POCONO STATE PARK

Camelback Mountain

Big Pocono State Park includes the top and slopes of Camelback Mountain, an area of more than 1,300 acres in Monroe County. Rim Road, a 1.4-mile-long paved road, loops around the ridge top at the end of the mountain; visitors delight in its spectacular views over a large area of Pennsylvania as well as sections of New Jersey and New York. The summit of Camelback Mountain is 2,133 feet above sea level and 900 to 1,100 feet above the surrounding terrain. The mountain itself points easterly as a thumblike projection of the Glaciated Pocono Plateau Section, the easternmost part of Pennsylvania's Appalachian Plateaus physiographic province. (On the province, see the sidebar in Chap. 2.)

The area at and inside the loop road provides many terrific spots from which to enjoy the views. Pick the crispest, clearest day, and stop at different places for magnificent vistas in all directions.

The views at the summit area parking lot are to the north and south on both sides of the ridge top. The northerly view is some 180 degrees wide, about 270 degrees west to 90 degrees east. Visible to the north are the large tan towers of a grain and flour mill, as well as the Pocono Mountain High School complex.

The view along the southern part of Rim Road, near the first parking area, is mainly to the south-southeast, about 105 degrees east-southeast to 225 degrees southwest. Near Parking Area 1, I-80 and PA Route 611 are visible to the southeast. Farther to the east (look left) in the distance is the Delaware Water Gap, about 12 miles away. The mountain along the horizon is Kittatinny Mountain. Wind Gap is visible to the south-southeast. Below Camelback Mountain, to the south, you will see Spring Mountain Lake, Trout Lake, and Blue Mountain Ski Area.

If you look northeasterly with powerful binoculars or a spotting scope, on a particularly clear day, you can see the High Point State Park monument, a 220-foot-high obelisk in New Jersey's High Point State Park. The marker, which stands about 38 miles away from Camelback Mountain, indicates New Jersey's

From Camelback Mountain, visitors can discern the Delaware Water Gap (on the left) about 12 miles away.

highest point. In addition, to the north and northeast on the clearest, brightest days, you may see New York State's Catskill Mountains, which appear as a dark band on the horizon. The Catskills are more than 70 miles away. About 21 miles away to the northeast is High Knob Fire Tower, west of Pecks Pond in Delaware State Forest (Pike County).

Visible to the west, about 8 miles away, is the Pohopoco Fire Tower, located on Pimple Hill in Delaware State Forest in the southwest corner of Monroe County (see Chap. 38). To the west, notice Pocono Raceway. On calm, clear days during races, you can see the "dust" of the racetrack and, in the best conditions, you might hear the roar of the race cars.

OPPORTUNITIES: Picnicking, hiking on 10 trail miles, horseback riding on 5 trail miles, hunting, downhill skiing, and wildlife-watching. Camelback Ski Area has thirty-three trails and thirteen lifts; it is accessible on Camelback Road on the way to the state park. A food concession and a restaurant near the top of the chairlifts are also available. The parking areas along Rim Road provide ample parking as well as picnic tables in wooded settings from which to enjoy the views. The parking area and picnic area at the summit are expansive and offer wonderfully scenic views.

ADMINISTRATION AND AMENITIES: The park is open from 8:00 A.M. to sunset. Water and rest rooms are available near the parking areas around Rim Road. The park is closed seven days after the antlerless deer season ends in December; it reopens in the spring as conditions permit. Camelback Restaurant (570-629-1661, ext. 2218) is near the top of the chairlifts.

DIRECTIONS: From Exit 299 on I-80, take PA Route 715 north about 0.25 mile to the next light, and turn left onto Sullivan Trail. Follow the signs to Big Pocono State Park: you will drive about 5 miles to reach the park entrance. After entering the park, drive 0.6 mile and turn right onto the one-way loop road. If you continue straight for 1.9 miles at the beginning of the loop road, you pass the state forest heliport and Big Pocono Fire Tower and arrive at the summit parking area, which has picnic tables and more magnificent views to the north and south.

FOR MORE INFORMATION: Contact Big Pocono State Park c/o Tobyhanna State Park, PO Box 387, Tobyhanna, PA 18466-0387 (call 570-894-8336 or e-mail tobyhanna@dcnr.state.pa.us), or visit its Web site at www.dcnr.state.pa.us/stateparks/parks/bigpocono.htm.

NEARBY OVERLOOKS: Pimple Hill (Monroe and Pike Counties); Delaware Water Gap National Recreation Area overlooks (Monroe and Northampton Counties); and High Rocks Vista (Bucks County).

OTHER NEARBY OPPORTUNITIES

Beltzville State Park (Carbon County). Activities include boating (with unlimited horsepower), fishing for trout and other species, ice fishing, hiking on 15 trail miles, hunting, picnicking, cross-country skiing, snowmobiling on 5 trail miles, lake swimming, and wildlife-watching. The park also offers boat launching and mooring [$], boat rental [$], environmental education, a food concession, pavilion rental [$], a playfield, and a playground.

Gouldsboro State Park, northwest of Tobyhanna (Pike and Monroe Counties). Activities include boating (with electric motors only), fishing for warm-water species, hiking on 10 trail miles, hunting, picnicking, cross-country skiing, lake swimming, and wildlife-watching. The park also offers boat launching and mooring [$] as well as boat rental [$]. It adjoins Tobyhanna State Park and State Game Lands #127.

Hickory Run State Park, east of White Haven (Carbon County). Activities include tent and trailer camping [$], organized group tent and trailer camping [$], fishing for trout, ice fishing, hiking on 45 trail miles, hunting, picnicking, ice skating, cross-country skiing, sledding, snowmobiling on 20 trail miles with trailhead, creek swimming, and wildlife-watching. The park also features the Boulder Field (a National Natural Landmark) and offers environmental education, a food concession, pavilion rental [$], playfield and playground facilities, and a visitors center.

Lehigh Gorge State Park (Luzerne and Carbon Counties). Activities include mountain biking, white-water boating, fishing for trout, hiking on 30 trail miles, hunting, cross-country skiing, and wildlife-watching.

Tobyhanna State Park, north of Tobyhanna (Pike and Monroe Counties). Activities include bicycling, boating (with electric motors only), tent and trailer camping [$], organized group tent camping [$], fishing for trout and other species, ice fishing, hiking on 12 trail miles, hunting, picnicking, ice skating, cross-country skiing, snowmobiling on 5 trail miles with trailhead, lake swimming, and wildlife-watching. The park also offers boat launching and mooring [$], boat rental [$], pavilion rental [$], a playfield, and a playground. It adjoins Gouldsboro State Park and State Game Lands #127 and #312.

The 25-mile *Lehigh Gorge State Park Trail* (Luzerne and Carbon Counties) is part of the Pennsylvania Rails-to-Trails program. Trailheads are located at White Haven and Glen Onoko. For more information, contact Lehigh Gorge State Park (570-443-0400) or visit its Web site at www.dcnr.state.pa.us/stateparks/parks/l-gor.htm.

40

DELAWARE WATER GAP NATIONAL RECREATION AREA

Resort Point Overlook, Point of Gap Overlook, and
Arrow Island Overlook

Created in 1965 and administered by the National Park Service,
the Delaware Water Gap National Recreation Area includes some
70,000 acres on the New Jersey and Pennsylvania sides of the
Delaware River, and it spans approximately 40 miles of the
Delaware River from about 5 miles north of Milford, Pennsylvania, to a few miles southwest of the Delaware Water Gap.

Resort Point Overlook, Point of Gap Overlook, and Arrow
Island Overlook are in the southernmost portion of the Delaware
Water Gap National Recreation Area. Each of these overlooks
stands about 100 to 200 feet above the Delaware River and
offers views of the river, the Delaware Water Gap, and the
mountains beyond in Pennsylvania and New Jersey. The
overlooks are pull-offs along PA Route 611, with ample
parking, and they are located just south of the borough of
Delaware Water Gap. From Resort Point Overlook, you can see
Kittatinny Mountain, about 1,400 to 1,500 feet high, on the
New Jersey side; Mount Minsi, on the Pennsylvania side, stands
1,463 feet high. Mount Minsi is part of Kittatinny Mountain.
Visible from Point of Gap Overlook and Arrow Island Overlook
is Mount Tammany in New Jersey. (Mount Minsi looms close
to the road on the Pennsylvania side.)

Around 1793, Antoine Dutot, a French colonial plantation
owner, bought the land that is known today as the Delaware
Water Gap. In 1820, area residents opened their homes to vaca-
tioners, and around 1829, Dutot built a hotel called "Kittatinny."
The hotel began operating in 1833; by the mid-1880s,
Kittatinny was enlarged to house about 275 guests. By 1900,
the Delaware Water Gap and Pennsylvania Poconos hosted some
500,000 visitors annually. Resort Point Overlook is the site of
Dutot's Kittatinny Hotel, although nothing of the hotel remains.
When you view the Delaware Water Gap and the river from this
overlook, I-80 and its bridge are the only main alterations to the
area in more than a century.

Resort Point Overlook. Except for the addition of I-80, this scene looks much as it did more than a century ago.

Flooding in 1955 caused Congress to authorize funds to build a dam at Tocks Island, located just downriver of the present-day Smithfield Beach Access. Conservationists led the effort to abandon the project, which was finally scuttled in 1975, keeping the Delaware River the only free-flowing waterway on the East Coast. In 1992, the Tocks Island project was "officially de-authorized." The Delaware River in the area of the Delaware Water Gap National Recreation Area became a designated National Wild and Scenic River in 1978, offering the area further protection from development and change.

Resort Point Overlook

The view at Resort Point Overlook is mainly to the southeast, about 45 degrees northeast to 195 degrees south-southwest. The view looks directly into the Delaware Water Gap itself. Visible are I-80 and its bridge between Pennsylvania and New Jersey; beyond, in New Jersey, Worthington State Forest can be seen. To the south-southwest is Mount Minsi.

Point of Gap Overlook

The view at Point of Gap Overlook is easterly, about 0 degrees north to 150 degrees south-southeast. Point of Gap Overlook is unique: you look up at the overlook's prominent feature, Mount Tammany in New Jersey, instead of looking down onto a landscape from a height.

Mount Tammany is 1,527 feet above sea level. In geological terms, Mount Tammany is called a "hogback." The visibly tilted rock layers are sandstone and conglomerate—hard, erosion-resistant rocks. Rocks beneath this layer are softer and erode more quickly. The steeply tilted resistant rock layer resembles a hog's back. Similar formations that look flatter and more like tables are called "mesas." ("Mesa" is the Spanish word for "table.")

Talus, the rock rubble at the base of the slopes beneath the rock layers, is formed by the action of water seeping between cracks in the rock. As the water freezes, it pushes the rock pieces apart. Ice acts as glue to hold the separated pieces together, but when the ice melts, the rock pieces tumble below. These broken rock pieces gather to form talus slopes, commonly seen here and on the sides and bases of many Pennsylvania mountains.

From this overlook, if you look behind you (westward), you will see Mount Minsi and its exposed rock layers.

Arrow Island Overlook

Arrow Island Overlook's view is mainly easterly with a direct northeast view of Mount Tammany. You can also see the river through the trees below. This overlook stands about 100 feet above the river. Like Point of Gap Overlook, Arrow Island Overlook features a view *up* at Mount Tammany in New Jersey, not down onto a landscape. Look westerly (behind you) to see towering Mount Minsi.

Arrow Island Overlook provides an eye-opening look at New Jersey's Mt. Tammany. At this overlook, visitors look up—not down—at the point of interest.

Mount Minsi in Pennsylvania and New Jersey's Mount Tammany are both part of Kittatinny Mountain. In Pennsylvania, Kittatinny Mountain extends southwestward, where it becomes Blue Mountain. It also extends northeastward through New Jersey and southeastern New York State, where it becomes part of the Shawangunk Mountains. Kittatinny Mountain, with all its different names, extends a total of some 260 miles.

OPPORTUNITIES: Road and mountain biking, bird-watching (eagles and other raptors), boating (see below), camping [$] (tent and RV sites available, as well as group camping [$] for nonprofit organizations), hiking and backpacking on 60 trail miles (including 25 miles of the Appalachian Trail, which reaches PA Route 611 at Resort Point Overlook), horseback riding on 9 trail miles in Pennsylvania, ice climbing (only for the experienced), ice fishing, rock climbing at Point of Gap Overlook, ice skating, cross-country skiing, snowmobiling on a 3-mile trail or 6-mile loop, swimming (Smithfield Beach and Milford Beach in Pennsylvania), tubing, and wildlife-watching. At these vistas, look in front of you for the easterly views and behind you, toward Mount Minsi, to spot raptors and other migrating birds.

Boating and fishing opportunities abound, and boat launching [$] is available. Canoe accesses to the Delaware River on the Pennsylvania side include Milford Beach, Dingmans Ferry Access, Smithfield Beach, Eshback, and the Bushkill Access.

Powerboating is also permitted, and small fishing boats and run-abouts can use some deeper portions of the river. The Delaware Water Gap Recreation Area offers excellent fishing for American shad, catfish, carp, smallmouth bass, muskellunge, and walleye.

Certain sections of the recreation area are open to hunting according to Pennsylvania and New Jersey regulations; federal hunting regulations also apply. The Recreation Area offers environmental education programs on weekends.

Visitors to the area may experience the magnificent views in a number of ways. Photographers will find opportunities for excellent scenic compositions (note, though, that commercial photography requires a permit). Spectacular overlook views are available on the trails of Mount Minsi, but reaching these places can require long hikes. There are also 200 miles of roads from which to appreciate scenic beauty, waterfalls, and historic sites. And those interested in picnicking will discover free sites in Pennsylvania, including the George W. Childs Recreation Site, Toms Creek, and Hialeah.

ADMINISTRATION AND AMENITIES: No services at these overlooks. At Resort Point Overlook there is ample parking and, under a big oak tree, a bench from which to enjoy the view at the overlook's stone barrier. User fees are collected at Milford Beach, Dingmans Ferry, Bushkill, and Smithfield Beach accesses. Stop at the Bushkill visitors center, on U.S. Route 209 in Bushkill, Pennsylvania, for detailed park information, regulations, maps, and activity and program schedules. The visitors center is open from May through October and has rest rooms, water, a picnic area, and a store with gifts and books. There is also the Kittatinny visitors center in New Jersey with similar facilities. It is located off the first exit from I-80, and it remains open during the winter on weekends.

DIRECTIONS: From I-80, take Exit 310 south to PA Route 611 south. (Heading eastbound, Exit 310 is the last exit in Pennsylvania.) Follow PA Route 611 south through the borough of Delaware Water Gap about 1.2 miles to Resort Point Overlook. The parking area is on the east side of PA Route 611. Point of Gap Overlook is 1.5 miles south of Resort Point Overlook, and its large parking lot is on the west side of PA Route 611. Walk about 50 yards up the paved walkway to the overlook. From Point of Gap Overlook, follow PA Route 611 south about 0.6 mile to Arrow Island Overlook. The parking area is on the east side of PA Route 611.

FOR MORE INFORMATION: Contact Delaware Water Gap National Recreation Area, 1 River Road, Bushkill, PA 18324-9999 (call the Pennsylvania visitors center and park headquarters at 570-588-2451 or 1-800-654-5984 [TDD], or e-mail dewa_interpretation@nps.gov), or visit its Web site at www.nps.gov/dewa.

NEARBY OVERLOOKS: Irving Cliff (Wayne County); Camelback Mountain (Monroe County); Pimple Hill (Monroe and Pike Counties); and High Rocks Vista (Bucks County).

OTHER NEARBY OPPORTUNITIES

The *Jacobsburg Environmental Center* near Belfast (Northampton County) offers indoor and outdoor programs and activities throughout the year, including mountain biking, fishing for trout, hiking on 7.5 trail miles, horseback riding on 12 trail miles, hunting, cross-country skiing, and wildlife-watching. It also features a historical center.

Two other nature centers and an environmental education center are nearby, each with exhibits and indoor and outdoor programs and activities throughout the year. Contact the Mariton Wildlife Sanctuary in Easton (610-749-2379); the Pool Wildlife Sanctuary, operated by the Wildlands Conservancy, in Emmaus (610-965-4397); and the Pocono Environmental Education Center at Dingmans Ferry (call 570-828-2319, e-mail peec@peec.org, or visit its Web site at www.peec.org).

State Game Lands #180, including Shohola Falls. Activities include boating (canoes, kayaks, and boats powered by electric motors only), fishing, ice fishing, hiking, hunting, picnicking, and wildlife-watching; boat launching is also available.

The Pocono Mountains Vacation Bureau provides details on *area accommodations and other attractions.* For details, call 1-800-POCONOS, or visit the Vacation Bureau's Web site at www.800poconos.com.

41

ROCKY RIDGE COUNTY PARK

North and South Observation Decks

Rocky Ridge County Park, largely a mature hardwood forest, encompasses some 750 acres on a ridge in York County. The park lies a few miles from the Susquehanna River in Hallam Township, about 2 miles north of U.S. Route 30 in eastern York County.

The north observation deck stands about 900 feet above sea level and about 400 feet above the surrounding lowland. The panoramic view is mostly northerly from 315 degrees northwest to about 75 degrees east-northeast. Visible to the northwest is Ski Roundtop. To the north, about 9.5 miles away, is Three Mile Island; beyond, you will see Dauphin County and Blue Mountain, some 25 miles away. Looking northeasterly, Elizabethtown lies about 9.5 miles away, and the heights of Mt. Gretna and Mt. Wilson, some 18 miles away, are also visible. The north observation deck is a hawk watch site. You will find hawk-watchers here every fall weekend and during the week from mid-August into December. A small wayside exhibit helps people identify a variety of raptors. Bring a lawn chair and your binoculars for bird-watching.

The south observation deck is 940 feet above sea level and some 400 feet above the low spots to the southeast. Its view is mainly to the southeast, 90 degrees east to 180 degrees south. U.S. Route 30 and the hills of Lower Windsor Township are visible.

The only drawback to the north and south overlooks is that the steel supports of power-line rights-of-way cross their views. But the observation decks at both overlooks are spacious, sturdy, and comfortable, and each has a picnic table with seats.

OPPORTUNITIES: Bird-watching (raptors and songbirds); mountain biking, hiking, and horseback riding on 12 miles of multi-use trails; hunting (requires special permit issued by the county parks office), and picnicking. The park also offers a 0.5-mile cinder fitness trail with twenty exercise stations, horseshoe pits, a playground accessible to people with disabilities, a softball field (contact the park office for availability), and a volleyball court.

Rocky Ridge County Park's north observation deck is accessible and provides comfortable viewing.

ADMINISTRATION AND AMENITIES: Park hours are from 8:00 A.M. to dusk. Rest rooms and water are available in the park.

DIRECTIONS: From U.S. Route 30, take Mt. Zion Road (PA Route 24) north about 1.2 miles to the top of the hill. Turn right onto Deininger Road and drive about 1 mile to the park entrance. After another 0.1 mile, take the right fork in the road toward the Oak Timbers Picnic Area, and drive another 0.7 mile to the parking lot at the power-line right-of-way.

To reach the north observation deck: Park immediately on the left near the rest rooms and follow the sign and path northwest along the right-of-way for the power line. The deck is about 200 yards beyond on a flat, groomed path. The north observation deck is accessible to people with disabilities.

To reach the south observation deck: Follow the signs at the other end of the parking lot, and follow the power-line right-of-way trail. The south observation deck is not accessible to people with disabilities. The site is a leisurely ten-minute walk from the parking lot.

FOR MORE INFORMATION: Contact the York County Department of Parks, 400 Mundis Race Road, York, PA 17402-9721 (call 717-840-7440 or e-mail parks@york-county.org), or visit its Web site at www.york-county.org.

NEARBY OVERLOOKS: Chickies Rock County Park overlooks (Lancaster County); Susquehannock State Park overlooks (Lancaster County); Holtwood Environmental Preserve overlooks (Lancaster County); Mt. Pisgah (York County); Negley Park (Cumberland County) and Reservoir Park, Harrisburg (Dauphin County); and Little Round Top (Adams County).

OTHER NEARBY OPPORTUNITIES

Gifford Pinchot State Park (York County). Activities include boating (with electric motors only), ice boating, tent and trailer camping [$], organized group tent and trailer camping [$], fishing for warm-water species, ice fishing, hiking on 18 trail miles, horseback riding on 4 trail miles, hunting, picnicking, ice skating, cross-country skiing, sledding, lake swimming, and wildlife-watching. The park also offers boat launching and mooring [$], boat rental [$], modern cabin rental [$], environmental education, a food concession, pavilion rental [$], a playfield, a playground, and a visitors center.

The Pennsylvania Fish and Boat Commission's *Fish Culture Station and visitors center at Huntsdale* (717-486-3419) is open to the public with tours available.

The 22-mile *Heritage Rail Trail County Park* (York County) is part of Pennsylvania's Rails-to-Trails program. It has trailheads at Hanover Junction and the

city of York. The trail connects with Maryland's North
Central Railroad Trail. For more information, contact
the York County Department of Parks (see the contact
information above).

The Pennsylvania Game Commission's *Middle Creek
Wildlife Management Area* near Klinefeltersville (Lebanon
and Lancaster Counties) features a waterfowl museum and
programs on wildlife; for information, call 717-733-1512.

Nolde Forest Environmental Education Center, operated by
the Pennsylvania Department of Conservation and
Natural Resources Bureau of State Parks, offers
programs and activities year-round. For information,
contact the center (call 610-775-1411 or e-mail
noldeforest@dcnr.state.pa.us).

The *Holtwood Environmental Preserve* includes the Lock 12
Historic Area, Kelly's Run Natural Area, and Shenk's
Ferry Wildflower Preserve. For more information, contact the Holtwood Environmental Preserve, owned by
the PPL Corporation. (See Chap. 44 for details.)

York County and the city of York are filled with historic
sites. Contact the York County Heritage Trust through
its Web site (www.yorkheritage.com). Farther east is the
Amish and Mennonite farm country in Lancaster County.

42

SAMUEL S. LEWIS STATE PARK

Mt. Pisgah

Samuel S. Lewis State Park and its 885-foot ridge, Mt. Pisgah, are located in York County some 12 miles east of the city of York. Mt. Pisgah is the area's highest point, overlooking the lower Susquehanna River Valley near Wrightsville. (Mt. Pisgah's elevation is some 600 feet above the Susquehanna River's elevation.) The mountain separates the Kreutz Creek Valley to the northwest and the East Prospect Valley to the southeast, and the ridge top provides a wonderful view of the river and the countryside.

Pavilion C offers a mainly easterly, nearly 180-degree panorama, and it surveys the area from Marietta, the western Lancaster County farmland, and Chickies Rock to the north to Conejohela Flats and Safe Harbor Dam to the south. Also visible are the Columbia-Wrightsville Bridge, the U.S. Route 30 bridge, the borough of Columbia, and East York High School. Nearer the parking area is a northwesterly view of the Kreutz Creek Valley.

A wayside exhibit at Pavilion C details the sights from this vantage point and reveals intriguing historical facts about the area. George Washington, for instance, appreciated the Wrightsville area for its location and beauty as well as its commanding view of the Susquehanna River and its strategic position on the river. These latter traits—as Washington pointed out to the Congress— made the area a perfect location for the new nation's capital. By only a small margin, Congress rejected Washington's proposal in favor of the Potomac River site. As you take in the view from the pavilion, consider how different this area would look if Washington had had his way!

Washington's plans aside, the Wrightsville area would probably have been part of the state of Maryland if it had been up to Lord Baltimore, who claimed the land to the fortieth latitude, just north of Mt. Pisgah. "Cresap's War," which was fought between 1730 and 1738, resulted from Baltimore's claim. . Thomas Cresap, an agent of Lord Baltimore, constructed a fort just south of the Wrightsville area on the river and conducted raids in the disputed territory. Pennsylvanians and the Maryland

Mt. Pisgah's 885-foot summit provides ample wind for kite fliers.

militia clashed over the land, and the war ended in 1738 with Cresap's arrest.

Samuel S. Lewis, after whom the park is named, was Pennsylvania's secretary of the Department of Forests and Waters from 1951 to 1954. He acquired the mountaintop's 35 acres and gave the land to the state. The Commonwealth later bought the rest of the park's land.

OPPORTUNITIES: Hiking on 1 trail mile to explore rock formations and the park's pine forest, kite flying, picnicking, cross-country skiing, sledding, and wildlife-watching. The park also features the George E. Stine Arboretum and offers pavilion rental [$], a playground, and playfield facilities. Star watches are sponsored at the park throughout the year for general stargazing and for observing the Leonid, Perseid, and Orionid meteor showers. (Call the park for schedule information and details.) Star watches are sponsored by the Astronomical Foundation of America, 2802 North George Street, York, PA 17402 (717-843-6032).

DIRECTIONS: From U.S. Route 30, take the PA Route 462 exit for Wrightsville and turn south. On the exit ramp you will see a small sign pointing the way to the state park. The sign says that it is 2 miles to the park, but it is actually nearly 3 miles from this exit on U.S. Route 30. Follow the road south and cross PA Route 462. You are now on Cool Creek Road and will pass a golf course and country club on your right. After about 2 miles, turn right onto Mt. Pisgah Road, following another sign to the state park. The park entrance is about 0.5 mile farther on the left. Park in the first parking lot and walk about 100 yards to the wayside exhibit and Pavilion C.

ADMINISTRATION AND AMENITIES: Rest rooms, water, and coin-operated binoculars are available at Pavilion C. Park hours are 8:00 A.M. to sunset.

FOR MORE INFORMATION: Contact Samuel S. Lewis State Park c/o Gifford Pinchot State Park, 2200 Rosstown Road, Lewisberry, PA 17339-9787 (call 717-432-5011 or e-mail gpinchot@dcnr.state.pa.us), or visit its Web site at www.dcnr.state.pa.us/stateparks/parks/sam.htm.

NEARBY OVERLOOKS: Rocky Ridge County Park (York County); Chickies Rock County Park overlooks (Lancaster County); Holtwood Environmental Preserve overlooks (Lancaster County); Susquehannock State Park overlooks (Lancaster County); Kings Gap Environmental Education and Training Center (Cumberland County); Little Round Top (Adams County); and Negley Park (Cumberland County) and Reservoir Park, Harrisburg (Dauphin County).

OTHER NEARBY OPPORTUNITIES

Gifford Pinchot State Park (York County). Activities include boating (with electric motors only), ice boating, tent and trailer camping [$], organized group tent and trailer camping [$], fishing for warm-water species, ice fishing, hiking on 18 trail miles, horseback riding on 4 trail miles, hunting, picnicking, ice skating, cross-country skiing, sledding, lake swimming, and wildlife-watching. The park also offers boat launching and mooring [$], boat rental [$], modern cabin rental [$], environmental education, a food concession, pavilion rental [$], a playfield, a playground, and a visitors center.

The Pennsylvania Fish and Boat Commission's *Fish Culture Station and visitors center at Huntsdale* (717-486-3419) is open to the public with tours available.

The Pennsylvania Game Commission's *Middle Creek Wildlife Management Area* near Klinefeltersville (Lebanon and Lancaster Counties) features a waterfowl museum and programs on wildlife; for information, call 717-733-1512.

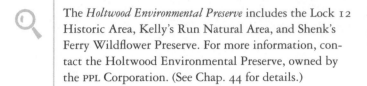 The *Holtwood Environmental Preserve* includes the Lock 12 Historic Area, Kelly's Run Natural Area, and Shenk's Ferry Wildflower Preserve. For more information, contact the Holtwood Environmental Preserve, owned by the PPL Corporation. (See Chap. 44 for details.)

Nolde Forest Environmental Education Center, operated by the Pennsylvania Department of Conservation and Natural Resources Bureau of State Parks, offers programs and activities year-round. For information, contact the center (call 610-775-1411 or e-mail noldeforest@dcnr.state.pa.us).

The 22-mile *Heritage Rail Trail County Park* (York County) is part of Pennsylvania's Rails-to-Trails program. It has trailheads at Hanover Junction and the city of York. The trail connects with Maryland's North Central Railroad Trail. For more information, contact the York County Department of Parks, 400 Mundis Race Road, York, PA 17402-9721 (call 717-840-7440 or e-mail parks@york-county.org), or visit its Web site at www.york-county.org.

York County and the city of York are filled with historic sites. Contact the York County Heritage Trust through its Web site (www.yorkheritage.com). Farther east is the Amish and Mennonite farm country in Lancaster County.

43

CHICKIES ROCK COUNTY PARK

Chickies Rock and Breezyview Overlook

Chickies Rock and nearby Breezyview Overlook are located in
Chickies Rock County Park. The park borders the Susquehanna
River between Marietta and Columbia and encompasses more
than 420 acres in western Lancaster County. Both overlooks stand
about 200 feet above the river and cover some 800 feet along the
Susquehanna River's eastern shore. The cliff is primarily
quartzite, a hard, brittle rock that has resisted the river's erosion
more than the surrounding land. (This hard rock also creates the
Susquehanna River's rapids below Chickies Rock.) The overlooks
are part of a geological formation called Chickies Ridge, which
stretches eastward from the Susquehanna River for a few miles.
If you look at a map of the river here, you will see that it turns
sharply away from Chickies Rock: the hard ridge resisted the
water's erosional forces, and the river, flowing easterly, turned
sharply south to take an easier erosional course. The park's name
derives from the American Indian word "Chiquesalunga," which
means "place of the crayfish."

The Susquehanna River Valley is a part of the major bird
migration route known as the Atlantic Flyway. Raptors (including American eagles), ducks, geese, tundra swans, shorebirds,
warblers, and other small birds fly through the area. The area is
also a permanent home for ample numbers of birds along the
river and in the nearby woods and fields.

Face Rock and Pinnacle Overlook in the PPL Corporation's
Holtwood Environmental Preserve and the Susquehannock State
Park overlooks offer similarly varied bird-watching opportunities
on the Susquehanna River. (For details, see Chaps. 44 and 45.)

Chickies Rock

From the Chickies Rock parking lot to the overlook is about 0.25
mile—a twelve-minute leisurely walk. At the parking lot, the
trail begins with a moderate-grade hill for a few hundred feet.
Then it levels off to the overlook on an old woods road on which
vehicles are no longer permitted. To get to the wooden fence at

Northwesterly view from Chickies Rock.

the overlook's edge, you have to climb a few feet down steep rocks, but you need not reach the fence to enjoy the overlook view.

The view from Chickies Rock is mostly westerly, spanning the Susquehanna River and York County beyond the river, from about 180 degrees south to 0 degrees north. Just north of the overlook, the river doglegs west and then north again. To the north, the borough of Marietta lies on the river's western shore. The plumes of white from the Three Mile Island cooling towers are occasionally visible from some 13 miles away. Looking toward Marietta, you will see the Pennsylvania Fish and Boat Commission's Marietta Access at the water's edge. Also visible to the north is the farmland of northwest Lancaster County. Looking south from either overlook, you can find Wrightsville on the river's eastern shore; beyond Wrightsville stands Mt. Pisgah, which is located in Samuel S. Lewis State Park.

At the Chickies Rock parking lot, six picnic tables are shaded by large trees.

Breezyview Overlook

The view from Breezyview Overlook is mainly northwesterly from 240 degrees south-southwest to 45 degrees northeast. A

Southwesterly view from Breezyview Overlook over the Susquehanna River toward the U.S. Route 30 bridge.

wooden fence marking the Breezyview precipice begins at the parking lot and extends some 50 yards along a flat, open grassy area. There are four picnic tables in a pavilion and two tables outside the shelter.

To the northwest, toward the borough of Marietta, you can see the large tan water tower about 3.5 miles away in Maytown (East Donegal Township). The tower reads "Maytown," with the town's name centered above "1999." The water tower is visible from either overlook; at Breezyview Overlook, with binoculars, you can make out part of the *n* in "Maytown." Some 26 miles to the far northwest is Blue Mountain. In Marietta, you can see a three-story red-brick building that appears to be a turn-of-the-century factory with a chimney. This former factory was built in 1897 and is now the Silk Mill Condominiums. Visible to the southwest, beyond the U.S. Route 30 bridge across the river, are Mt. Pisgah and Samuel S. Lewis State Park.

From the Breezyview Overlook, the line of low hills toward the southwest is called Mine Ridge, and it is located in southern York County. Far to the north are the Furniss Hills, including Mt. Hope and Mt. Gretna (the more easterly rise on the horizon).

In another part of the park—the field next to the parking lot—you can observe enthusiasts operating radio-controlled airplanes. The Lancaster County RC Club members frequently visit the park when steady winds blow from the west. The parking lot can be crowded on weekends.

Also at the parking lot is the entrance to the Chickies Trail, part of a series of trails through Chickies Rock County Park.

OPPORTUNITIES: Boating, fishing, hiking, horseback riding, hunting, model-airplane flying, picnicking at individual sites and two pavilions, rock climbing, cross-country skiing, sledding, snowmobiling, and wildlife-watching. The park also offers a ball field, historic sites, playgrounds, and a volleyball court.

ADMINISTRATION AND AMENITIES: No services at Chickies Rock. Breezyview Overlook has portable toilets. Both overlooks are open year-round from sunrise to sunset.

DIRECTIONS: Both overlooks are accessible from PA Route 441 between Marietta and Columbia. You know that you are approaching Chickies Rock because PA Route 441 climbs uphill from Marietta (to the north) *and* from Columbia (to the south). The entrance to Breezyview Overlook appears suddenly on the left about 0.5 mile from the intersection of U.S. Route 30 and PA Route 441. The entrance is marked with a sign. From the entrance, drive about 100 yards on an improved dirt road to the gravel parking lot. You can see the overlook's edge and enjoy the view from the parking lot.

The parking lot for Chickies Rock is unmarked but obvious. It is on the west side of PA Route 441, about 0.5 mile north of the Breezyview Overlook entrance. The parking area for Chickies Rock is ample but unimproved. Watch for potholes and broken chunks of pavement as you leave and return to PA Route 441.

FOR MORE INFORMATION: Contact Lancaster County Parks and Recreation Department, 1050 Rockford Road, Lancaster, PA 17602 (call 717-299-8215 or e-mail mikowycj@co.lancaster.pa.us), or visit its Web site at www.co.lancaster.pa.us/parks.htm.

NEARBY OVERLOOKS: Rocky Ridge County Park overlooks (York County); Mt. Pisgah (York County); Holtwood Environmental Preserve overlooks (Lancaster County); Susquehannock State Park overlooks (Lancaster County); and Little Round Top (Adams County).

OTHER NEARBY OPPORTUNITIES

Gifford Pinchot State Park (York County). Activities include boating (with electric motors only), ice boating, tent and trailer camping [$], organized group tent and trailer camping [$], fishing for warm-water species, ice fishing, hiking on 18 trail miles, horseback riding on 4 trail miles, hunting, picnicking, ice skating, cross-country skiing, sledding, lake swimming, and wildlife-watching. The park also offers boat launching and mooring [$], boat rental [$], modern cabin rental [$], environmental education, a food concession, pavilion rental [$], a playfield, a playground, and a visitors center.

The *Holtwood Environmental Preserve* includes the Lock 12 Historic Area, Kelly's Run Natural Area, and Shenk's Ferry Wildflower Preserve. For more information, contact the Holtwood Environmental Preserve, owned by the PPL Corporation. (See Chap. 44 for details.)

The Pennsylvania Game Commission's *Middle Creek Wildlife Management Area* near Klinefeltersville (Lebanon and Lancaster Counties) features a waterfowl museum and programs on wildlife; for information, call 717-733-1512.

Nolde Forest Environmental Education Center, operated by the Pennsylvania Department of Conservation and Natural Resources Bureau of State Parks, offers programs and activities year-round. For information, contact the center (call 610-775-1411 or e-mail noldeforest@dcnr.state.pa.us).

HOLTWOOD ENVIRONMENTAL PRESERVE

Face Rock Overlook and Pinnacle Overlook

On some 5,000 acres on both sides of the Susquehanna River in Lancaster and York Counties, the PPL Corporation manages the Holtwood Environmental Preserve. At the preserve, Face Rock Overlook surveys the Susquehanna River and Holtwood Dam, and Pinnacle Overlook provides spectacular views of Lake Aldred, the lakelike part of the Susquehanna River created by Holtwood Dam.

Face Rock Overlook

Face Rock Overlook stands 520 feet above sea level and some 400 feet above the Susquehanna River, and it offers a panoramic view of Holtwood Dam and the Holtwood Hydro/Steam Plants. The view is mainly westerly, 345 degrees north-northwest to 180 degrees south. Holtwood Dam, 55 feet high and 2,400 feet long, is one of four major main-stem Susquehanna River obstacles to migratory fish that are now overcome by fish passage facilities. The yellow-topped structure on the dam's east end is a fish lift. The lift gives American shad, river herring, eels, striped bass, and other migratory fish the ability to reach native spawning grounds. Construction of the fish lift was completed in 1997 at a cost of $20 million. When the lift was completed, it was the largest-capacity fish lift in the United States.

Fish passage facilities at Holtwood and at the three other major main-stem dams—York Haven and Safe Harbor Dams in Pennsylvania and Conowingo Dam in Maryland—were built in partnership with the dam owners and federal and state government agencies. The completion of the York Haven Dam fish passage facility in 2000 (the last of the four obstacles to overcome) gave migratory fish access to native spawning grounds for the first time in about a century.

At the overlook are wayside exhibits on the Susquehanna River's water level from Harrisburg to the Chesapeake Bay as well as an exhibit on shad restoration at Holtwood Dam.

Face Rock Overlook has wayside exhibits on Holtwood Dam and its fish passage facility.

Another exhibit identifies fourteen overlook features with letter-coded illustrations.

Visible just north of the dam is the high ground of State Game Lands #181. Looking downriver, you can see the Norman Wood Bridge (PA Route 372). Visible just north of the Norman Wood Bridge on the west side of the river is the Lock 12 Historic Area. Consider the islands and boulders below the Face Rock Overlook to a point just south of the Hawk Point Overlook in Susquehannock State Park (see Chap. 45). This area is probably how the entire river looked in the 1500s and 1600s, before dams created deeper, lakelike river sections.

Pinnacle Overlook

Pinnacle Overlook is a spectacular, mainly northwesterly view from o degrees north to about 270 degrees west. The overlook is about 700 feet above sea level and some 530 feet above the Susquehanna River. Note the two islands visible from Pinnacle Overlook. The smaller island closest to the overlook is Reed Island; Duncan Island is the larger one. These two islands are the only visible ones among the islands and boulders inundated by Lake Aldred, the lake created by Holtwood Dam. Notice, just below the overlook, that the river is contained in a narrow, steep, wooded area. This area is one of the deepest stretches of the Susquehanna River. Otter Creek enters the Susquehanna upriver on the western shore. From the formal constructed overlook, a

Northwesterly view from Pinnacle Overlook of Lake Aldred on the Susquehanna River.

fenced area of about 75 yards also provides views of the river before the trail begins.

On a Sunday afternoon in April, I watched a bald eagle and an osprey duel in midair over the river. Face Rock Overlook and Pinnacle Overlook are great sites for watching raptors and other birds.

OPPORTUNITIES: Boating, tent and trailer camping [$], group tent camping [$], fishing for trout and other species, hiking on 39 trail miles, hunting, picnicking, water skiing, and wildlife-watching; boat launching, historic sites, and pavilion rental [$] are also available.

The Holtwood Environmental Preserve includes the Lock 12 Historic Area, Kelly's Run Natural Area, and Shenk's Ferry Wildflower Preserve. For more information, contact the Holtwood Environmental Preserve (see below).

ADMINISTRATION AND AMENITIES: Face Rock Overlook is open from 9:00 A.M. to 4:00 P.M. weekdays; on Saturdays, Sundays, and holidays, it is open from 9:00 A.M. to 6:00 P.M. No services are available at this overlook. At Pinnacle Overlook, water and pit toilets are available from April through October. The Pinnacle Overlook area opens at 8:00 A.M. and closes at 7:00 P.M.

DIRECTIONS: Face Rock Overlook is about 1 mile from the intersection of River Road and Old Holtwood Road in Holtwood. From River Road, turn westerly onto Old Holtwood Road. Pass

Holtwood Arboretum on the right and the Holtwood Environmental Preserve Office on the left. Watch for a small wooden sign on the left that reads "Welcome to Holtwood" with an arrow directing you to the Face Rock Observation Area. At this turn, in addition to the wooden sign, there is a large green turbine runner. From the turbine runner and Face Rock Observation Area sign, it is about 0.4 mile to the overlook parking lot.

To reach Pinnacle Overlook: From River Road near Tucquan, turn west onto Pinnacle Road for about 1.1 miles. Turn right at the Pinnacle Overlook sign and continue 0.2 mile to the parking area. The overlook is about 1.2 miles from this intersection. If the gate is locked at the overlook, park at the gate and walk to the overlook. It is only about 150 yards from the gate to the overlook, and the walk is level on a paved road.

FOR MORE INFORMATION: Contact PPL, Holtwood Environmental Preserve Office, 9 New Village Road, Holtwood, PA 17532 (717-284-2278).

NEARBY OVERLOOKS: Chickies Rock County Park overlooks (Lancaster County); Susquehannock State Park overlooks (Lancaster County); Mt. Pisgah (York County); Rocky Ridge County Park overlooks (York County); Negley Park (Cumberland County) and Reservoir Park, Harrisburg (Dauphin County); and Little Round Top (Adams County).

OTHER NEARBY OPPORTUNITIES

Near Pinnacle Overlook is the *Tucquan Glen Nature Preserve,* Lancaster County Conservancy. Tucquan Creek is in the Pennsylvania Scenic Rivers System.

The *Indian Steps Museum,* off Route 425, features Native American artifacts (717-862-3948).

The Pennsylvania Game Commission's *Middle Creek Wildlife Management Area* near Klinefeltersville (Lebanon and Lancaster Counties) features a waterfowl museum and programs on wildlife; for information, call 717-733-1512.

Nolde Forest Environmental Education Center, operated by the Pennsylvania Department of Conservation and Natural Resources Bureau of State Parks, offers programs and activities year-round. For information, contact the center (call 610-775-1411 or e-mail noldeforest@dcnr.state.pa.us).

The *Pennsylvania Dutch region* surrounding Lake Aldred has museums, historic sites, and other points of interest. Contact the Pennsylvania Dutch Tourist Bureau, 1800 Hempstead Road, Lancaster, PA 17601 (717-299-8901) or the York County Convention and Visitors Bureau, 1 Marketway East, York, PA 17402 (717-848-4000).

45

SUSQUEHANNOCK STATE PARK

Hawk Point Overlook and Wissler Run Overlook

In 1608, Captain John Smith first described the Susquehannock American Indians in his journal. No one knows what the Susquehannock people actually called themselves, but this name—given to the people, the river, and Susquehannock State Park—derived from Smith's American Indian interpreter's name, "Sasquesahanough." Translated from the interpreter's Algonquian language, the word means "roily water people" or "people at the falls."

Susquehannock State Park occupies a plateau on the Susquehanna River's eastern shore in southern Lancaster County. The 224-acre park has two magnificent overlooks: Hawk Point and Wissler Run.

Hawk Point Overlook

Hawk Point Overlook, some 400 feet above the Susquehanna River, provides a mainly south-southwesterly view from about 135 degrees southeast to nearly 315 degrees northwest. A wayside exhibit identifies fourteen sights from the overlook. Look about 2.5 miles downriver near the eastern shore for a round, moundlike island: that is Mt. Johnson Island, dedicated in 1945 as the world's first bald eagle sanctuary. Eagles nested on Mt. Johnson Island until 1949. Pesticides caused the eagle eggshells to grow so thin that the eggs broke before they could hatch. Since then, eagles have nested successfully on some of the other river islands nearby. Eagles can be seen most often from winter into spring.

Right below the overlook is the Chestnut Island Group and the Upper and Lower Bear Islands. These belong to the Conowingo Islands, more than sixty islands that are erosional remnants. Other islands in the Susquehanna are alluvial—that is, they formed from deposits that the river brought. Native Americans camped, fished, and hunted here. The islands' mature forests show that the timber was never harvested. Look below Holtwood Dam to the north (visible from either overlook) to a spot just below the Hawk Point

Looking south from Hawk Point Overlook—400 feet above the Susquehanna River.

Overlook: this is how the river probably looked in the 1500s and 1600s. Far to the south on the river's western shore is the Peach Bottom Power Plant, one of the largest power plants in the world. Looking southwest, directly across the river from the overlook, you will see the mouth of Muddy Creek; looking northwesterly (upriver), you can see the Norman Wood Bridge (PA Route 372), which is 3,504 feet long. Also upriver is Holtwood Dam—note the white water flowing over the dam—and above Holtwood Dam is Lake Aldred. Westerly across the river is the Pennsylvania Fish and Boat Commission's Muddy Creek Access.

Wissler Run Overlook

Like Hawk Point, Wissler Run Overlook stands about 400 feet above the Susquehanna River, but it offers a mainly northwesterly view from about 225 degrees southwest to about 0 degrees due north. Visible upriver is the Norman Wood Bridge (PA Route 372) and, in the distance, Holtwood Dam and Lake Aldred. Below the overlook is the Philadelphia Electric Company's Muddy Run Pump/Storage Plant. Across the river on the western shore is the Pennsylvania Fish and Boat

Northerly view from Wissler Run Overlook. Holtwood Dam and the Norman Wood Bridge (PA Route 372) can be seen in the distance.

Commission's Muddy Creek Access. Little Chestnut Island is southwest of the overlook.

The 0.5-mile Overlook Trail leads you on a leisurely ten-minute walk to Wissler Run Overlook from Hawk Point Overlook.

The Wissler Run Overlook could offer some interesting early morning photos in winter, with a low sun angle coming downriver from the northeast. Sunset shots here could also be intriguing, with the sun setting to the northwest over an expansive river scene. At Wissler Run Overlook, photographers will have to negotiate a chain-link fence that is nearly 5 feet high. Do not set up or venture beyond the fence.

OPPORTUNITIES: Hiking on 4 trail miles, horseback riding on 1 trail mile, picnicking, cross-country skiing, sledding, and wildlife-watching; pavilion rental [$] and playfield and playground facilities are also available.

ADMINISTRATION AND AMENITIES: Pit toilets and water are available near the Hawk Point Overlook parking area, and coin-operated binoculars are available at the overlook itself. Day-use areas are open from 8:00 A.M. to dusk.

DIRECTIONS: From Quarryville, follow PA Route 372 west and turn left onto River Road at the sign that reads "Susquehannock State Park 4.5 miles." The road follows the Muddy Run

Reservoir dam breast. From River Road, turn right onto Furniss Road and follow the sign ("Susquehannock State Park 2 miles"). A third sign will lead you to the state park, and yet another park sign will indicate a right turn into the park entrance in 200 feet. At the park hours sign (8:00 A.M. to sunset), continue 0.4 mile to the parking area for the overlooks. Park and then follow the signs for the river overlook and scenic view trail; about 100 yards from the parking lot, the trail forks. Hawk Point Overlook is another 100 yards down the left fork. The right fork is the trail to Wissler Run Overlook. From the parking lot to Hawk Point Overlook is a four-minute walk on an easy path.

FOR MORE INFORMATION: Contact Susquehannock State Park c/o Gifford Pinchot State Park, 2200 Rosstown Road, Lewisberry, PA 17339-9787 (call 717-432-5011 or e-mail gpinchot@dcnr.state.pa.us), or visit its Web site at www.dcnr.state.pa.us/stateparks/parks/susque.htm.

NEARBY OVERLOOKS: Chickies Rock County Park overlooks (Lancaster County); Holtwood Environmental Preserve overlooks (Lancaster County); Mt. Pisgah (York County); Rocky Ridge County Park overlooks (York County); Negley Park (Cumberland County) and Reservoir Park, Harrisburg (Dauphin County); and Little Round Top (Adams County).

OTHER NEARBY OPPORTUNITIES

The Pennsylvania Game Commission's *Middle Creek Wildlife Management Area* near Klinefeltersville (Lebanon and Lancaster Counties) features a waterfowl museum and programs on wildlife; for information, call 717-733-1512.

The *Holtwood Environmental Preserve* includes the Lock 12 Historic Area, Kelly's Run Natural Area, and Shenk's Ferry Wildflower Preserve. For more information, contact the Holtwood Environmental Preserve, owned by the PPL Corporation. (See Chap. 44 for details.)

Nolde Forest Environmental Education Center, operated by the Pennsylvania Department of Conservation and Natural Resources Bureau of State Parks, offers programs and activities year-round. For information, contact the center (call 610-775-1411 or e-mail noldeforest@dcnr.state.pa.us).

46

RALPH STOVER STATE PARK

High Rocks Vista

High Rocks Vista is a sheer cliff some 200 feet above Tohickon Creek. The viewing area is a path along the cliff's edge, marked by a barrier (a chain-link fence) at the center of Tohickon Creek's horseshoe bend. Several spots at this site provide breathtaking views of Tohickon Creek and its surroundings. The geological features and excellent view attract overlook lovers, and the cliff's steep rock face lures experienced rappellers. The viewing area at the center of the horseshoe bend is located only about 100 yards from the parking lot, and it is accessible on a well-traveled, easy trail.

Observe the warning sign near the parking lot. Rappelling is only for those who are properly equipped, trained, and experienced. Use extreme caution along the barrier, and watch children carefully.

The view is surprisingly pleasant in the winter. Through leafless tree branches, you can see much of the creek and its surroundings. (In warmer weather, the tree leaves obscure part of the view.) When I visited High Rocks Vista on a cold, brisk, clear Sunday afternoon in mid-February, eight vehicles stood in the parking lot, people were walking the trail, and several rappellers were scaling the cliff.

At the center of the horseshoe bend, the nearly 180-degree view is primarily southeast: it runs from 60 degrees north-northeast to 225 degrees west-southwest. The vista provides a commanding view of the Tohickon Creek Valley. The High Rocks Vista is a great place for photographs, particularly in the winter, when the leaves have fallen. Try shooting photographs in the mornings, when the sun angle produces less glare off the western bend of the creek.

The 45-acre Ralph Stover State Park, located in Bucks County, is named after Ralph Stover, a prominent eighteenth-century businessman who used water from Tohickon Creek to power a grain mill. Park visitors can still see the remnants of the mill and mill race.

In 1931, the Stover family heirs gave this property to the Commonwealth for use as a state park. In 1935, recreational

The view from High Rocks Vista is surprisingly pleasant in the winter. The vista spans a sheer cliff some 200 feet above a horseshoe bend in Tohickon Creek.

facilities developed by the federal Works Progress Administration opened. Author James A. Michener donated the High Rocks property. The High Rocks area and the main Ralph Stover State Park are separated by Tohickon Valley Park, which is operated by Bucks County.

OPPORTUNITIES: In Ralph Stover State Park, activities include white-water boating, fishing for trout and other species, hiking on 1 trail mile, picnicking, and wildlife-watching. Boat launching, rustic cabin rental [$], pavilion rental [$], and playfield and playground facilities are also available.

ADMINISTRATION AND AMENITIES: There is a portable toilet at the High Rocks Vista parking lot. Water and more rest rooms are available near the picnic area. The park closes at sunset.

DIRECTIONS: Reach the High Rocks Vista via Cafferty Road in Point Pleasant. From Cafferty Road, turn west onto Tory Road (a dirt road) and drive about 1 mile to the parking lot, where a sign identifies the "High Rocks Vista" and Ralph Stover State Park.

To reach the vista, cross the road and walk down the trail to the chain-link fence barrier.

FOR MORE INFORMATION: Contact Ralph Stover State Park c/o Delaware Canal State Park, RR 1, Box 615-A, Upper Black Eddy, PA 18972-9540 (call 610-982-5560 or e-mail delaware@dcnr. state.pa.us), or visit its Web site at www.dcnr.state.pa.us/ stateparks/parks/ralph.htm.

NEARBY OVERLOOKS: Delaware Water Gap National Recreation Area overlooks (Monroe and Northampton Counties); Camelback Mountain (Monroe County); and Militia Hill (Bucks County).

OTHER NEARBY OPPORTUNITIES

Delaware Canal State Park (Bucks and Northampton Counties). Activities include mountain biking, boating (with canoes only), fishing for trout and other species, hiking on 60 trail miles, horseback riding on 60 trail miles, picnicking, cross-country skiing, and wildlife-watching. The park also offers boat launching, environmental education, and a historical center exploring the Delaware Canal (a National Historic Landmark).

Nockamixon State Park (Bucks County). Activities include bicycling, boating (with a 10 hp limit), ice boating, fishing for warm-water species, ice fishing, hiking on 3 trail miles, horseback riding on 20 trail miles, hunting, picnicking, ice skating, cross-country skiing, sledding, pool swimming [$], and wildlife-watching. The park also offers boat launching, boat rental [$], modern cabin rental [$], environmental education, a food concession, a playground, and a visitors center.

Adjoining Ralph Stover State Park is *Tohickon Valley Park* (Bucks County). Activities include camping [$], fishing, hiking, picnicking, pool swimming [$], and wildlife-watching; ball fields and playgrounds are also available. Contact the park at 215-757-0571 or visit its Web site at www.bctc.org/parkmain.html.

Nine nature centers, wildlife sanctuaries, and environmental education centers in eastern Pennsylvania present exhibits and offer indoor and outdoor programs and activities

throughout the year. For details, contact Churchville
Nature Center, Churchville (215-357-4005); Great
Valley Nature Center, Devault (610-935-9777); Honey
Hollow Environmental Education Center, New Hope
(215-297-5880); John Heinz National Wildlife Refuge,
Philadelphia (610-521-0662); Mariton Wildlife Sanctu-
ary, Easton (610-749-2379); Mill Grove Wildlife Sanctu-
ary, Audubon (610-666-5593); Pool Wildlife Sanctuary,
Wildlands Conservancy, Emmaus (610-965-4397);
Schuylkill Center for Environmental Education,
Philadelphia (215-482-7300); and Silver Lake Nature
Center, Bristol (215-785-1177).

47

FORT WASHINGTON STATE PARK

Militia Hill

In July 1776, the thirteen British colonies in North America declared independence from England. At that time, British colonies could be found all across the globe, and England was a most formidable adversary. George Washington assumed command of the Continental Army on July 3, 1776, and he trained its fourteen thousand men, preparing the soldiers for battle. After several encounters with the British in New York State and in the city of New York, Washington retreated across New Jersey and into southeast Pennsylvania.

Washington crossed the Delaware River and launched a surprise attack on Trenton on Christmas night, 1776, which allowed the Continental Army to take Trenton. But the Continentals were defeated at the Battle of Brandywine in September 1777 and at the Battle of Germantown, in Philadelphia, in October 1777.

After these defeats, Washington retreated northwestward through present-day Montgomery County to the area then known as Whitemarsh. Today, this high ground is known as Militia Hill and Fort Washington. Washington chose this area because the Continental Army could defend its vantage point and easily observe British troop activity. The encampment for Washington and the Continental Army began November 2, 1777.

In December 1777, the British marched westward from Philadelphia to attack, but the Continental Army's strong position prevented a full-force British onslaught. Both armies engaged only in skirmishes. As winter set in, Washington knew that his army needed better supplies and more substantial quarters. He was also concerned about the possibility of a British surprise attack on the encampment, and he wanted to move closer to the foundries and iron forges along the Schuylkill River so that he could defend these vital interests. On December 11, 1777, the Continental Army left Whitemarsh and marched some 15 miles westward. A week later, Washington and the Continental Army arrived at Valley Forge. There—as history has recorded—fate tested Washington's resolve and the fortitude of the Continental Army.

The Wyncote Audubon Society sponsors the Militia Hill Hawk Watch at the observation platform. The hawk watch begins in September and operates daily through November.

Militia Hill, in Fort Washington State Park, is about 360 feet above sea level and about 140 to 200 feet above the surrounding area. At the observation deck, the view is mainly southeast from 45 degrees northeast to about 180 degrees south. Militia Hill rises above the Wissahickon Creek Valley. The ridge along most of the viewing area to the southeast is Edge Hill Ridge, about 3 miles away.

A small wayside exhibit at the observation platform explains the actions of the American Revolutionary soldiers in the fall of 1777. Pamphlets at the observation platform include "A Visitor's Guide to Fort Washington State Park" (provided by The Friends of Fort Washington State Park), "Birds of Fort Washington State Park," and "Butterflies of Fort Washington State Park." These last two publications are provided by the Militia Hill Hawk Watch.

Militia Hill's observation platform is a great place for bird- and butterfly-watching. Nests and feeders dot the area. Volunteers from the Wyncote Audubon Society have documented some 198 bird species and 58 butterfly species at the site, and the Society holds bird and butterfly walks throughout the year. In addition, the Society sponsors the Militia Hill Hawk Watch at the observation platform. The hawk watch begins in September and operates daily through November, and details of the hawk migration are forwarded to the Hawk Migration Association of North America (HMANA) and Cornell University. The information gathered from this hawk watch and others can help scientists understand more about bird migration and aid in conservation and restoration efforts. For more information, contact the Wyncote Audubon Society (visit http://hometown.aol.com/sialia1/index.htm) or HMANA (www.hmana.org).

OPPORTUNITIES: Organized group tent camping [$], fishing for trout and other species, hiking on 5 trail miles, picnicking, cross-country skiing, sledding, and wildlife-watching; a mobile food concession, pavilion rental [$], and playfield facilities are also available.

ADMINISTRATION AND AMENITIES: The park hours are 8:00 A.M. to sunset. Water and pit toilets are available at the observation deck parking area.

DIRECTIONS: From Exit 339 of the Pennsylvania Turnpike, continue straight after paying the toll—do not turn off onto PA Route 309 either north or south. This road becomes Pennsylvania Avenue. Follow Pennsylvania Avenue 0.5 mile to Bethlehem Pike, and turn left. Follow Bethlehem Pike for about 1.1 miles and turn right onto PA Route 73 west (Skippack Pike). Drive 0.3 mile and turn left at the Fort Washington sign for the Militia Hill Picnic Area. Turn left again in another 0.1 mile, and enter the park. The road winds uphill. Park in the parking lot across the road from the observation deck.

FOR MORE INFORMATION: Contact Fort Washington State Park, 500 Bethlehem Pike, Fort Washington, PA 19034 (call 215-591-5250 or e-mail fortwashingtonsp@state.pa.us), or visit its Web site at www.dcnr.state.pa.us/stateparks/parks/ft-was.htm.

NEARBY OVERLOOKS: High Rocks Vista (Bucks County) and Delaware Water Gap National Recreation Area overlooks (Monroe and Northampton Counties).

OTHER NEARBY OPPORTUNITIES

Evansburg State Park (Montgomery County). Activities include fishing for trout and other species, hiking on

6 trail miles, horseback riding on 15 trail miles, hunting, picnicking, cross-country skiing, and wildlife-watching. The park also offers environmental education, a historical center, pavilion rental [$], a playfield, a playground, and a visitors center.

Marsh Creek State Park (Chester County). Activities include boating (with electric motors only), fishing for warm-water species, hiking on 6 trail miles, horseback riding on 6 trail miles, hunting, picnicking, cross-country skiing, sledding, and wildlife-watching. The park also offers boat launching and boat mooring [$], boat rental [$], a food concession, and playground facilities.

Tyler State Park (Bucks County). Activities include bicycling, boating (with canoes only), fishing for warm-water species, hiking on 4 trail miles, horseback riding on 9 trail miles, picnicking, cross-country skiing, sledding, and wildlife-watching. The park also offers boat launching and mooring [$], boat rental [$], environmental education, a mobile food concession, pavilion rental [$], and playfield and playground facilities.

Ten nature centers, wildlife sanctuaries, and environmental education centers in eastern Pennsylvania present exhibits and offer indoor and outdoor programs and activities throughout the year. For details, contact Churchville Nature Center, Churchville (215-357-4005); Great Valley Nature Center, Devault (610-935-9777); Honey Hollow Environmental Education Center, New Hope (215-297-5880); John Heinz National Wildlife Refuge, Philadelphia (610-521-0662); Mariton Wildlife Sanctuary, Easton (610-749-2379); Mill Grove Wildlife Sanctuary, Audubon (610-666-5593); Nolde Forest Environmental Education Center, Reading (610-775-1411); Pool Wildlife Sanctuary, Wildlands Conservancy, Emmaus (610-965-4397); Schuylkill Center for Environmental Education, Philadelphia (215-482-7300); and Silver Lake Nature Center, Bristol (215-785-1177).

In Valley Forge, the National Park Service administers *Valley Forge National Historic Park* (610-783-1077). For information on other opportunities and attractions in the area, contact the Valley Forge Convention and

Visitors Bureau (610-834-1550), or visit its Web site at www.valleyforge.org.

The *Schuylkill River Trail* is part of the Pennsylvania Rails-to-Trails program. Its 11.5 completed miles run from Philadelphia to Montgomery County, with trailheads at Philadelphia and Valley Forge. Some 25 trail miles are planned. For more information, contact the Montgomery County Planning Commission at the Montgomery County Courthouse in Norristown (610-278-3736).

For *Philadelphia opportunities and attractions,* contact the Philadelphia Convention and Visitors Bureau (215-636-3300) or visit its Web site at www.pcvb.org.

GENERAL INTERNET RESOURCES

Consult these Internet resources for general information on overlooks and other nearby opportunities. (Note, however, that Web sites can disappear without warning.) Web addresses connected to specific parks, forests, museums, and so on appear in the main text.

Allegheny National Forest
www.fs.fed.us/r9/allegheny

Allegheny National Forest
Vacation Bureau
www.allegheny-vacation.com

Bedford County Visitors Bureau
www.bedfordcounty.net

Cameron County Tourist
Promotion Agency
www.pavisnet.com/camtpa

Centre County Convention and
Visitors Bureau
www.visitpennstate.org

Clinton County Economic
Partnership
www.clintoncountyinfo.
com/tourism.htm

Crawford County Convention
and Visitors Bureau
www.visitcrawford.org

Duquesne and Monongahela
Inclines
www.portauthority.org/ride/
incline.asp

Elk County Visitors Bureau
www.ncentral.com/~elkcovb

Endless Mountains Visitors
Bureau
www.endlessmountains.org

Erie Area Convention and
Visitors Bureau
www.eriepa.com

Forest County Industrial
Development Corporation
www.forestcounty.com

Gettysburg National Military
Park
www.nps.gov/gett

Greater Johnstown/Cambria
County Convention and
Visitors Bureau
www.visitjohnstownpa.com

Greater Pittsburgh Convention
and Visitors Bureau
www.visitpittsburgh.com

Hawk Migration Association of
North America (HMANA)
www.hmana.org

Hawk Mountain Sanctuary
www.hawkmountain.org

Horseshoe Curve National
Historic Landmark
www.railroadcity.com
www.trainweb.org/horseshoe
curve-nrhs/Altoona_
area.htm#6

Indiana County Tourist Bureau
www.indiana-co-pa-
tourism.org

Jennings Environmental
Education Center
www.dcnr.state.pa.us/state
parks/parks/jenn.htm

Johnstown Inclined Plane
www.inclinedplane.com

Keystone Trails Association
www.kta-hike.org

Lackawanna County
www.visitnepa.org

Laurel Highlands Visitors Bureau
www.laurelhighlands.org

Lawrence County Tourist
Promotion Agency
www.lawrencecounty.com/
tourist

Lehigh Valley Convention and
Visitors Bureau
www.lehighvalleypa.org

Luzerne County Convention and
Visitors Bureau
www.tournepa.com

Lycoming County Visitors Bureau
www.williamsport.org/visitpa

Maryland Hang Gliding
Association
www.mhga.com

Mercer County Convention and
Visitors Bureau
www.mercercountypa.org

National Park Service
www.nps.gov

National Register of Historic
Places
www.cr.nps.gov/nr

National Wild and Scenic Rivers
System
www.nps.gov/rivers

Northern Alleghenies Vacation
Region
www.northernalleghenies.com

Oil Heritage Region Tourist
Promotion Agency
www.oilregiontourist.com

Pennsylvania Association of
Convention and Visitors
Bureaus
www.pacvb.org/tpa.html

Pennsylvania Audubon Society
www.audubon.org/chapter/pa

Pennsylvania Department of
Conservation and Natural
Resources
www.dcnr.state.pa.us

Bureau of Forestry
www.dcnr.state.pa.us/
forestry

Bureau of State Parks
www.dcnr.state.pa.us/
stateparks

Bureau of Topography and
Geologic Survey
www.dcnr.state.pa.us/
topogeo

Conservation Volunteer
Program
www.dcnr.state.pa.us/cons/
cv.htm

Pennsylvania Rails-to-Trails
Program
www.dcnr.state.pa.us/rails

Pennsylvania Rivers
Conservation Program
(Scenic Rivers System)
www.dcnr.state.pa.us/
rivers/newrconhome.htm

Pennsylvania Department of
Transportation
www.dot.state.pa.us

Pennsylvania Dutch Convention
and Visitors Bureau
www.padutchcountry.com

Pennsylvania Fish and Boat
Commission
www.fish.state.pa.us

Pennsylvania Game Commission
www.pgc.state.pa.us

Pennsylvania Historical and
Museum Commission
www.phmc.state.pa.us

Pennsylvania Lumber Museum
www.lumbermuseum.org

Pennsylvania's Capital Region
Visitors Bureau
www.pacapitalregions.com

Pennsylvania Tourism and
Lodging Association
www.patravel.org

Philadelphia Convention and
Visitors Bureau
www.pcvb.org

Pocono Environmental
Education Center
www.peec.org

Pocono Mountains Vacation
Bureau, Inc.
www.800poconos.com

Potter County Visitors
Association
www.pottercountypa.org/
home.html

Reading and Berks County
Visitors Bureau
www.readingberkspa.com/
home.asp

Shaver's Creek Environmental
Center
www.shaverscreek.org

Susquehanna Valley Visitors
Bureau
www.visitcentralpa.org

Tioga County Visitors Bureau
www.visittiogapa.com

U.S. Army Corps of Engineers
Baltimore District. www.nab.
usace.army.mil
Philadelphia District: www.
nap.usace.army.mil
Pittsburgh District: www.lrp.
usace.army.mil

USDA Forest Service
www.fs.fed.us

Western Pennsylvania
Conservancy
www.wpconline.org

Wildwood Lake Sanctuary and
the Olewine Nature Center
www.wildwoodlake.org

INDEX